THE ECCENTRIC DESIGN

The Eccentric Design

Form in the Classic American Novel

MARIUS BEWLEY

> . . . *a law of inherent opposites,*
> *Of essential unity, is as pleasant as port,*
> *As pleasant as the brush-strokes of a bough,*
> *An upper, particular bough in, say, Marchand.*
>
> WALLACE STEVENS
>
> *It was when the trees were leafless first in November*
> *And their blackness became apparent, that one first*
> *Knew the eccentric to be the base of design*
>
> WALLACE STEVENS

COLUMBIA UNIVERSITY PRESS

NEW YORK

1959

PUBLISHED IN GREAT BRITAIN BY
CHATTO AND WINDUS LTD

PRINTED IN GREAT BRITAIN BY
BUTLER AND TANNER LTD
FROME AND LONDON

To John Garry Mackenzie

Contents

Preface

SEVERAL years ago in a book called *The Complex Fate* I pointed to Cooper, Hawthorne, Melville, and Henry James as composing the centrally significant tradition of fiction in America, and I said that 'the largest problem that confronted the artist in nineteenth-century America, and which still occupies him' might be defined as 'the nature of his separateness, and the nature of his connection with European, and particularly with English, culture'. As with all tidy formulations applied to a highly complex reality, the possibilities of misunderstanding were present, but not, I thought, insistent. However, in a brief notice accorded the book in an American weekly widely known for its crisp sophistication, if not urbanity, it was accused of betraying the United States for the United Kingdom out of snobbery and general servility. In another American weekly, equally well known for its wilted politics, it was accused in a second notice, appearing in the same week, of insulting Our Old Home in the interests of an America First programme in literature. This was gratifying as Our Old Home had rarely been accorded such respectful consideration in the pages of this magazine before. A year or so later, taking the higher retrospective line for the purpose of surveying what he called 'new horizons', a writer in the TLS rather wincingly noted that *The Complex Fate* had received some attention 'in certain quarters'. Although this literary ghetto was not further specified, the implication was clearly not salubrious, and it was not surprising to learn that *The Complex Fate* was more than suspected of genteel traditionalism. These critics are welcome to whatever confirmation they can find in the present book of their earlier distinguished insights. But to the less creatively gifted reader the argument of *The Eccentric Design* should be clear enough. It is an attempt to enlarge upon, to corroborate with additional evidence, and define more rigorously, certain general statements made in the opening chapter of *The Complex Fate*, one of which has been quoted here. If I speak of national attitudes, my interest is still in literature, not passports. Finally,

9

I am not convinced that a certain distaste for the humour of Petroleum V. Nasby necessarily identifies one with Barrett Wendell. Such simplifications are nearly as frequent in literary journalism of a particular type as they are deeply vicious. It will be found that the 'new horizons' they are faced towards open into the valley of dry bones after all.

The genteel tradition is not a simple thing. In the nineteenth century when the wealthy mercantile interests of New England and New York based their commercial prosperity on trade reciprocity with Great Britain, it was in the economic interests of the 'men of property and talents' to advocate an art and literature that created an ambience of Anglophiliac servility and flattery. It paid off well in helping to keep commercial relations well lubricated, and the 'men of property' found their admiration for the power image Britain provided trickled down, quite naturally, to a taste for American art that imitated British models. Hence the genteel tradition, grounded in privileged economics and partisan politics, and nourished by the snobbism of the newly wealthy, came into being. America has her 'men of property' (who are no longer 'men of talents') in the twentieth century no less than in Hamilton's time, but in other respects the scene has changed. Money no longer flows into privileged American pockets through happy reciprocal trade relations with England. In fact the current is in the other direction. The old genteel tradition, solidly grounded in the prosperous business interests of the country, is now defunct, and nothing has come to replace it because the contemporary 'men of property' have no literary preferences at all. Modern literature means as little to them as modern England. No doubt if they ever read books they would prefer something in the realistic line, stressing the hard facts and 'spiritual' dynamism of America. That would encourage enterprise. They might go as far afield lyrically as Carl Sandburg, who once gave a boost to the Chicago meatpacking industry. The most subtle of them might even go highbrow, as Otto Kahn did when he subsidized a celebration of the mystic possibilities of American capitalism in Hart Crane's *The Bridge*. But the fact remains that there is no modern equivalent for the old genteel tradition, and somewhat paradoxically this is not wholly a good sign. It has ceased to exist, but for the wrong reasons.

I shall speak of the genteel tradition in some detail in the pages that follow, but as formal judgements on what a book says are sometimes based on the preface rather than the later chapters, it has seemed advisable to make my attitude towards the genteel tradition explicit as early as possible. This book deals with literature in which the American artist has endeavoured to confront and understand his own emotional and spiritual needs as an American. He cannot, after all, confront them as an Englishman or a Welshman. But the focus is on his achievement as an artist, not on any patriotic or expatriate commitments he may make. The only commitment I am interested in is the commitment of the original artist to the integrity of his own creative act. Where this integrity is not violated any question about the genteel tradition is totally irrelevant.

I should like to acknowledge my great obligations to Professor David Daiches and Professor Arthur Mizener, who painstakingly read the manuscript of this book more than once, and offered valuable suggestions and comments. I am deeply grateful to them. I wish to thank the Rockefeller Foundation, and particularly Mr. John Marshall of the Humanities Division, for a grant that assisted me in completing this study. My debt to F. R. and Q. D. Leavis is both comprehensive and personal.

Parts of this book have appeared in *American Literature*, *The Hudson Review*, *Mandrake*, *Scrutiny*, and *The Sewanee Review*. I am grateful to the editors for permission to publish them here. I also wish to thank Messrs. Charles Scribner's Sons for permission to quote from *The Great Gatsby* and *The Diamond as big as the Ritz* by F. Scott Fitzgerald.

MARIUS BEWLEY

St. George, S.I.
April, 1957

I

The Question of Form

FORM is an elusive, even a frightening, word. A word that stands for so much sometimes ends up by meaning little, and therefore at the outset I wish to define the limits within which I shall use it in this book. Sir Herbert Read has written that we should realize that 'form is the natural effect of the poet's integrity', and that we should be concerned not so much with ' "the life of form," . . . but rather the form of life'.[1] I doubt if an investigation of aesthetic form that tried to push beyond these sensible boundaries would lead us very far towards understanding the peculiar constitution and problems of the American novel.

'The form of life' results from emotions and ideas coming together in various combinations in the moulds provided by the conventions and manners of a given society. As the novelist's subject is man in society, his subject must also be the texture of manners and conventions by which social man defines his own identity. In saying this I do little more than paraphrase the arguments of two illuminating essays by Mr. Lionel Trilling, 'Manners, Morals, and the Novel', and 'Art and Fortune'. It is at this point, as Mr. Trilling makes clear, that a distinction between the American and the European novel becomes evident. In the earlier of the two essays he writes:

> Now the novel as I have described it has never really established itself in America. Not that we have not had very great novels but that the novel in America diverges from its classic intention, which, as I have said, is the investigation of the problem of reality beginning in the social field. The fact is that American writers of genius have not turned their minds to society. The reality they sought was only tangential to society.[2]

And enlarging on this in the second essay, 'Art and Fortune', Mr. Trilling says that 'In this country the real basis of the novel has never existed—that is, the tension between a middle class and an aristocracy which brings manners into observable relief as the living representation of ideals and the living comment on ideas.' The American novel has sheered towards abstraction.

Even its great characters, Natty Bumppo and Captain Ahab, 'tend to be mythic because of the rare finesse and abstractness of the ideas they represent; and their very freedom from class gives them a large and glowing generality'.[3]

These remarks suggest that the matrix of form for the American novel is not manners or society. 'Many of us forget', Mr. Trilling continues, 'how in the novel ideas may be as important as character and as essential to the given dramatic situation.' There was that in the American ethos which gave an emotional primacy to ideas, which made them the proper subject-matter of the novelist's art, while at the same time the novelist was deprived of that richness of nuance and tone which a traditional society alone can provide. The American novelist was necessarily at a disadvantage when he attempted to create character. The traditional codes and manners by which the European novelist creates his men and women were not at his disposal; but before the middle of the nineteenth century he had discovered his great alternative in symbolism. It is a gross simplification to say that symbol in art stands in relation to idea as character in fiction stands in relation to the values represented by traditional social patterns, but the statement has its measure of truth. If the American novelist, deprived of an adequate social density, has never been able to approach nearer to Emma Bovary than poor Sister Carrie, it is also true to say that no English or French novelist has ever come so near to the White Whale. *Moby Dick* and *Madam Bovary* may be taken as examples of contrasting modes of fiction, each representative (in so far as a masterpiece can ever be representative) of its particular world, and of different ways of searching out truth in art. Therefore, when I say that I am chiefly concerned in the following pages with ideas rather than with manners it is not with any intention of minimizing the overwhelming importance of the latter for the European tradition, nor of maintaining that the absence of a rich texture of manners in American life may not have resulted, on many levels, in artistic impoverishment. But the most casual reading of Fenimore Cooper, Hawthorne, or Melville—the most significant American novelists before Henry James—is sufficient to indicate that they did not draw on social observation to achieve their profoundest effects, nor search traditional social forms for their values. If the case of Cooper will call for certain qualifications later, it will be found nevertheless that his deepest meaning is at variance with anything he was able to read in patterns of American social behaviour. The popularity of such writers as Scott and Dickens in the United States was responsible for a large number of American imitators, but where the American novelist was successful enough to create genuine art it will usually be found that it is a deep and emotional concern with abstractions which is the controlling factor in the motives and organization of his work.

This should not surprise us, given the conditions under which the American writer had to create. Jane Austen, to take the ideal example, was able to move progressively into her values in the course of any given novel, to reveal them in the very circumstances of her story, in the inflections of her characters' speeches, or the way they wore their inherited manners. Her values *pre-existed* in the materials and conditions of her art, even if it took her genius to reveal them. Her art is essentially an art of ironic illumination, of revealing in a new light what had been there all along. Her judgements and insights have the sureness and strength that come from the corroboration of traditional sanctions. But the American novelist had only his *ideas* with which to begin: ideas which, for the most part, were grounded in the great American democratic abstractions. And he found that these abstractions were disembodied, that there was no social context in which they might acquire a rich human relevance. For the traditional novelist, the universal and the particular come together in the world of manners; but for the American artist there was no social surface responsive to his touch. The scene was crude, even beyond successful satire, as Dickens was to discover. There was really only one subject available to the nineteenth-century American novelist— his own unhappy plight. And the essence of that plight was his isolation. The American novelist before James, in his most successful work, turns his back on manners and society as such. In doing so he confronts his own emotional and spiritual needs which his art becomes the means of comprehending and analys- ing. Under such circumstances these novelists ran the risk of becoming exponents of the romantic agony; it is to the credit of certain elements in the American intellectual climate, as well as to their personal stature as artists, that they became metaphysical novelists instead. Obviously such a description must apply to the artists treated here in widely different ways and in different degrees, but when they were writing most intensely they were intent on discovering and defining a reality that the traditions and orthodoxy of the Old World had pre-sented pre-packaged to the European novelists to do with what they would. If the American novelists were deprived of great riches, it is also true that the starkness of their situation invited extraordinary creative originality. It was a situation in which the artist had to be great or abdicate his role entirely. And it is true that America produced several of the greatest novels written in English in the nineteenth century (in *Moby Dick* quite probably the greatest), but no minor novels that we can take very seriously.

I hope I have not suggested that what the great American novelists of the period in question have in common is mainly a matter of deprivation, though it is, of course, in the shadow of deprivation that the truly great ones have made their beginning. Our concern in the following pages is with common problems growing out of that common deprivation; problems which the novelists with whom we shall be dealing could not have shirked without a loss of intellectual integrity or stature. If we agree with Sir Herbert Read that form is the natural effect of the poet's integrity, then it is also the stance in which, as a creative artist, he meets and resolves those problems that form the medium in which he lives his intellectual and emotional life.

The American novelists whose works we shall consider in the following pages are Cooper, Hawthorne, Melville, and Henry James. Under the wide diversity of types their art represents, we are aware of a concealed fellowship among them. I have already suggested, somewhat obliquely, the nature or the grounds of the resemblance, but I should like to be more explicit. The likeness does not exist in the texture of their writings, or their enthusiasms or aversions, though these elements may, on occasion, play their parts. It is not even, strictly speaking, rooted in their technical equipment as artists, although it colours that equipment and enriches it. Mr. Allen Tate has a passage that is suggestive in his essay, 'Techniques in Fiction':

> There are 'good' popular novelists who have done much to make us physically at home in our own country; they have given us

our scenes, our people, and above all our history; and these were necessary to the preliminary knowledge of ourselves, which we have been a little late in getting and which must be got and assimilated if we are going to be a mature people. Possibly the American novel had to accomplish the task that in Europe had been done by primitive chronicle, memoire, ballad, strolling player. The American novel has had to find a new experience, and only in our time has it been able to pause for the difficult task of getting itself written. That is an old story with us, yet beneath it lies a complexity of feeling that from Hawthorne down to our time has baffled our best understanding.[4]

The American novel has had to find a new experience and discover how to put that experience into art. And the process by which it has been done was one of progressive self-discovery for the nation. Mr. Tate is speaking of 'popular' novelists, and perhaps he is thinking more of the surfaces of American life then of the more inaccessible problems and conflicts. But the preliminary knowledge of ourselves out of which mature art grows is no more a sense of one's own people and history than of one's own tensions and inner struggles. Indeed, these *are* one's history and one's sense of racial self. And yet the deepest tensions that have contributed to establishing the American identity are extremely elusive. They are ultimately grounded in the sense of deprivation I spoke of before, the sense of being without certain kinds of reality that men ought to have: the sense that there is a world of abstract ideas and ideals, and a world of bitter fact, but no society or tradition or orthodoxy in which the two worlds can interact and qualify each other. If we are justified in searching 'popular' American fiction in the nineteenth century for a mirror image of ourselves, shall we be less justified in searching the works of the great American novelists for some clue to what those characteristic spiritual problems—intensified by the deprivations of American society —may have been, and possibly are? Referring to this deeper and more complex question, Mr. Tate names Hawthorne as a significant starting point. But I think the problem may be presented on a more elementary and unambiguous level if we move a step farther back in time to Hawthorne's greatest predecessor in American fiction, James Fenimore Cooper.

Behind much of Cooper's writing there is a fundamental conflict or tension that grows out of his sense of American society and history. In successive novels he tried to solve this tension, but without complete success. This tension was inherited later by such novelists as Hawthorne, Melville, and James, who saw it in different lights and colours, and they too tried to resolve it—each in his own way. It is, then, at this point of crucial strain in American experience that the writers to be treated here resemble each other. Each great, or even successful, work of art is an attempt to surmount a crisis in experience. The crisis is both private and impersonal; both cruelly one's own, and participating in the wide cycle of history. This tension which passed down from Cooper through Hawthorne and Melville to James is, at bottom, a matter of American history; and yet each writer felt it intimately as his own. It is because each suffered it privately in his unique way that we sometimes lose sight of how they also suffered it in common. The tension I am speaking of has grown more complex with time, and it is therefore worthwhile to trace it back, if we can, to its earliest distinguished expression in our literature.

In its most basic definition this tension was the result of a struggle to close the split in American experience, to discover a unity that, for the artist especially, almost sensibly *was not there*. The nature of the division that supported this conflict was partly determined by those deprivations in American society I have discussed above: deprivations of which the practising American novelist was deeply aware, for they confronted him with a society in which the abstract idea and the concrete fact could find little common ground for creative interaction. From a more positive point of view the division took on many different forms concurrently: it was an opposition between tradition and progress, between democratic faith and disillusion, between the past and the present and future; between Europe and America, liberalism and conservatism, aggressive acquisitive economics and benevolent wealth. These same divisions existed in Europe also, but there they were ballasted by a denser social medium, a richer sense of the past, a more inhibited sense of material possibilities. At bottom the tension is political in character. But it is in Cooper that we are able to trace its political grounding most clearly, and to

see how the tension in its political sense is at one with the tension
in its social, economic, and international senses.

At this point I should like to offer some explanation of the
apportionment of space allotted to the novelists treated in
the following chapters. I am not concerned with presenting
here a series of critical evaluations of each novelist in his turn,
but in discovering what elements, if any, common among them
all, may be isolated as characterizing a tradition in the novel
that is distinctly American. I have looked for these common
elements, not in American manners, conventions, or language,
but in the very structure of thought and in the nature of the
emotional drive out of which each novelist created. I have
done this because, as I said above, the absence of a traditional
social medium in America compelled the original American
artist to confront starkly his own emotional and spiritual
needs which his art then became the means of comprehending
and analysing. It is in this hidden and comparatively inaccessible area that we must look for the roots of any generalization
about form in the American novel. In the following pages it
will be found that I treat the work of Fenimore Cooper at
somewhat greater length than that of Melville, or Henry James,
but no comparative evaluation is implied thereby. Although I
believe with Joseph Conrad that Cooper 'is a rare artist' [5] and
that he can sometimes reach 'the heights of inspired vision', [6]
my purpose in treating him at greater length in the present
context than the other writers is practical: he touches the argument at more points than they.

In writing of Hawthorne my principal concern will be the
tension between isolation and social sympathy which is,
perhaps, the dominant theme of his work. Melville touches my
argument principally in the conflict between democratic faith
and despair; James, in the everlasting dialectic between Europe
and America. These respective tensions are all reflections, at
different levels, of the basic split or tension in American experience. But Cooper reflects this basic tension not in one, but in
various ways. His work shows us, for example, the creative
tension between aristocracy and democracy, but operating in
a very different mode from that 'tension between a middle class
and an aristocracy' which Mr. Lionel Trilling, in an earlier
quotation, mentioned as 'the real basis of the novel'. We also

find the tension between acquisitive economics and benevolent wealth—one of the most persistent of the American historical tensions—becoming a structural idea out of which he shapes the form of at least one of his novels. Most fundamental of all, he celebrates the tension between the American wilderness (which emotionally corresponds to the solitude of Hawthorne) and the new American industrial civilization. He endeavours to resolve these tensions artistically in specific novels in ways that make them ideal platforms on which to demonstrate how abstractions rather than manners became the material out of which the American novelist constructed the form of his art. Intellectually he was far more deeply and sensitively aware of the political grounding of these tensions he was dealing with in his novels than any of his successors, and by virtue of that awareness we are able to see more clearly the relation between certain abiding factors in American history and the disturbing problems which became the substance of his fictions, and of other writers' fictions later on. Chronologically he stands at the beginning. 'He wrote', as Conrad said, 'before the great American language was born,' [7] and in that clear and simple light one is able to trace the outlines of the problems dealt with here, more unambiguously and more simply in their relations, than in Melville's metaphysical shadows or James's nuanced atmosphere. In his modest way he stands at or near the beginning of the symbolist tradition in American fiction—that tradition by which the American artist was able to overcome, in a handful of great books, the impoverishment of his social milieu. This is a role with which Cooper has rarely, if ever, been credited,[8] but Natty Bumppo is, as I shall endeavour to show, a beautifully realized symbol through which Cooper expresses his highly complex reaction to American civilization.

But before proceeding to an analysis of Cooper's novels I should like to sketch in very briefly the background against which these tensions developed. To do so adequately would require a much longer study than is possible here, but even a slight sketch may add weight to our later discussion of the novels. As the tensions I have been speaking of are, in some considerable part, a reflection of tensions that existed in the early intellectual climate of America, it may be possible to avoid a random discursiveness by concentrating on the writings of those political theorists of the national formative period whose political and social doctrines, meeting in polemical hostility, not only established the shape of the Republic, but generated that variegated pattern of tensions that are to be so largely the subject of the present argument.

II

A Sketch for an
Historical Background

I

ALTHOUGH I have stated this theory of a creative tension
in American experience in a way I have not encountered
elsewhere, the idea in some form or other is by no means a new
one. It cropped up, for example, some twenty years ago in
Parrington's *Main Currents in American Thought*. In his 'Introduction' to Volume I, Parrington traces the formation of
America to the confluence of contrary tendencies that ultimately
exhibit a democratic or a conservative bias. There is little
point in discussing Parrington here except to say that any
resemblance between his position and that of the present book
is only momentary. Mr. Lionel Trilling's criticism of Parrington
in his essay, 'Reality in America', reprinted in *The Liberal
Imagination*, offers a definition of this 'tension' that is more nearly
in accord with my own meaning:

> Parrington's characteristic weakness as a historian is suggested
> by his title, for the culture of a nation is not truly figured in the
> image of the current. A culture is not a flow, nor even a con-
> fluence; the form of its existence is struggle, or at least debate—it
> is nothing if not a dialectic. And in any culture there are likely
> to be certain artists who contain a large part of the dialectic within
> themselves, their meaning and power lying in their contradic-
> tions; they contain within themselves, it may be said, the very
> essence of the culture, and the sign of this is that they do not sub-
> mit to serve the ends of any one ideological group or tendency. It
> is a significant circumstance of American culture, and one which
> is susceptible of explanation, that an unusually large proportion
> of its notable writers of the nineteenth century were such re-
> positories of the dialectic of their times—they contained both the
> yes and the no of their culture, and by that token they were
> prophetic of the future.[1]

In speaking of a 'resolution' of tensions in the pages that
follow, I shall not mean by that a progressive excursion into,

and colonization of, some discovered 'truth'—political, social or whatever; but the achievement of that vital point within the given work of art at which divergent energies reverse themselves towards a moment of creative balance and harmony, at least for the duration of our response.

The 'Preface' of a popular book on the American novel begins with a 'safe' confession of faith that, since Parrington, has become merely conventional: 'The bias of the book is democratic, its belief is in the potential of democratic society, and especially American society, as the only mature form of our communal life.' [2] Such an attitude, which is common today, cancels out any sensitive awareness of those complicated urgencies that have motivated the best of classical American literature. The great classical American writers were too seriously concerned with the frightening range of their political and social alternatives to be capable of any such facile or electioneering statements. If their predilections were for democracy, there were cross currents at work in their times and their consciousness that contributed depth and complexity to their attitudes.

For the purpose of the present chapter I wish to isolate only one of these complexities: their sense that what was good in the American democratic ideal was defined and guarded by its relation to a European aristocratic ideal of which, they, as the offspring of European, and particularly British, ancestry, were no less the heirs. In later chapters I shall analyse the several ways in which this tension between the democratic and the aristocratic attitudes helped to shape the form of the American novel, and refined its texture in the work of the greatest practitioners of American fiction. The Americans of the opening nineteenth century had one great advantage over their descendants, of course: the word 'democracy' had not yet become the slightly obnoxious shibboleth that it is today. It was still possible to investigate its claims seriously and critically. It did not induce narcosis, but an imaginative intensity that stimulated creative effort.

The sensibilities of the novelists we are to consider here were sharpened by their knowledge of the urgency of issues that were ultimately political in nature, although they may not always have defined them under that term. To understand the intellectual and moral climate on which the novelists drew it is important to understand the genesis of this tension, and we may do so most easily in the writings of those political theorists who helped to form the fabric of the American government during its great formative period. The three figures I have chosen to consider here are John Adams, Alexander Hamilton, and Jefferson. The writings of these three men are germinal sources of three great conflicting attitudes that run through the best American fiction of the nineteenth century up to James. In the regal republicanism of John Adams we find the most complete expression of that aristocratic bias which was to stiffen the democratic principles of Cooper, Hawthorne, and James. In Hamilton we find the ground of this bias shifting from birth, merit and landed property, to money, and thereby introducing a feeling of insecurity and guilt that was to run through novels as far removed from each other as *The Bravo* and *The Ivory Tower*. In Jefferson we have the swing towards democracy in the modern sense, but in him it is a credo, at least on the practical and administrative levels, that is controlled by his sense of the opposite values. In the final view, the antagonism between Jefferson and Adams is more apparent than real; but both are equally the enemies of Hamilton. The best tradition in the American novel incorporates tensions that are the expression of the antagonism between the fundamental attitudes expressed in the writings of these men. It is in their writings, if anywhere, that we shall find 'the yes and the no' of American culture, and find it in its starkest expression. Cooper certainly knew the writings of Adams and Jefferson, and it is safe to assume that Hawthorne and James did also; but it is not my purpose to establish a direct relation. The important thing is that certain problems occurred and recurred in the intellectual climate of America, and these were present in their own way to her greatest novelists hardly less than to her greatest political writers. And these problems shaped the form of American fictional thought no less than of American political thought.

II

John Adams's substantial contribution to the formation of the national American government is summed up succinctly in this sentence: 'Without Adams, the preservation of the dignified ideal of lawful, representative government and a great example of Bolingbroke's ideal "Patriot King" who comes to guard like an "angel" the destiny and long range interests of his country might not have been realized.' [3] But the effect of Adam's political wisdom on the government itself was slighter than the impact of his writings on the imagination of his contemporaries. If Adams was a Tory after the fashion of Samuel Johnson, that fact was not always considered a virtue by his fellow Americans. It was certainly of John Adams that the writer in William Duane's *National Gazette* was thinking when he wrote:

> British habits, British affections, ideas, attachments, prejudices, and even resentments, have vegetated rapidly in this country since the late war. No better evidence of this truth is wanting than the torrent of abuse daily poured from many of the American presses by the vile tools of British ministerialism and British king-worshippers against the republicans and patriots of France. . . . If the enlightened citizens of America know not how to venerate the French, and would not be considered in Europe, and by every consistent character here as degenerate from their manly principles of 1776, they will turn in abhorrence from the men, who by the aid of the press are endeavouring to prejudice the community against France, and to excite the sympathy of the public in favour of royalty, eternally extirpated as it is from this country, and from the hearts of all true Americans. [4]

When that was written Adams had just shortly discontinued his long series of papers in Fenno's *Gazette of the United States* which were marked by strong monarchical sympathies. *Discourses on Davila*, written as they were by the first Vice-President, caused such a storm of protest that Adams had thought it politically expedient to cut them short, but a good deal of damage had already been done as the *Discourses* continued to supply ammunition to Adams's enemies for years to come. Nevertheless, *Discourses on Davila*, along with *Defense of the Constitutions of Government of the United States of America*, helped to define a tone of mind and an attitude which has persisted, although the role of John Adams in shaping and perpetuating it is not commonly recognized.

'I only contend', wrote Adams in the first volume of the *Defense*,

that the English Constitution is, in theory, the most stupendous
fabric of human invention, both for the adjustment of the balance,
and the prevention of its vibrations, and that the Americans
ought to be applauded instead of censured for having imitated it
as far as they have. Not the formation of languages, not the whole
art of navigation and shipbuilding, does more honour to the
human understanding than this system of government.[5]

In all likelihood the true base of Adams's admiration for
the British Constitution was a natural affinity with, and an
honest love for, England. Jefferson certainly placed Adams
among those 'characters . . . high in office . . . hostile to France
and fondly looking to England as the staff of their hope', who
only tolerated republicanism as 'a stepping stone to monarchy'. [6]
But perhaps a more reliable explanation of his admiration for
the British is to be found in Adams's conception of human
nature, and the pattern of its operation in society. Out of this
grew Adams's insistence on the necessity of aristocratic government as the only safeguard, when correctly checked and
balanced, of human liberties. For Adams, unlike Jefferson,
thought of liberty not as an abstraction imposed on life from
without, but as a condition of practical living that could only
be achieved by a due regard for human conditions as they
were. At no moment was he ever capable of the non-human,
abstracting fanaticism of the French Revolutionary heroes
whom Jefferson, especially in his private utterances, liked to
honour. His cousin, Samuel Adams, who was troubled by a pro-
pensity to mouth revolutionary slogans, received an exemplary
correction at his hands:

'The love of liberty,' you say, 'is interwoven in the soul of man.'
So it is, according to La Fontaine, in that of a wolf, and I doubt
whether it be much more rational, generous, or social, in the one
than in the other, until in man it is enlightened by experience,
reflection, education, and civil and political institutions, which
are at first produced, and constantly supported and improved by
a few; that is, by the nobility.[7]

Adams does not favour an élite because he has contempt for
the people or their liberties. It is because he understands that
the human heart, however good its intentions, cannot be trusted
long:

Though we allow benevolence and generous affections to exist in the human breast, yet every moral theorist will allow the selfish passions in the generality of men to be the strongest. There are few who love the public better than themselves, though they all may have some affection for the public. We are not, indeed, commanded to love our neighbour better then ourselves. Self-interest, private avidity, ambition, and avarice, will exist in every state of society, and under every form of government.[8]

It is not, then, we gather from this passage (and there are many others that might be quoted equally well), the people considered as a class who are to be distrusted, but the basic constitution of human nature in *all* classes. Self-interest is at the heart of all human activity, and the only way to curb and discipline it in government is to organize government in a tripartite way, in such a manner that each division, devoted to its own power and interests, will continually balance off the others, the two weaker components regularly forming a defensive alliance against the third factor which may happen to be the strongest at any given moment. It is the great achievement of the English Constitution that it has balanced these divisions in the Sovereign, the Lords and the Commons.[9]

Just as human nature is governed in all its actions by self-interest, one of the most important considerations of self-interest in promoting aristocracy is vanity and the desire for esteem. Adams confessed in his old age that he was a vain and a weak man, and that was the opinion of a large number of his contemporaries. But his vanity was of the most amiable kind. It was undoubtedly a very personal perception when Adams declared :

> The desire of the esteem of others is as real a want of nature as hunger; and the neglect and contempt of the world as severe a pain as the gout or stone. It sooner and oftener produces despair, and a detestation of existence; of equal importance to individuals, to families, and to nations. It is a principal end of government to regulate this passion, which in its turn becomes a principal means of government.[10]

This desire for distinction naturally recommended a government in which royal insignia, orders, garters, ribbons, etc., were widely used.

What is it that bewitches mankind to marks and signs? A

ribbon? a garter? a golden key? a marshal's staff? or a white hickory stick? Though there is in such frivolities as these neither profit nor pleasure, nor anything amiable, estimable, or respectable, yet experience teaches us, in every country of the world, they attract the attention of mankind more than parts of learning, virtue or religion. They are, therefore, sought with ardour, very often, by men possessed in the most eminent degree, of all the more solid advantages of birth and fortune, merit and services, with the best faculties of the head, and the most engaging recommendations of the heart.[11]

Adams particularly admired the Romans on this score, and through the prose of the following passage, written while Adams was Vice-President, we can hear the somewhat naïve tone of ardent espousement which has remained a perpetual possibility for nostalgic American republicans since Adams's day:

Has there ever been a nation who understood the human heart better than the Romans, or made a better use of the passion for consideration, congratulation, and distinction? . . . *Distinctions* of *conditions*, as well as of ages, were made by differences of clothing. The laticlave or large flowing robe, studded with broad spots of purple, the ancient distinction of their kings, was, after the establishment of the consulate, worn by the senators through the whole period of the republic and empire. The tribunes of the people were, after their institution, admitted to wear the same venerable signal of sanctity and authority. The augusticlave, or smaller robe, with narrower studs of purple, was the distinguishing habit of Roman knights, and was not permitted to be worn by any other citizens. The praetext, or long white robe, reaching down to the ankles, bordered with purple, which was worn by the principal magistrates, such as consuls, praetors, censors, and sometimes on solemn festivals by senators. The chairs of ivory; the lictors; the rods; the axes; the crowns of gold; of ivory; of flowers; of herbs; of laurel branches; and of oak leaves; the civil and mural crowns; their ovations; and their triumphs; everything in religion, government, and common life, among the Romans, was parade, representation and ceremony. . . . And this was the true spirit of republics, in which form of government there is no other consistent method of preserving order, or procuring admission to the laws.[12]

And Adams, as is well known, was notorious for his devotion

to titles. It is easy enough to interpret all this, in the light of some of the personal anecdotes we have of his character, as mere pomposity. But on the most serious level of his thought, Adams was intensely aware of the eternal fact of inequality, and with a classic taste for order, he saw no better way of dealing with it than by admitting that hieratic status existed. Adams could speak with the full weight of the eighteenth century at its best:

> Nature, which has established in the universe a chain of being and universal order, descending from archangels to microscopic animalicules, has ordained that no two objects shall be perfectly alike, and no two creatures perfectly equal.[13]

In America, Adams said, there are three kinds of inequality —wealth, birth, and merit. Surveying his native province, Massachusetts, Adams beholds a state of moral and political equality, with no artificial distinctions. But looking closer he is struck by how deeply people are divided on the score of property, and even by the various ways in which they come into the possession of their fortunes. The rich men inevitably have, according to their degree of wealth, large numbers of the poor dependent on them, and this gives them influence. But even apart from obligation and dependence, Adams argues, 'among the wisest people that live, there is a degree of admiration, abstracted from all dependence, obligation, expectation, or even acquaintance, which accompanies splendid wealth . . .' [14] As an old man, his eye still testily focused on this fact, Adams could write in a private letter of the power of wealth in America: 'Would Washington have ever been commander of the revolutionary army or president of the United States, if he had not married the rich widow of Mr. Custis? Would Jefferson ever have been president of the United States if he had not married the daughter of Mr. Wales?' [15]

In dealing with inequalities of birth, Adams argues that advantages deriving from this are greater in free republics than in monarchies. Even the free villages in New England tend to elect their offices from the same families over a succession of generations. If hereditary legal descent is avoided, as in America,

> a nobility must and will exist though without the name, as really

as in countries where it is hereditary; for the people, by their elections, will continue the government generally in the same families from generation to generation. Descent from certain parents, and inheritance of certain houses, lands, and other visible objects, will eternally have such an influence over the affections and imaginations of the people, as no arts or institutions of policy will control.[16]

And in still another place Adams argues that Chancellor Livingston inherited a name, a fine manor house, and influential family connections that gave him more influence in America than the Duke of Norfolk possessed in England.[17]

Adams did not believe that, simply because an aristocracy was 'natural' and not hereditary it was not also possessed of external insignia and artifical signs of rank. He noted with a good deal of shrewdness what has since been frequently observed —that Americans are much impressed by titles:

> The pompous trumpery of ensigns, armorials, and escutcheons are not, indeed, far advanced in America. Yet there is a more general anxiety to know their originals, in proportion to their numbers, than in any nation in Europe; arising from the easier circumstances and higher spirit of the common people. And there are certain families in every state equally attentive to all the proud frivolities of heraldry.[18]

The natural aristocracy arising out of the inequalities of wealth, descent, and merit or talent—to which, on occasion, Adams also adds beauty and grace of movement—[19] is seen to be, in his argument, based on human nature itself. But although Adams differentiates between the natural and the hereditary aristocracies, in practice he tends to merge them in the tone in which he deals with them. The distinction that remains is only a logical one, and this is also true of the Federalist political newspapers of the day: 'Take away thrones and crowns from men and there will soon be an end of all dominion and justice,' was a theme of a leading article in Fenno's *Gazette of the United States*.[20] The whole Federalist temper during the first decade of the government was not disinclined to elevate John Adams's 'natural aristocracy' into a more organized and secure class than the phrase itself suggests.

Although titles might be abolished, Adams maintained that

distinctions would never be, that to be well-born was as important in America as in Europe. Years later he was to write
to John Taylor of Caroline:

> Has not the experience of six thousand years shown that the
> common people submit more easily and more quietly to birth
> than to wealth, genius, fame or any other talents? . . . There is
> nothing, Mr. Taylor, to which the vulgar, in general, so quietly
> and patiently and cordially submit as to birth.[21]

Adams realized that an aristocracy of wealth did not represent the values he wanted, and it was this, one guesses, that led
him to stress birth and illustrious descent more and more :

> As the pride of wealth produced nothing but meanness of senti-
> ment and a sordid scramble for money; and the pride of birth
> produced some degree of emulation in knowledge and virtue; the
> wisdom of nations has endeavoured to employ one prejudice to
> counteract another; the prejudice in favour of birth to moderate,
> correct, and restrain the prejudice in favour of wealth.[22]

That, indeed, was written as early as *Discourses on Davila*,
but as Adams grew older he came more and more to see that
the prejudice in favour of wealth was sweeping everything
before it; that the new financial aristocracy was destroying
all other values. His opposition to the financial measures of
Hamilton, which were designed to give overwhelming power
to the aristocracy of wealth, was instrumental in causing the
downfall of the Federalist party, and Adams found himself
moving, with his aristocratic prejudices still intact, towards his
final reconciliation with Jefferson.

The aristocratic bias which one finds in the novels of Cooper
and James clearly has an important intellectual antecedent in
the political philosophy of Adams. And just as the aristocratic
bias in the novelists is subtly counterpointed with democratic
principles and sentiments, so we find this oscillation between the
two poles in Adams also. In 1811, when Benjamin Rush was
endeavouring to bring about a reconciliation between the two
men whom political divergences had caused to drift apart,
Adams outlined the differences between his and Jefferson's
views of life, and it is apparent that Adams realized that a
large part of their political quarrel was more apparent than
real. 'Jefferson and Rush were for liberty and straight hair,'

Adams wrote. 'I thought that curled hair was as republican as straight.' [23]

Reviewing Adams's theory of government one may conclude that he kept America closer than anyone else to the model provided by the English Constitution, and at a time when the American imagination was in danger of turning towards France. It held up to that imagination those patterns of dignified and hieratic behaviour which were as native to American as to English blood. If Adams's contribution to the actual fabric of government itself was surpassed by that of some others, the dignity and power of the *tone* with which he invested his doctrine of regal republicanism has had a permanent effect on the sensibility of a culturally important minority. 'The Prince of Orange, William V,' Adams wrote, 'in a conversation with which he honoured me in 1788, was pleased to say, that "he had read over our new constitution", and he added, "Monsieur, vous allez avoir un roi, sous le titre de président." ' [24] The sense one finally has of Adams is the degree to which, while retaining his republican convictions undiminished, such a remark was capable of pleasing him. He guaranteed that the American imagination should not be cut off from the refreshment and stimulus of aristocratic conceptions, and this alone was a great gift to the American creative artist in later generations.

Adams's own attitude towards the fine arts in America was sensible, but a little unexciting :

> It is not indeed the fine arts which our country requires; the useful, the mechanic arts are those which we have occasion for in a young country as yet simple and not far advanced in luxury, although perhaps much too far for her age and character. . . . I must study politics and war, that my sons have liberty to study mathematics and philosophy, geography, natural history and naval architecture, navigation, commerce, and agriculture, in order to give their children a right to study painting, poetry, music, architecture, statuary, tapestry, and porcelain. [25]

But despite the modesty of his disclaimer, Adams was serving the arts better than he knew by demonstrating the reconciliability of his liberal republicanism, as sturdy as that of any of the Founding Fathers, with aristocratic manners of thought and conduct. The aristocracy he favoured was English.

'England alone was the Europe of the Americans,' Talleyrand wrote in 1796;[26] and working with, shaping, this natural inclination in the Americans, Adams created a strong and enduring bias which was to find its reflection on other levels in the pages of some of the greatest American novelists.

III

As an old man Adams wrote to Benjamin Rush concerning Jefferson: 'I know of no difference between him and myself relative to the Constitution, or to forms of government in general.' [27] That was more than either of them could have said of Hamilton. It is for this reason that the relation between Adams and Jefferson is particularly interesting. In Adams we see how the English bias gradually finds itself at ease with the democratic philosophy of Jefferson—a fact of importance for the future of American literature; whereas the English bias, as represented by Hamilton, rigidifies itself in the business interests of America, and finally loses all traces of dignity in the Republican vulgarity of the Gilded Age. Mr. H. B. Parkes, with perhaps a touch of optimism, has written: 'Of all great men who have contributed to the development of the United States, Hamilton was the least American.' [28]

Basing his philosophy of government on postulates and attitudes that began by resembling Adams's, in effect Hamilton subtly distorted the vocabulary and meaning of Adams's writings until the old division between the rich and the poor, marshalled against each other in Adams's tripartite state for their mutual benefit and security, was placed in an entirely new perspective, and one for which Adams himself had no sympathy. For Adams, property meant land, and behind his talk of an aristocracy there still persisted the High Tory ideal (already a little old-fashioned) of a class invested with landed wealth and alive to its traditional responsibilities in society. In practice Adams found that this ideal tended to sink its differences with Jefferson's conception of an agrarian republic. But what was to happen to Adams's view when the nobles, no longer landed aristocrats but factory owners, counted their wealth not in acres but in men employed at the lowest possible wage? Adams's view of wealth and social structure was in danger of becoming quaint in Hamilton's America. Instead, it was meta-morphosed into a kind of sphinx with aristocratic head and shoulders and a speculator's body.

England was at the beginning of the Industrial Revolution, and when Hamilton became first Secretary of the Treasury in March, 1790, the United States, with a little encouragement, was ready to follow suit. There was a strong and wealthy Federalist merchant class in America who already identified their interests with those of England, and if America was still mainly agrarian, the moment was rapidly approaching when new capitalist interests were to be created, with a consequent transfer of power and influence from land to industry and finance. Backed by the extreme pro-British party, Hamilton's series of financial reforms changed the economic face of America in a few years to an extent hardly paralleled by the political revolution which the country had recently undergone.* These new capitalist interests were able to seize the vocabulary which Adams had used with such purity, even with such nobility of motive, and subvert it to their own uses. Hamilton endowed Adams's vocabulary with a new set of meanings which the second President in a long series of letters written later in life was to disavow. Mr. Zoltán Haraszti sums up the differences between the two men very clearly:

> He [Adams] uses the words 'the rich and well born' almost as often as Hamilton. But there was a difference. For Hamilton the 'rich' meant primarily the capitalists, whereas Adams hated the banks and paper money and, like Jefferson, hoped that America would remain agrarian for centuries to come. He could see, he wrote to John Taylor, no more impropriety in well born 'than in the epithets *well bred, well educated, well brought up, well taught*' and so on, pouring out some thirty such combinations.[29]

I should like to glance here at one or two passages which illustrate both the similarity and the difference of Hamilton's terminology as compared with Adams's. Here is Hamilton on the well born:

> All communities divide themselves into the few and the many. The first are rich and well born, the other the mass of the people. The voice of the people has been said to be the voice of God; and,

* See Appendix A.

however generally this maxim has been quoted and believed, it is not true to fact. The people are turbulent and changing; they seldom judge or determine right. Give, therefore, to the first class a distinct permanent share in the government. They will check the unsteadiness of the second; and as they cannot receive any advantage by a change, they therefore will ever maintain good government. Can a democratic assembly, who annually revolve in the mass of the people, be supposed to pursue steadily the public good? Nothing but a permanent body can check the imprudence of democracy. Their turbulent and uncontrollable disposition requires checks.[30]

At the Constitutional Convention in 1787 he had desired a First Magistrate and an upper house elected for life, or at least during good behaviour, and nothing chagrined him more than the republican form which emerged from that assembly. If he supported the Constitution vehemently during the fight for ratification, it was because he saw, from an early date, that no other form would be acceptable to the people to whom it must be presented. In the passage just quoted, Hamilton speaks of checks, but he is interested in checks for the lower house only. And the phrase, 'the mass of the people', is peculiar to the first Treasurer. There is an implication of the proletarian nature of the masses in the nuance. In the opposition between classes as envisaged by Hamilton there is no idea of functional co-operation, as was the case in Adams's theory. The mass of the people exist mainly as human raw material to be exploited by the new capitalists whom his reforms were creating:

Besides this advantage of occasional employment to classes having different occupations, there is another, of a nature allied to it, and of a similar tendency. This is the employment of persons who would otherwise be idle, and in many cases, a burden on the community, either from bias of temper, infirmity of body, or some other cause, indisposing or disqualifying them for the toils of the country. It is worthy of particular remark, that, in general, women and children are rendered more useful, and the latter more early useful, by manufacturing establishments, than they would otherwise be. Of the number of persons employed in the cotton manufacturies of Great Britain, it is computed that four sevenths, nearly, are women and children; of whom the greatest proportion are children, and many of them of a tender age.[31]

With this conception of the predominant importance of manufactures Adams was no less out of sympathy than Jefferson. But above all Adams had a conception of individual dignity that was in direct contrast with the ugly attitude that peers through Hamilton's prose. The differences between Adams and Hamilton are not merely superficial differences of temperament. They lead into radically different views on the most pressing questions of the day. Yet even on the question of banking and paper capital the vocabulary which Adams had used in *Discourses on Davila* and *Defense of the Constitutions* was so skilfully appropriated by Hamilton that it did service for both. An enemy of Hamilton's financial reforms, John Taylor of Caroline, wrote of the Bank which Hamilton had established as the keystone of his entire financial programme: '. . . a design for erecting aristocracy and monarchy is subsisting—that a *money impulse*, and not the public good, is operating on Congress; and that taxes are imposed upon motives other than the general welfare'.[32] I quote this here only to indicate how an opponent of the Bank could take over the vocabulary which Adams had used in the *Defense* (of which book Taylor was a profound student) and apply it to the very different economic reality with which Hamilton was concerned.

The importance of Hamilton's programme from our point of view is that the financial interests he created, deriving their prosperity from commercial relations with England, guaranteed the perpetuation of a strong pro-British strain of feeling among the wealthy American business classes throughout the nineteenth century. The whole subject is an extremely unwieldy one to treat under the best circumstances, but where space is so limited the difficulty becomes nearly insuperable. The proclivity of the early American business class, as Talleyrand pointed out in his *Memoir concerning Commercial Relations of the United States with England*, was already in the direction of Britain even before Hamilton came on the scene. All that he did was to utilize a bias and construct it into an enduring policy. The whole history of the period, from Hamilton's influence in securing the passage of the Jay Treaty, which secured peace with England at a critical juncture, to Timothy Pickering's plan for bringing about the secession of New England in the interests of commercial amity with Great Britain—the whole history of the period points to a state of affairs perfectly designed to promote Hamilton's schemes. Summing up the period, Henry Adams wrote, 'As a force in the affairs of Europe, the United States had become an appendage to England.' [33]

Hamilton's programme was assured of permanency when it was able to consolidate in one great party all those scattered economic interests in the country, but primarily in New England and New York, which thrived on trade with Great Britain. John Adams was devoted to the spiritual and intellectual heritage of England; Hamilton admired British power and sovereignty in the world, and he was more interested in the successful operation of British finances than he was in English political philosophies or those essential decencies which Adams thought he found in English law more than anywhere else in the world. Through these two men, so radically opposed in most respects, Great Britain made her greatest impact on American life and thought. Their respective conceptions of what constituted the fineness of England were different, but both conceptions have entered into the pattern.

It may be objected that what I have said here hardly applies to the post-Civil War period. But during the Gilded Age the economic reciprocity between England and America was greater than ever before, and the design which had been laid in the days of Hamilton was suddenly enlarged and strengthened in the aftermath of the War Between the States. To understand how this happened it is necessary to glance, however briefly, at the economic history of the period.

Just before the middle of the century England overhauled her whole economic pattern by repealing the ancient Corn Laws which had imposed protective duties on grain. Protective tariffs, impoverished soil, and high rents had automatically curtailed the growth of an industrial labouring class by the imposition of an agrarian economy which had for centuries kept in view the welfare of the landowning classes. But when it became possible to import cheap grain and large numbers of agricultural labourers were freed from the soil, capitalistic enterprise suddenly entered a period of extraordinary growth.

During the 1870's England turned to America more than to any other country for her supply of food. S. S. Cox, a New York Congressman, writing in 1879, said: 'By the repeal of the Corn

Laws, England enlarged the area of her agricultural resources. Free interchange annexed the food-growing acres of other nations. . . . The United States became practically a part of England.' England thus encouraged American agriculturists to put an increasing amount of land under cultivation, and encouraged the vast expansion of cattle raising. This sudden acquisition of a great new market led immediately to the building of railroads, the development of the steel industry, the manufacture of farm machinery, and this in turn promoted the growth of the American industrial class. To insure its food supply, English capital was eager to invest largely in American enterprise, and thus that reciprocity which Hamilton had seen as the basis of America's future wealth bore out his most sanguine hopes.[34]

But this new prosperity which was made possible by the English market for American products, by investments of English capital, and the extension of English credit, loosened an avalanche of materialism and vulgarity in American life that made reciprocity on any but a commercial level extremely difficult. Still, the new American moneyed classes were strengthened in their admiration for British institutions; but by this time it was a snob appeal of the worst sort that England held out to the American millionaires. Henry Adams, in his brilliant little novel, *Democracy*, which is a scathing indictment of the United States during the period, describes the attraction of English things for American capitalists:

In the middle of April a sudden social excitement started the indolent city of Washington to its feet. The Grand Duke and Duchess of Saxe-Baden-Hombourg arrived in America on a tour of pleasure, and in due course came on to pay their respects to the Chief Magistrate of the Union. The newspapers hastened to inform their readers that the Grand-Duchess was a royal princess of England, and, in want of any other social event, every one who had any sense of what was due to his or her own dignity, hastened to show this august couple the respect which all republicans who have a large income derived from business, feel for English royalty. New York gave a dinner, at which the most insignificant person present was worth at least a million dollars, and where the gentleman who sat by the Princess entertained her for an hour or two by a calculation of the aggregate capital represented. New York also gave a ball at which the Princess appeared in an ill-fitting black silk dress with mock lace and jet ornaments, among several hundred toilets that proclaimed the refined republican simplicity of their owners at a cost of several hundred thousand dollars.[35]

The economic reciprocity between the two countries in the 'seventies and 'eighties ended by destroying the conditions necessary for that great native art which was represented in the tradition of Hawthorne, Thoreau, and Melville. Deprived of a stage of operation at home, the American artist more than ever turned his eyes to Europe, and particularly to England. Thus we are faced with this paradox: that it was in England, whose gold had been instrumental in financing the Gilded Age, that the American artist sought spiritual solace. If to the American millionaires of business and finance England was the power image on which they wished to model their own enterprises, and if it represented the ideal of their most snobbish social aspirations, it also held out to the disinterested imagination a finer range of values. With little exaggeration England might be said to have been both the cause of and the medicine for the diseased American culture of the Gilded Age.

We have not come as far from Hamilton's financial programme in this discussion as might appear at first, for Hamilton is the very embodiment of the acquisitive spirit in the American tradition; or rather, he is its philosopher. Mr. Russell Kirk in *The Conservative Mind* remarks that 'industrialization of America which Hamilton promoted was burdened with consequences the haughty and forceful new aristocrat did not perceive',[36] and he proceeds to exercise a generosity towards him that seems to me misplaced. There is nothing in Hamilton's character that suggests he could not easily have adjusted his tastes to the worst excesses of his financial doctrines as they developed later.

To sum up some of the things that have been said here: from Adams we have the generous spirit of aristocracy, a taste for tradition, for English values that have been proved through generations; and he subtly blends these values into a ground of liberal republican sentiment. But from the first it was, or should have been, clear that Hamiltonianism would encourage a fatal imitativeness of English models. Literature was to be the handmaid of a wealthy commercial class whose taste in the arts was economically directed. It represented a class whose status was publicized by its servility to Britain—a servility that was uncreative in essence. *The Port Folio*, for example, published in Philadelphia from 1801, was not only America's first important literary magazine: it represented a deliberate attempt to blend Hamiltonianism and English taste into a native literary flavour that would be christened the genteel tradition in due course.* The intellectual distance that separates Barrett Wendell's *Literary History of America* from *The Port Folio* is considerably less than the century that separates it in time.

Hamilton's contribution to American letters, we may conclude, was none of the purest. But one element he did contribute that paid off better than the rest. He implanted a doubt in the minds of some of the artists who came later as to the innocence of wealth and large incomes. It was a problem that Cooper had to face, that troubled Hawthorne, and that James never quite satisfactorily resolved. And yet the mere presence of this doubt in their works is one of the marks by which we can separate the best American writers from the mere literary mouthpieces of the genteel tradition.

IV

The decline in John Fiske's reputation as an historian need not prevent us from conceding the truth in such a passage as the following:

> The swiftly and radically centralizing measures of Hamilton soon carried the Federalists onward to a new position, so that those who agreed with them in 1789 had come to dissent from them in 1793. It was thus in Washington's first administration that the seeds of all party differences hereafter to bear fruit in America were sown and sedulously nurtured. All American history has since run along the lines marked out by the antagonism between Jefferson and Hamilton. Our history is sometimes charged with lack of picturesqueness because it does not deal with the belted knight and the moated grange. But to anyone who considers the moral impact of events, it is hard to see how anything can be more picturesque than the spectacle of these giant antagonists contending for political measures which were so pro-

* See Appendix B.

foundly to affect the lives of millions of human beings yet unborn. Coleridge once said, with as fair an approximation to truth as is likely to be reached in such sweeping statements, that in philosophy all men must be Aristotelians or Platonists. So it may be said that in American politics all men must be disciples either of Jefferson or Hamilton.[37]

Fortunately, Hamilton is not the only embodiment of the alternative Fiske sees him as symbolizing, but the passage does personify, in terms of historical characters, a great basic tension in the American experience. Jefferson himself was aware of this tension, but from a somewhat different point of view. He wrote to Elbridge Gerry in 1797:

> Our countrymen have divided themselves by such strong affections to the French and the English, that nothing will secure us internally but a divorce from both nations; and this must be the object of every real American, and its attainment is practicable without much self-denial.[38]

Historically, Jefferson's statement places that 'split in American experience' of which we have already spoken at its simplest level, and in one of its most graphic guises. It comes from that period when the *Gazette of the United States* could describe a banquet held in Philadelphia for the French Ambassador at which the Liberty cap was handed from head to head, while at another tavern in the same city a group of gentlemen met to celebrate the birthday of His Britannic Majesty with toasts to George III, Queen Charlotte, George Washington, the prosperity and commerce of Great Britain and America, the Constitution of Great Britain, and 'the red coats and the wooden walls of Old England'.[39] It was that period when, as Jefferson wrote to Edward Rutledge, 'Men who have been intimate all their lives cross the streets to avoid meeting, and turn their heads another way, lest they should be obliged to touch their hats.'[40]

This, of course, is merely another way of putting it. All these conflicts and divisions between Jeffersonians and Hamiltonians, Francophiles and Anglophiles, democrats and aristocrats, agrarians and capitalists, progressives and conservatives, are ultimately only *one* division. Among themselves they represent 'the yes and the no' of American culture by examining it from opposed points of view as its central problems are continuously restated in shifting historical terms up to the present. The greatness of Adams and Jefferson lies in this: that while each was stubbornly what he was, each was endowed with a flexibility of mind and sensibility that carried with it the wonderful creative power of organically reshaping itself to meet the exigencies of change. This is not the shiftiness of expediency, but the expression of a disinterested intelligence and integrity that is animated by the processes of life. It is the faculty of reconciling opposites, of discovering new unities and new harmonies that are not discontinuous with the old. In short, it is the mark of creative intelligence, whether it is exercised in politics, in science, or in art. Today there is a kind of democratic American literature that has embalmed the axioms of Jefferson, and until we learn to distinguish between the creative principle in Jefferson's mind and the numerous pretenders to his tradition, we shall possess but little of that 'liberal imagination' on which Americans profess to draw larger drafts than anyone else in the world. And it is equally important that we should assess accurately the stereotyped conservatism, cut off from validly aristocratic roots, that represents the Hamiltonian tradition. What is alive and significant in American art is equally remote from either of these extremes, which are forms of intellectual and emotional death: it exists in a dialectical middle ground to which both extremes contribute, but which is essentially different from either.

Although Jefferson in 1797 was wishing to divorce the United States from affection to both France and England, few had done more than he to emphasize, during the opening years of the decade, that emotional division in the Americans. His letters of this period are filled with expressions of affection for the French and with hatred for the English. To take only one example from among many, he wrote of the French Revolution to William Short on January 3, 1793:

> The liberty of the whole earth was depending on the issue of the contest, and was ever such a prize won with so little blood? My own affections have been deeply wounded by some of the martyrs to this cause, but rather than it should have failed, I would have seen half the earth desolated. Were there but an Adam and an Eve left in every country, and left free, it would be better than as it now is. I have expressed to you my sentiments because

they are really those of 99 in an hundred of our citizens. The universal feasts and rejoicings which have lately been had on account of the successes of the French shewed the genuine effusions of their hearts. . . . There are in the United States some characters of opposite principles; some of them are in high office, others possessing great wealth, and all of them hostile to France and fondly looking to England as the staff of their hope. . . . Their prospects have certainly not brightened. Excepting them, this country is entirely republican, friends to the constitution, anxious to preserve it and to have it administered according to its own republican principles. The little party above mentioned have espoused it only as a stepping stone to monarchy, and have endeavoured to approximate it to that in its administration in order to render its final transition more easy. The successes of republicanism in France have given the *coup de grâce* to their prospects, and I hope to their projects.[41]

Certain things stand out about this passage. Jefferson, we notice, is in no danger of underestimating the strength of his own party, and there is a vivid emotional colouring throughout ; the issues, probabilities, and emphases are recreated in the medium of his imagination. It would be difficult to discover an American prose more remote, both in its vividness and warmth, from Hamilton's with its calculated line-treading air of impartiality and logical precision. The prose burgeons with exhilarated images that always entice Jefferson a little further than he really wants to go. The first half of the passage is dominated by the evocative image of a set of racial Adams and Eves that cast a glow of primal innocence over the revolutionary enterprise, and there is a sound of 'universal feasts and rejoicings' that give an air of gaiety and springtime to the 'rebirth' ceremony that is about to populate the earth with democrats. Then the prose takes on, in high spirited fashion, an almost operatic tone as the little conspiratorial group of 'characters of opposite principles' ('high in office'!) advance from the background hatching monarchical plots. Despite his deep earnestness, Jefferson reserved this freehanded style for his private correspondence, and part of its charm is that there is a kind of implicit self-raillery usually around the corner of the next sentence.

I have commented on the qualities of Jefferson's prose because they give the secret of his influence. Impressive as his writings are—and they are more so than Hamilton's, or even Adams's—they have, in spite of their volume, a certain desultory quality. Their strength is not in their consistency or coherence taken as a whole, but in their appeal to the imagination, to the warmth of life they are able to impart to ideas, to the sense of humanity they convey. His writings and attitudes do not readily submit to the kind of analysis to which Adams and Hamilton prove amenable. The acts of his administration frequently seem at odds with what we think of as Jeffersonianism. 'Jefferson's own administration,' as Arthur Schlesinger puts it, 'became a series of notations on the doom of his Utopia.' [42] In the end what we think of as Jeffersonianism is a kind of living presence that is capable of informing circumstances and situations that constantly change. What we have to understand is not a systematized body of writings, but a complex personality that brings to the shifting events of history a set of attitudes that is variable, but always centred in generosity of mind and faith in humane values. At the same time, it can be an insidious set of attitudes unless submitted to constant vigilance.

One of the most famous passages Jefferson ever wrote is from *Notes on Virginia*. Not only does this passage glow with the warmth of some pastoral American dream; it also suggests why, in a world and a nation rapidly becoming industrialized, Jefferson could not have afforded the virtue of consistency:

> Those who labour in the earth are the chosen people of God, if ever He had a chosen people, whose breasts He has made His peculiar deposit for substantial and genuine virtue. It is the focus in which He keeps alive that sacred fire, which otherwise might escape from the face of the earth. Corruption of morals in the mass of cultivators is a phenomenon of which no age nor nation has furnished an example. . . . While we have land to labour then, let us never wish to see our citizens occupied at a workbench, or twirling a distaff. . . . The mobs of great cities add just so much to the support of pure government, as sores do to the strength of the human body. [43]

This passage bears hardly more relation to a realistic assessment of American economics in Jefferson's day than Natty Bumppo's view of wealth and urban life. Essentially, it is a poetic evocation, and it scarcely contains a fact that is not suspect under scrutiny. Nevertheless, it is an expression of the American conscience at its best. It is a metaphorical affirmation of human integrity, a ritualistic gesture of dissent from the industrial philosophy that was taking over, and with which Jefferson himself would come to practical working arrangements without much difficulty. But its very quality of archaism illuminates that irreducible element of selfhood and personal dignity to which all societies, however remote in time, are entitled, and which the new industrial philosophy would presently threaten.

But Jefferson was also a practical administrator, and despite the partisan passion of his private utterances, few statesmen in power have been more moderate in dealing with opponents or in shaping policy. Hamilton's influence was of the most material kind: it consisted in raising up a moneyed machine, and a class of financial aristocrats capable of wresting power to themselves. As the good philosopher of regal republicanism, Adams's influence was intellectual. But Jefferson's has proved at once the most impalpable and the most valuable of all. It is, in the last analysis, an attitude of the spirit, and a profound faith in the possibilities of life.

Today it is commonly maintained by a certain class of writers that Jeffersonianism marks the beginning of the national genius. Thus, Claude G. Bowers in the 'Preface' to *The Young Jefferson* remarks that Jefferson 'definitely determined that ours should be a democratic republic'; and that 'The social and political theories that have come to be synonymous with what we call "Americanism" had been set forth by Jefferson before the inauguration of Washington.' [44] What Jefferson really did was to give form to that ambivalence which the conditions of American history had implanted in the national mind and sensibility by defining for the American imagination the democratic and 'French' side of the tension, and by demonstrating in a practical manner that if the two sides were opposed, they could also discover a *modus vivendi*. '. . . every difference of opinion is not a difference of principle', Jefferson had said in his First Inaugural. 'We are all Republicans, we are all Federalists.' Although the statement became one of the standing jokes of the administration, particularly in the pages of *The Port Folio*, it had its measure of truth. It was in creating a climate and a situation in which the aristocratic and the democratic principles, the English and the French bias, the traditionalist and the progressive, could have their latitude and play, that Jefferson made his real achievement. It is too finely orchestrated with theirs—particularly with Adams's—to be considered on its own merits alone. Nathan Schachner has remarked that in the clash of personalities and political ideas of three key figures—Hamilton, Aaron Burr, and Jefferson—'the formative years of the American nation may be studied to advantage'.[45] For our purposes, if we substitute Adams for Burr, in the interplay of *these* figures it will be possible to study certain basic tensions in the pattern of American experience that are reflected on levels of creative activity with which we are more immediately concerned.

I said in Chapter I that there was a tension in American experience that 'took on many forms concurrently: it was an opposition between tradition and progress, or between the past and present or future; between America and Europe, liberalism and reaction, aggressive acquisitive economics and benevolent wealth'. It will hardly be necessary to enlarge on the ways in which these tensions, as I have noted them here, are exemplified in the writings of the three statesmen who have been considered above. In some degree I have done so already. If there is a 'new American experience', there cannot be a deeper source in which to look for it than in the writings of these three men. In the following chapters I shall attempt to show the way in which these tensions, basically political in nature, enter into the fabric of American fiction. In themselves they constitute a style, an architecture of the American sensibility which, with minor modifications from decade to decade, keeps its ground throughout the nineteenth century, and is capable of being transposed, with its identifying characteristics intact, from one medium of expression to another.

III

Fenimore Cooper and
the Economic Age

I

COOPER has been consistently underestimated as an artist. He ranks with Hawthorne, James, and Melville as one of the four greatest novelists America produced in the nineteenth century. Conrad called him a rare artist and one of his own masters, and his words deserve more attention than they have ever received. But the novels that must be considered in this chapter are by no means his masterpieces, interesting as they are in many respects. The European political novels with which I shall be concerned first, greatly enlarged, or would have done had their example been heeded, the scope of the political novel as it then existed. In them Cooper presents a strikingly original analysis of history and of his own times, the brilliance of which has never received any recognition. In a day such as our own when the political novel largely concerns itself with the threat to democracies from the outside, it is salutary to consider Cooper's political novels, which are concerned with threats to democracy that arise from abuse of its own nature. The European political novels are, in effect, a manifesto of Cooper's ardent democratic principles. But at this point the tension which we have been considering in the last two chapters asserts itself. Ten years later, in the Littlepage trilogy, Cooper wrote three novels whose political philosophy seems diametrically opposed to that he had previously expressed. And yet Cooper had not really changed his views. The aristocratic Cooper of *The Chainbearer* and *The Redskins* is the democratic Cooper who had written *The Heidenmauer* and *The Bravo*. These two sets of novels exemplify the polarity in American experience. Cooper never really succeeded in resolving this polarity or conflict artistically in any one novel. The best he could do was to shift his attention back and forth from one aspect to the other, and in doing so he often gives what appears to be a contradictory performance. Out of this tension or spiritual conflict, Henry James was to evolve at

47

last the structural dialectic of the international novel in which opposites are brought together, skilfully juggled or held in suspension, and at last resolved by mutually qualifying each other, as in *The Europeans*.[1] No one before James was equipped, either with the worldly knowledge or creative tact, to achieve so much, but many American writers had been brought face to face with the devastating problem. Two of them had been among America's greatest writers, and if Cooper and Hawthorne partially failed where James was later to succeed, it is possible that James himself would not have succeeded if Cooper and Hawthorne had not struggled with the tension before him. To revert to Mr. Tate's terminology, quoted in Chapter I, Cooper and Hawthorne helped James to that preliminary knowledge of America—not indeed a knowledge of the mere surfaces of American life, but of her profoundest spiritual trials which was the necessary prelude of the full maturity of Jamesian art. In the following pages I wish to explore this basic tension as it occurs in Cooper's novels. If we can understand it fully in Cooper, we shall have a touchstone that may well prove helpful in guiding our critical explorations through the American novel as it developed after him.

II

The three European political novels are *The Bravo* (1831), *The Heidenmauer* (1832), and *The Headsman* (1833). It will be convenient to discuss *The Heidenmauer* first, and we may omit discussion of *The Headsman* altogether. Considered simply as a work of fiction *The Heidenmauer* is far from a success, but it must occupy an important place in any consideration of Cooper's intellectual powers. The story deals with the Palatinate in the sixteenth century. The village of Duerckheim is dominated by the wealthy Benedictine Abbey of Limburg, whose powers and exactions the villagers resent. Encouraged and led on by the neighbouring nobleman, Emich, Count of Hartenburg, they sack and burn the monastery; then, having been motivated by no religious impulse higher than that of greed, and fearing that they have trespassed too far for their personal safety, the villagers hedge the issues by making a penitential pilgrimage.

Mr. Robert E. Spiller comments on *The Heidenmauer* in these terms:

> In thus showing the effect of Lutheranism in liberating the mind of man from superstition, and the social order from corruption and hypocrisy, Cooper draws an obvious parallel to his own time in the effect of the American ideal in liberating the modern mind from the corruption of the world controlled by the ancient régime. He does not state this in so many words, however, and there is small reason to suppose that anyone in his own day understood the point of his conclusion.[2]

Nothing, I think, could be more remote from Cooper's intention than this description of it. One looks in vain for any enthusiastic support of the reformers in *The Heidenmauer*. There are no obvious villains, but the three who might be considered as embodying nobility, disinterestedness, and that magnanimity of character that Cooper admired so much, are Father Arnolphe of Limburg, the devout Ulrike, and Odo von Ritterstein, the penitent nobleman whose integrity and virtue are revealed through many years of cheerfully accepted penance for having committed an offence against the Church in his youth. Cooper's 'noble' characters, in short, prove the opposite of Mr. Spiller's contention. All three are products and ardent adherents of the old régime, and no evidence that they were ever to change their allegiance is either given or implied.

The brilliance of *The Heidenmauer* as a piece of intellectual analysis lies in the fact that Cooper presented a convincing economic interpretation of the Reformation as early as 1832. There was, of course, a deliberate analogy intended between the subject of Cooper's novel and the situation in America, but the analogy was not between the 'liberating' effect of the Reformation and American democracy. Cooper drew it, rather, in a sphere to which Tawney points in his *Religion and the Rise of Capitalism*: 'The modern world has seen in America the swift rise of combinations controlling output and prices by the power of massed capital. A somewhat similar movement took place in the generation before the Reformation. Its centre was Germany, and it was defended and attacked by arguments almost identical with those which are familiar today.'[3]

One may begin with Cooper's passionate detestation of the new financial aristocracy in America, which, often allying its interests with the old landed aristocrats of New York like the Van Rensselaers and the Livingstons, ended up by changing the character of the whole class from that of a civilized gentry into that of a financial oligarchy. It was a hatred of this class, and the vulgarity of its values, that persuaded Cooper, when the old aristocratic Federalist party, of which his father had been a prominent state leader, dissolved, to become a Democrat rather than a Whig, which he logically should have done.

As we shall see later, Cooper ardently believed in inherited wealth as the basis of a cultural élite which would be the dispensers of civilized values, but he saw no such function being performed by the pretentious upstart financial aristocracy which had been the end product of Hamilton's financial programme. The life of Hamilton by John Williams describes the aristocracy in terms that Cooper would readily have endorsed:

> The aristocracy which he would have formed would have been an aristocracy of wealth, the most repulsive of all, as it would have embraced the pride of distinction without its refinement. We should have had an equestrian order, but no *generosi*: haughty bipeds decked with armorial trappings, but no graceful examples of high taught endowment and mellowed dignity: arrogant *fungi*, a forced fruit that would have borne the appearance of patricians without the inward zest and ripeness. Having knowledge enough to be vain and insolent, but not enough to be wise and forbearing, we should have been annoyed with saucy ignorance and bloated rank.[4]

It was precisely such a false aristocracy that Cooper saw in the Whig party, and it was the more insidious because it cloaked its self-interest in patriotic language. In this coupling of patriotic pretension and self-interest Cooper sensed great danger to the nation, for he believed, as many had done before him, that the American Constitution was an instrument capable of being seriously perverted by those in power. In *The American Democrat* Cooper attempted to show that its weakness as well as its strength lay in its great flexibility:

> . . . the federal government has no fixed character, so far as the nature of its constituency is concerned, but one that may constantly vary, and which has materially varied since the commencement of the government, though, as yet, its changes have always been in the direction of popular rights. . . .

Any state of this Union, by altering its own constitution, may place the power of its own government, and, by consequence, its representation in the government of the United States, in any dozen families, making it perpetual and hereditary.[5]

The brilliance of Cooper's analysis of the American political situation as he focused it in his European novels exists in the fullness of his economic recognitions. He believed that the shifting of economic power in the United States into the hands of a small moneyed class might mean a radical reshaping of government under the Constitution. He appreciated both the manœuverability of that document and the existence of a powerful body of vested interests which tended to identify the good of the country with their private prosperity. Cooper knew that if man had a fallen nature economics was the science in which one encountered it first. In the European novels he determined, therefore, to analyse the dangers he believed confronted America, but to do so in terms of a larger historical context than concentration on the national scene would permit, for he saw that these dangers had their roots and their counterparts in the cycle of European history.

The economic base of the Protestant Reformation was no new discovery in the nineteenth century, but it was soft-pedalled for at least half a century after *The Heidenmauer*. It was not, indeed, until Brooks Adams published his brilliant treatise, *The Law of Civilization and Decay*, in 1895, that an American was to be so outspoken again. 'The soldier and the priest were overpowered; and from the Reformation downward, the monied type possessed the world,' writes Adams,[6] and that is the thesis of Cooper's novel. But in Cooper's eyes this did not represent, as Mr. Spiller thinks, a liberating 'of the mind of man from superstition, and the social order from corruption and hypocrisy'. On the contrary, the point of *The Heidenmauer* is that the economic motive is always an element of dangerous impurity, that it works in disguises and moves towards goals which are other than the ones professed. Describing the Lollard movement in England, Brooks Adams wrote two short paragraphs that outline, in effect, the motive of action in *The Heidenmauer*:

The Lollards were of the modern economic type, and discarded the miracle because the miracle was costly and yielded an uncertain return. Yet the mediaeval cult was based upon the miracle, and many of the payments due for the supernatural services of the ecclesiastics were obligatory; besides, gifts as an atonement for sin were a drain on savings, and the economist instinctively sought cheaper methods of propitiation.

In an age as unscientific as the sixteenth century the conviction of the immutability of natural laws was not strong enough to admit of the abrogation of religious formulas. The monied class, therefore, proceeded step by step, and its first experiment was to suppress all fees to middlemen, whether priests or saints, by becoming their own intercessors with the deity.[7]

The resentment of the villagers of Duerckheim against the Abbey of Limburg is solely financial. Lutheranism has not yet penetrated into this remote district, except by rumour, and the destruction of the Abbey springs entirely from the profit motive. Theological considerations enter, if at all, only as an after-thought. So much, indeed, is this the case that the Count of Hartenburg no sooner beholds the blackened walls and knows that his object is attained than he welcomes the opportunity of making a pilgrimage of penance to the holy shrine of Our Lady of the Hermits. Cooper describes his disposition in these words:

Bold, haughty, and audacious, he was also deeply artful and superstitious. For years his rude mind had been tormented by conflicting passions—those of cupidity and religious dread; and now that the former was satisfied, he had begun to reflect seriously of appeasing his latent apprehensions in some effectual manner. Plans of various expiatory offerings had already crossed his mind, and so far from hearing the declaration of the Benedictine with resentment, he entertained the idea with pleasure. It seemed an easy and cheap expedient of satisfying all scruples; for the re-establishment on the hill of Limburg was a condition he knew to be entirely out of the question in the present state of the public mind of Germany.

Having arrived at last at Our Lady of the Hermits, the Count is received by the Prior, from whom he has the miraculous story of the shrine. In replying to the Prior, the Count is made to reveal that strange tangle of religion and cupidity out of which Cooper, like Brooks Adams so much later, saw the Reformation, at least in its material aspects, as growing:

Emich crossed himself devoutly, having listened in perfect

faith, and with deep interest;—for at that moment early impressions were stronger than modern doubts.

'It is good to be here, father,' he reverently answered. . . . 'But are there any special favours accorded to those who come hither in a fitting temper, in the way of temporal gifts or political considerations? since, being before a shrine so holy, I would fain profit by the sore pains and privations by which the grace is gained.'

The Prior seemed mortified, for, though he lent the faith required by the opinions of the age to the tradition he had recounted, he was too well instructed in the true doctrines of his Church not to perceive the false bias of his companion's mind.

Inasmuch as the Count is the representative of the Lutheran spirit in the novel, if it may be said to have one at all, Mr. Spiller's description of Cooper's purpose seems widely off the mark. As a moral person, and as a liberated mind, the Prior decidedly has the better of it here, and this is true throughout the book. It is always the old régime which Cooper, whether deliberately or not, presents as morally admirable. It has its unattractive representatives in such persons as the Abbot Bonifacius, but he is explicitly presented as the most intelligent person in the book, and the faults in his life are matched or surpassed by the opposite side.

The following exchange between the Count and his friend Heinrich Frey, the Burgomaster of Duerckheim, demonstrates beyond argument, I think, the quality Cooper wished to show as the moving force behind these social and religious changes. The two men are discussing masses for the repose of the soul of a young man who was, supposedly, killed during the attack on the Abbey:

'I could wish that poor Berchthold, after all, had the virtue of masses from these servitors of Our Lady of the Hermits,' said the Count. . . .

'. . . to own the truth, I have thought of little else, while going through the Aves, but to devise the means of persuading the holy Abbot, at a reasonable rate, to change his mind, and honestly to let the youth's soul benefit by his intercessions.'

'Thou hast not well bethought, thee altogether, friend Heinrich, of thine own errand here!'

'Sapperment! what would you, Herr Emich, from a man of my years and education? One gets to be so ready with words by oft

repeating, that going through the beads is much like tapping with
a finger while the eye looks over an account. But to speak of the
boy—were we to bid higher for these masses, it might raise the
present price, and we be uselessly losers. . . .'

'Heinrich!' returned the Count, musingly, 'they say that
Brother Luther denounces these *post mortem* prayers as vain of
none avail.'

'. . . one could wish to be sure in an affair of this delicacy; for
if the monk of Wittenberg hath reason of his side, we lose our gold;
and if he hath wrong, the soul of Berchthold may be none the
better for our doubts.'

'We laymen are sorely pressed between the two opinions,
worthy Burgomaster. . . . By the mass! there are moments when
I am ready to throw away the rosary, and to take Duke Friedrich
of Saxony's side of the question as being the most reasonable and
manly. But, then, again, should he prove wrong, thou knowest
Heinrich, we lose the benefit of chapels built, of Aves said, of gold
often paid, and the high protection of Rome.'

'Nowhere', Brooks Adams argued, 'has faith withstood the
rise of the mercantile class.'[8] Even though the presentation is
clumsy here, the way in which Cooper illustrates the supplant-
ing of the imagination that governed an earlier order of things
by the mercantile mentality constitutes a remarkable insight.
'The crime of the English monks, like the crime of the
Templars,' to quote Brooks Adams once more, 'was defenceless
wealth.'[9] That is substantially the crime which the villagers of
Duerckheim cannot forgive in the monks of Limburg; and we
see this motive, decorously disguised, in the following speech of
the Burgomaster to the village blacksmith, Dietrich, delivered
while the two are walking side by side in the night march which
is to end in the spoliation of the monastery:

"'Tis said, neighbour Dietrich,' commenced the Burgomaster,
speaking to a sturdy smith, who acted on this occasion as a lieu-
tenant to the commander-in-chief, an honour that was mainly due
to the power of his arm, and who, emboldened by his temporary
rank, had advanced nearly to Heinrich's side, ''Tis said, neighbour Dietrich, that these Benedictines are like bees, who never go
forth but in the season of plenty, and rarely return without rich
contribution to their hive. Thou art a reflecting and solid towns-
man, one that is little moved by the light opinions of the idle, and
a burgher that knoweth his own rights, which is as much as to say,

his own interests, and one that well understandeth the necessity of preserving all our venerable usages and laws, at least in such matters as touch the permanency of the welfare of those that may lay claim to have a welfare. I speak not now of the varlets who belong, as it were, neither to heaven nor earth, being condemned of both to the misery of houseless and irresponsible knaves, but of men of substance, that, like thee and thy craft, pay scot and lot, keep bed and board; and are otherwise to be marked for their usefulness and natural rights; and this brings me to my point, which is neither more nor less than to say, that God hath created all men equal, and therefore it is our right, no less than our duty, to see that Duerckheim is not wronged, especially in that part of her interests that belong, in particularity, to her substantial inhabitants.'

The tortuous quality of this speech is of course deliberate. It is laboriously overdone, but Cooper does succeed in making the true character and motives of the speaker embarrassingly evident under the nervous, hedging sentence constructions. The Abbey of Limburg is about to be burned, not by the aroused moral enthusiasm of insurgent Lutherans, but by the petty greed of the new mercantile mentality whose essential timorousness is fully revealed in the periphrastic phrasings of Heinrich Frey. Commenting explicitly on this mentality a few pages further on, Cooper says:

We have already said that Heinrich Frey was a stout friend of the conservative principle, which, reduced to practice, means little more than that

'They shall get who have the power
And they shall keep who can.'

There is accomplished irony in the fact that when the attack on Limburg is made, the monks are celebrating a Mass of reparation for the penitent Odo von Ritterstein, who, many years before in that same Abbey, had been guilty of an act of sacrilege. Rejected for this crime by the righteous burghers, he has spent the intervening years in exemplary penance. Odo, it should be insisted, is one of the most positive norms of value in the book, along with the saintly Father Arnolphe. He is a man of chivalry, imagination, and profound sensibility, to whom economic motives mean so little that he gives away his large

estates in the final chapter—and it is not entirely owing to the
necessities of plot that the recipient of the gift is the daughter
of the Burgomaster and her young husband. The mercantile
order has taken over. It is characteristic of the Burgomaster's
cloddishness that he observes: '. . . as for Odo von Ritterstein,
his crime would be deemed all the lighter in these days'. But the
Burgomaster is brought to this charitable utterance only by
realizing that his own active participation in the sack of
Limburg has amounted to comparable sacrilege. He is now
prepared to reassess the guilt of such an act.

Heinrich Frey, having been moved by the hope of profit
alone, a motive which he has regularly endeavoured to conceal
behind a screen of suffocating respectability—or, more correctly, has justified by equating it with respectability—brings
his role in the novel to a close with this exchange with the
Count of Hartenburg:

> 'Our minds once fairly enlightened, it is no easy matter to
> throw them into the shade again. . . . There is naught so potent
> in an argument, as a little apprehension of losses or of plagues
> thrown into the scale. Wisdom weighs light against profit or fear.
> 'It is well as it is, though Limburg roof will never again cover
> Limburg wall, friend Heinrich, while an Emich rules in Harten-
> burg and Duerckheim.'—The count saw the cloud on the Burgo-
> master's brow as he uttered the latter word. . . .

Incapable of disinterestedness, the Burgomaster is nevertheless eager to interpret his activities against the monks as a fight
against superstition—now that a stand on Lutheran principles
is likely to confirm and enlarge his profits. But there is a hint
that Duerckheim, if it has got rid of the Abbey, has secured
another master whose exactions may not be less galling.

It should be insisted that while the Reformation in the
Palatinate is the ostensible subject of this novel, religion is not
its primary concern. It is not to be interpreted as an attack on
Rome or on Lutheranism. Its interest is centred in the shifting
grounds of action from the world of the imagination to the
world of profit which characterized the sixteenth century. Read
in this way, *The Heidenmauer* may still not be an exciting or a
successful novel, but it may claim its importance as a brilliant
intellectual analysis far in advance of its time. But it should

be remembered that in establishing the predominance of the intellectual motive, Cooper had his eye on the American scene and on the Whig aristocrats with their drive towards a financial oligarchy. He was aware, as Tawney was in a quotation given above, that there were significant parallels between the economic situation in Germany in the sixteenth century, and modern America. It was because Brooks Adams wished to warn against the usurpation of government by the vested interests during the Gilded Age—usurpations that he saw presaged through the whole course of European history, with a critical turning point for the worse at the time of the Reformation—that he wrote *The Law of Civilization and Decay.* In his concluding chapter, Adams sums up the picture by commenting on modern Europe. What he saw there, he saw on a smaller, but no less intense scale, in the United States. In the following paragraphs Adams is speaking of France after the fall of the Second Empire:

Only after 1871 came the new era, an era marked by many social changes. For the first time in their history the ruler of the French people passed admittedly from the martial to the monied type, and everywhere the same phenomenon appeared; the whole administration of society fell into the hands of the economic man. . . . Since the capitulation of Paris the soldier had tended to sink more and more into a paid official, receiving his order from financiers with his salary, without being allowed a voice even in questions of peace and war. The same fate has overtaken the producing classes; they have failed to maintain themselves, and have become subjects of the possessors of hoarded wealth. Although the conventions of popular government are still preserved, capital is at least as absolute as under the Caesars, and, among capitalists, the money-lenders form an aristocracy. Debtors are in reality powerless, because of the extension of that very system of credit which they invented to satisfy their needs. Although the volume of credit is gigantic, the basis on which it rests is so narrow that it may be manipulated by a handful of men. That basis is gold: in gold, debts must be paid; therefore, when gold is withdrawn, the debtor is helpless and becomes the servant of his master. The elasticity of the age of expansion has gone.

The aristocracy which wields this autocratic power is beyond attack, for it is defended by a wage-earning police, by the side of which the legions were a toy; a police so formidable that, for the first time in history, revolt is hopeless and is not attempted. The only question which preoccupies the ruling class is whether it is cheaper to coerce or bribe.[10]

Adams is speaking of the French, but he is thinking of the United States. And so was Cooper when he wrote *The Bravo*, the first of the three political novels to be published. The flexibility which Cooper found in the American Constitution, and which he commented on in the passage from *The American Democrat* quoted earlier, led him to conceive the possibility, even as early as 1831, of a situation similar to, or even more advanced, than the one Brooks Adams described in the passage just cited. *The Bravo*, which deals with the government of Venice at the beginning of her decline in power, was written as a warning of the kind of oligarchy that might, under the cover of nominally republican institutions, get control of the government of the United States. Such apprehensions were not entirely original with Cooper. Brooks Adams's great grandfather, John Adams, had warned in accents that Cooper would have appreciated: 'This aristocracy of wealth is now destroying the aristocracy of genius, talent, and merit too.'[11] And in his *Defense of the Constitutions of Government* in which he warns his country of those fallacies of European governments that were to be particularly avoided by the new nation, he discussed the Venetian Republic as a particularly horrible example of the insidious encroachments of a tyrannical financial oligarchy, and in doing so he wrote a description that sounds like a preliminary sketch for *The Bravo*.[12]

Unpleasant as the potentialities of such a class might be, Cooper's imagination presented a picture of a society that has a closer relation with the sinister atmosphere of Kafka's *The Castle* or Orwell's *1984* than with anything that was due to develop in his own century. It is, in fact, the totalitarian flavour that comes through *The Bravo* that should make it particularly interesting today. The real subject of *The Bravo* is the way a financial aristocracy in a republic keeps itself in power. The Council of Three is the impersonal force at the centre of the story—the anonymous and powerful disciplinarians and protectors of vested interest. We are given an intimate picture of its unlimited powers in operation, of its criminal practices; we are shown the devious and tortuous ways in which it secretly guides and protects the policies of the aristocratic state; and we understand the impersonality even more than the inhumanity that is required of those who serve in this capacity. Cooper takes us into the inner workings of the secret police and spy systems; shows us the way mutual mistrust is implanted in the various classes; the way that the state forces services and confessions from its victims by alternate threats and promises of rewards: 'I was sworn to serve the state, as its secret agent, for a certain time. The reward was to be my father's freedom. . . . They whispered to me of racks and wheels, and I was shown paintings of dying martyrs, that I might understand the agony they could inflict.' He describes the state's perpetual, incantatory praise of its own justice and liberality. 'Mark me, Antonio,' the hero of the novel says to another, 'thy language has given offence, and thou art not safe in Venice. They will pardon complaints against all but their justice. That is too true to be forgiven.' And it should be remarked, incidentally, that Cooper describes the traditional pageants and ceremonies of Venice with a success that one might have thought would have recommended the novel to contemporary neo-romantics. His descriptions of the Bucentaur, the marriage of Venice and the sea, the regatta on the Grand Canal, have the colour and splendour of Carpaccio with some of the ominous overtones of Eugene Berman.

Romantic and violent as the details of the plot are, it adheres with strict economy to the central theme which I have already described. The capitalist colouring of the Venetian Republic is kept systematically in the foreground. Here, for example, is a representative passage of dialogue between two members of the Council of Three:

'For a state in decline, Venice is to the last degree prosperous. Our ships are thriving; the bank flourishes with goodly dividends; and I do assure you, Signore, that, for many years, I have not known so ample revenues for most of our interests, as at this hour. All cannot thrive alike!'

'You are happily connected with flourishing affairs, Signore, but there are many that are less lucky. Our form of government is somewhat exclusive, and it is a penalty that we have ever paid for its advantages, to be liable to sudden and malevolent accusations, for any evil turn of fortune that besets the Republic.'

'Can nothing satisfy these exacting spirits? Are they not free—are they not happy?'

'It would seem that they want better assurance of these facts, than our own feelings, or our words.'

'Man is a creature of envy! The poor desire to be rich—the weak, powerful.'

'There is an exception to your rule, at least, Signore, since the rich rarely wish to be poor, or the powerful, weak.'

'You deride my sentiments tonight, Signore Gradenigo. I speak, I hope, as becomes a senator of Venice, and in a manner that you are not unaccustomed to hear.'

I said that Cooper, in writing the European political novels, had his eye steadily on the American scene, but this is a point which was not acknowledged in his own day, and which is still very little recognized. Among more percipient critics, Mr. Russell Kirk stated in an article published a few years ago:

> Cooper's precise purpose in writing the European novels still is in doubt. Lounsbury holds that he intended to instruct Europeans in the advantages of American democracy; Boynton maintains that he was attacking European political systems 'for the edification of American democracy'; and Spiller contends that he was defending America against a hostile world. Although in some measure all these intentions were Cooper's, a most important aspect of his thought was forgotten by each of his biographers; that Cooper was holding up the failings of European systems as a warning to America that her free institutions, too, could perish—as he had elsewhere expressed his fear for real liberty in America.[13]

The motive which Mr. Kirk assigns Cooper in these novels is one which we know moved John Adams to write the *Defense of the Constitutions of Government*. To that extent it was a traditional motive, although it had not previously been utilized in fiction. There is no doubt Mr. Kirk is right as far as he goes. Cooper's political novels present a powerfully argued caveat to the complacency of American democracy. But Mr. Kirk does not go far enough. Cooper's novels are not only a warning of what might come to America—to a large extent they are a bitter satire on what he believed already existed in America, and which he saw the Democratic party alone as opposing. I do not propose in this chapter to discuss Cooper as a devout Democrat lashed into fury by the Whig oligarchy. That aspect of Cooper has had complete justice in Dorothy Waples's admirable monograph, *The Whig Myth of James Fenimore Cooper*.[14] But I think it will be useful here to examine in some detail the political views and vocabulary of the two Venetian senators in the passage quoted above with a view to discovering how completely they embody the views and vocabulary of the early political philosophy of the Federalists and their Whig heirs. This can only be done by juxtaposing items from Cooper's dialogue with relevant representative passages from the contemporary political writers with whom Cooper was familiar. Cooper's senator declares, 'All cannot thrive alike!' It was one of the basic propositions of both the Federalists and the Whigs, and dominated their thought. Cooper could write dialogue such as he did in the passage quoted because all his life the American 'aristocracy' had been talking in the same way. I have already quoted that specious show of logic by which Hamilton eternally divided the rich from the poor. If one keeps this school of American political thought in mind as one reads *The Bravo*, Cooper achieves a really biting irony. I have already described how the flourishing mercantile interests had skyrocketed into huge fortunes through channels of speculation Hamilton's financial programme had opened up in the closing years of the eighteenth century. His creation of the Bank of the United States had become the focus of this new moneyed class, and in 1831, when *The Bravo* was published, the renewal of the charter of the Second Bank of the United States was being vigorously fought in Congress by the Jackson men. It is significant that in a long pamphlet called *A Letter to His Countrymen*, published in 1834, Cooper took occasion to offer a defence of Jackson's withdrawal of the public funds from the Bank, almost in the same breath with which he defended *The Bravo* against unscrupulous attacks in the Whig press. If it were not fully evident from the text of *The Bravo* that Cooper was describing the Whig financial oligarchy rather than the Venetian aristocracy, such extraneous considerations would help to establish the real target of Cooper's criticisms. 'Our ships are thriving; the bank flourishes with goodly dividends.' They may be given to us as the words of a Venetian senator, but they carry strong American implications, at least for Cooper's time. 'Our government is somewhat exclusive,' says the Venetian senator in a masterpiece of understatement.

But Chancellor Kent could write with equal conviction, as representing the opinion of his class: 'I wish those who have an interest in the soil to retain the exclusive possession of a branch in the Legislature. . . . The men of no property . . . may perhaps at some future date, under skilful management, predominate . . . and yet we should be perfectly safe if no laws could pass without the free consent of the owners of the soil.'[15] And even old Judge Cooper, the novelist's father, had gone around the country 'preaching the old and musty doctrine that government had better be left to gentlemen, and that simple folk should vote as they were told.'[16] In recommending exclusiveness of government, Cooper's senator is speaking less for Venice than for the America of the Whigs. 'Man is a creature of envy! The poor desire to be rich—the weak, powerful,' argues the senator, and in doing so he voiced one of the commonplaces of the American conservatives. John Adams had formulated the position with more fairness than anyone else was to do:

> The great question will forever remain, *who shall work?* Our species cannot all be idle. Leisure for study must ever be the portion of a few. The number employed in government must forever be very small. Food, raiment, and habitations, the indispensable wants of all, are not to be obtained without the continual toil of ninety-nine men in a hundred of mankind. . . . The controversy between the rich and the poor, the laborious and idle, the learned and ignorant, distinctions as old as the creation, and as extensive as the globe, distinctions which no art or policy can ever wholly destroy, will continue, and rivalries will spring out of them.[17]

As usual, John Adams made sense. He saw the division of classes as functional to good government and instrumental in obtaining a disciplined liberty for all. His position was very much that which Cooper himself was to champion a decade after *The Bravo*, as we shall see. But the opposition between the rich and the poor (and it is this that Cooper is thinking of in the Venetian senator's speech, and throughout the novel) came out as something very different, as we have already seen, in Hamilton's view of it. The absurdity of these 'gold bugs', as Henry Adams was to call them later, thinking of themselves in terms of a traditional aristocracy, made Cooper, who considered himself an aristocrat as well as a Democrat, gag. But he knew the power of such a class, once it was firmly intrenched in government. He held essentially the same views of its methods and abuses that Brooks Adams saw in the French government after 1871.

One of the basic assumptions out of which the American Constitution grew was the right of property to be protected. The first scholar to give this assumption its due weight was Charles A. Beard, but it had been generally recognized that the Constitution was capable of being manipulated as a class document from Jefferson down through a series of writers in the nineteenth century, among whom we may count Cooper. This assumption, good or bad according to the way it was used, was capable of being brought to a very narrow and selfish focus in the hands of the men of property. The American man of property had originally existed as a large landed proprietor, but the term was widened under Hamiltonian stimulus to include the men whose wealth was based on commerce and speculation. The man of property became a national type. He was the patriot, the pillar of society. He was different from the exploiting generations that came after the Civil War, but the later excesses provide an ironic commentary on his political philosophy. Cooper gives us one of the most scathing analyses of the type that we have in American literature. He is describing one of the Council of Three, Senator Gradenigo:

> The Signor Gradenigo was born with all the sympathies and natural kindnesses of other men, but accident, and an education which had received a strong bias from the institutions of the self-styled republic, had made him the creature of a conventional policy. To him Venice seemed a free state because he partook so largely of the benefits of her social system; and, though shrewd and practised in most of the affairs of the world, his faculties, on the subject of the political ethics of his country, were possessed of a rare and accommodating dullness. A senator, he stood in relation to the state as a director of a monied institution is proverbially placed in relation to his corporation; an agent of its collective measures, removed from the responsibilities of the man. He could reason warmly, if not acutely, concerning the principles of government, and it would be difficult, even in this money-getting age, to find a more zealous convert to the opinion that property was not a subordinate, but the absorbing interest of civilized life. He

would talk ably of character, and honour, and virtue, and religion, and the rights of persons, but when called upon to act in their behalf, there was in his mind a tendency to blend them all with worldly policy, that proved as unerring as the gravitation of matter to the earth's centre. As a Venetian he was opposed to the domination of one, or of the whole; being, as respects the first, a furious republican, and, in reference to the second, leaning to that singular sophism which calls the dominion of the majority the rule of many tyrants! In short, he was an aristocrat; and no man had more industriously or more successfully persuaded himself into the belief of all the dogmas that were favourable to his caste. He was a powerful advocate of vested rights, for their possession was advantageous to himself; he was sensitively alive to innovations on usages, and to vicissitudes in the histories of families, for calculation had substituted taste for principles; nor was he backward, on occasion, in defending his opinions by analogies drawn from the degrees of Providence. With a philosophy that seemed to satisfy himself, he contended that, as God had established orders throughout his own creation, in a descending chain from angels to men, it was safe to follow an example that emanated from a wisdom that was infinite. Nothing could be more sound than the basis of his theory, though his application had the capital error of believing there was any imitation of nature in an endeavour to supplant it.

This is really brilliant, and in the face of it one cannot pretend that it applies only, or even primarily, to the Venetian Republic. Nor is its application merely historical. It is as relevant to the contemporary political scene as it was to the America of Cooper's own day. It is not my contention that these novels are successful works of art, but they are distinguished expressions of the liberal viewpoint in American fiction—and what is more, a liberalism grounded in a sense of history that is rare. They are not only Cooper's democratic novels—in a quite real sense they are also documents of the Democratic party, though they have never, I believe, been accepted as such. But these novels did not express the whole of Cooper's attitude or sensibility. Perhaps they did not even express the most important part. In the aristocratic Littlepage trilogy we can see what was eliminated from the European political novels, and we must now turn our attention to them.

III

The Littlepage trilogy was written in the 'forties. The first novel in the series, *Satanstoe* (1845), is perhaps Cooper's best novel after the Leatherstocking tales. The pastoral picture it gives of colonial life, particularly among the Dutch settlers at Albany, reminds one of *The Pioneers*. *The Chainbearer*, also published in 1845, is almost as good; but *The Redskins* of the following year is a declamatory failure. The Littlepage trilogy traces the history of a single family through some three or four generations as they live their lives on their New York estates. The Littlepage family are landed proprietors, and the basis of interest in these novels is the way we see them acquiring their lands, surveying them, and building substantial houses on them, settling their thousands of acres with tenants, passing them on from father to son, and watching them rise in value as New York becomes more prosperous. Not least among the successes of these novels is the way in which one feels the lands acquire, not only greater money value, but an endowment of richer values through human association as they pass successively from heir to heir. Cooper's aim, of course, was to praise landed wealth, transmitted through families, at the expense of wealth gained by speculation or industrial enterprise. Landed wealth had a dignity, and carried certain values and responsibilities with it, that no other kind of wealth could claim. 'The vulgar, almost invariably in this country, reduce the standard of distinction to mere money,' Cooper had written in *The Chainbearer*. His trilogy is intended as an illustration of everything, in addition to money, that land means when it becomes the focal point for the activities and interests of a family. His ideas on land and inheritance are adequately suggested in the following paragraph from *Satanstoe*:

'You see,' continued Herman Mordaunt, as we walked together conversing on this subject, 'that my twenty thousand acres are not likely to be of much use to myself, even should they prove to be of any to my daughter. A century hence, indeed, my descendants may benefit from all this outlay of money and trouble; but it is not probable that either I or Anneke will ever see the principal and interest of the sums that will be expended in the way of roads, bridges, mills, and other things of that sort. Years may

C

go by before the light rents which will only begin to be paid a year or two hence, and then only by a few tenants, can amount to a sufficient sum to meet the expense of keeping up the settlement to say nothing of the quit-rents that must be paid to the Crown. . . .

'Every man who is at his ease in his moneyed affairs, Corny, feels a disposition to make some provision for his posterity. This estate, if kept together, and in single hands, may make some descendant of mine a man of fortune. Half a century will produce a great change in this colony; and at the end of that period, a child of Anneke's may be thankful that his mother had a father who was willing to throw away a few thousands of his own, the surplus of a fortune that was sufficient for his wants without them, in order that his grandson might see them converted into tens, or possibly into hundreds of thousands.'

We are confronted here with something that looks like a contradiction. If Cooper was embattled against the men of property, it was only when they were financiers or tycoons of the new class, men whose sources of wealth he distrusted, and whose desire to influence government for the welfare of vested interests he considered subversive of democratic principles. But the democratic principles Cooper championed were not broad enough to include a levelling interpretation of democracy. 'The tendency of democracies is, in all things, to medocrity,' he had written in *The American Democrat*.[18] Like John Adams, Cooper was intensely conscious of the inequality of natural endowments, and he was never guilty of perverting the doctrine of equality of rights into equality of opportunity. He realized that such a formulation can only mean the suppression of opportunity for the specially talented. In words that sound remarkably like John Adams, he wrote:

The rights of property being an indispensable condition of civilization, and its quiet possession everywhere guaranteed, equality of condition is rendered impossible. One man must labour, while another may live luxuriously on his means; one has leisure and opportunity to cultivate his tastes, to increase his information, and to reform his habits, while another is compelled to toil that he may live. One is reduced to serve, while another commands, and, of course, there can be no equality in their social conditions.[19]

That was part of Cooper's explanation of what it meant to be a democrat in America—or, perhaps, what it ought to have meant. It is not surprising, then, that he once told the editor of the Albany *Argus* that he was a good Democrat because he was a good aristocrat.[20] When Cooper used the word 'aristocratic' in a benign sense, as when he applied it to himself, he interpreted it in its imaginative and chivalric mode, a sense which the romanticism of the day made popular, but which the economic trends of the past hundred years had drained of much practical meaning. Cooper believed that there must be a cultural élite at the top of society who functioned as custodians and dispensers of civilized values. It was his distinction that he recognized that such an élite was as becoming to a democracy as it was to a monarchy. He saw it as the guardian of democracy, not as a threat to it. Part of his indignation against the Whigs sprang from his perception of how they failed as guardians of any values beyond the most selfish economic ones. This role of the civilizing function of a cultivated upper class comes out very clearly in the Littlepage trilogy. In *The Chainbearer*, for example, we have this speech, perfectly representative of the values that are recommended throughout these three books, in which Mordaunt Littlepage's father is speaking to him:

'You will naturally think of marrying ere long, and your mother and I were just saying that you ought to build a good, substantial dwelling on this very spot, and settle down on your own property. Nothing contributes so much to the civilization of a country as to dot it with a gentry, and you will both give and receive advantages by adopting such a course. It is impossible for those who have never been witnesses of the result, to appreciate the effect produced by one gentleman's family in a neighbourhood, in the way of manners, tastes, general intelligence, and civilization at large.'

Or again, in *The Redskins*, which brings the trilogy down to Cooper's own day, we have this passage on New York City:

Will New York ever be a capital? Yes—out of all question, yes. But the day will not come until after the sudden changes of condition which immediately and so naturally succeeded the revolution, have ceased to influence ordinary society, and those above again impart to those below more than they receive. This restoration to the natural state of things must take place as soon as society gets settled; and there will be nothing to prevent a town living under our own institutions—spirit, *tendencies* and all—from obtaining the highest tone that ever yet prevailed in a capital. The folly is in anticipating the natural course of events. Nothing will more hasten these events, however, than a literature that is controlled, not by the lower, but by the higher opinion of the country; which literature is yet, in a great degree, to be created.

Nothing could be more charming or superficially more plausible than this combination of democratic and aristocratic tendencies in their purity as they coalesced in Cooper's imagination. But the type of American democrat he looked forward to has failed to develop, at least in any numbers, while levellers and Babbitts have multiplied. The fact is that Cooper's American democrat was not a creature of the economic age in which he was compelled to take his place. Set down in the middle of nineteenth-century America there was something contradictory in his nature. His great virtues were to find an adequate stage only in literature—but here he was to be a complete success. The tensions that he could not resolve in politics were finally to make him into an artist. In the last analysis, it is not only Cooper, but Hawthorne and James who may be taken as the finest examples of what Cooper meant by being an American democrat.

There is a passage in Cooper's *Gleanings in Europe* which it will be well to bear in mind at this point. He and his family had just arrived in England, through which they were passing on their way to France, when they made a visit to the ruins of Netley Abbey:

> The Abbey was fine, without being a very imposing ruin, standing in the midst of a field of English neatness, prettily relieved by the woods. . . . The effect of these ruins on us proved the wonderful power of association. The greater force of the past than of the future on the mind can only be the result of questionable causes. Our real concern with the future is incalculably greater, and yet we were dreaming over our own graves, and the events and scenes which throw a charm around the graves of those who have gone before us.[21]

Cooper was one of the most astute politico-social critics America has ever had. But if he understood the new economic man so well, his clarity of vision was partly induced by hate. Of the elder Mr. Goldencalf in *The Monikins*, Cooper said: 'With him, to be born was but the commencement of a speculation, and to die was to determine the general balance of profit and loss.' It was a despicable way of life for a man as civilized as Cooper. The violence of his reaction was so great that in searching for an alternative he failed at times to preserve intact the precision of his critical judgement. To escape the financial aristocracy and its degraded image of the economic man, he embraced the remnants of feudal tenure in the New York land laws which were presently to be repealed under the new state constitution. In doing so he was dreaming over his own grave and the graves of those who had gone before him in a more literal sense than he had ever done while viewing the ruins of Netley Abbey.

It will not be necessary to discuss the nature of these feudal land laws except to say that they guaranteed the vast manorial system that New York had inherited from colonial days, and which was dominated by the great estate of Rensselaerwyck on the Hudson, covering an area of nearly eleven hundred square miles, and containing a number of villages and thousands of small farms which were rented on a basis of feudal tenure.[22] The evolving pattern of American society foredoomed the whole system to extinction, and Cooper, if anyone, should have known it. But at this point we encounter that crucial strain or tension which, if we probe deeply enough into their works, characterizes so many of the great American writers. Although he was always a devout Democrat, Cooper was also a man of an older and more imaginative order of things. In fact, this apparent paradox often exists in Americans—that men of High Tory mentality become Democrats, espousing the popular party, which they understand as the party of chivalry and the opponent of those vested interests that represent the triumph of a financial pseudo-aristocracy. Therefore, when Cooper turned from his criticism of Whig oligarchy, the position that attracted him most strongly was the feudalism of the landowners. The fervour of his attraction, based partly on his memory of his childhood on his father's great estate, prevented him from examining it with the same keen eye he had turned on the moneyed class who looked to speculation and commerce rather

than to land for wealth. As for the feudal aspects of the land-
owners, by that date Cooper didn't care (if he ever had—which
is doubtful). In the Preface to *The Redskins* he wrote: 'It is pre-
tended the durable leases are feudal in their nature. We do not
conceive this to be true; but, admitting it to be so, it would
only prove that feudality, to this extent, is a part of the institution of the state.'

Cooper saw in the great landowning interests the last bulwark
against the new financial mentality. It had been suggested that
the Van Rensselaers sell the farms they rented to their tenants
outright. In *The Redskins*, two of the characters, speaking for
Cooper, comment on this:

> 'Do you suppose the Rensselaers would take their money, the
> principal of the rent at 7 per cent, and buy land with it, after the
> experience of their uncertainty of such possessions among us?'
> 'Not they,' said my uncle Ro laughing. 'No, no! They would
> sell the Manor House at Beverwyck, for taverns; and then one
> might live in them who would pay the principal sum of the cost
> of a dinner; bag their dollars, and proceed forthwith to Wall
> Street, and commence shaving the notes—that occupation having
> been decided to be highly honoured and esteemed accordingly.'

As I said, Cooper was dreaming 'on the events and scenes
which throw a charm around the graves of those who have gone
before us' when he wrote the Littlepage novels, and a man of
his incisive intelligence ought to have known it: ought to have
known that in so far as the old estates had a chance of surviving
it was in that degree to which their interests had become allied
with the new financial class. Nevertheless, if Cooper's grasp of
reality seems momentarily relaxed in these novels, the idyllic
scenes of American aristocratic life, the benevolent High Tory-
ism that Cooper depicts in his landlords, is as agreeable as
anything he ever wrote, saving only the Natty Bumppo series.
But it is astonishing that Cooper, who had described Signor
Gradenigo so brilliantly, should suppose that in an age dominated by such men the relationship represented in the following
passage from *The Chainbearer* could long endure:

> A rumour had gone forth among the people that their landlord
> had arrived, and some of the older tenants, those who had known
> 'Herman Mordaunt' as they called my grandfather, crowded

around me in a frank hearty manner, in which good feeling was blended with respect. They desired to take my hand. I shook hands with all who came, and can truly say that I took no man's palm into my own that day, without a sentiment that the relation of landlord and tenant was one that should induce kind and confidential feelings.

Cooper failed to examine New York feudal society critically because he was enamoured of a way of life that, in imagination at least, it seemed to foster and protect. He could never have been convinced that the impoverished outlying farms of Rensselaerwyck were really open-air sweat shops. He remembered his own childhood in Otsego County too vividly to believe any such thing.

IV

When we contrast the democratic European political novels with the aristocratic Littlepage novels, we see that Cooper was faced with a difficult dilemma. It was one he could not solve, at least by any of the courses that suggested themselves as possible. Wedded to an older imaginative order, and cherishing the values that flourished under such an order no less than the democratic principles in which he believed, he looked in vain for a practical position in which to ground his values in his own time. And it is doubtful if he would have fared any better in ours. This dilemma which I have tried to isolate from two sets of his novels is important because it represents a recurrent tension that we meet in later writers, and on many levels of American thought. At the somewhat elementary level at which it occurs in Cooper we are able to understand it in relation to the surrounding intellectual context in which it occurs more easily than we can with Hawthorne and James. Considered merely as a political statement, Cooper's Littlepage novels represent the desperation of his plight, and of those who came later. How were a cultured élite who were the dispensers of civilized and moral values to reconcile themselves to the economic framework which alone provided the leisure and opportunities for the discharge of their elegant responsibilities? And was not the purity of the democratic dogma, for example, its insurance against demagoguery, guaranteed alone by disciplines that were most readily fostered in aristocratic societies? And although America looked to the future for the fulfilment of her destiny, wasn't it the future, as things were going in the economic age, that gave the lie to the hopes the past had cherished? And finally, wasn't it old, guilt-ridden Europe that, over and over again, whispered insidious intimations to the startled imaginations of these democratic New World writers, that some—perhaps an important part—of the answers they were looking for were to be found in her ancient institutions and seasoned manners?

Form in Fenimore Cooper's Novels

I

IN the first part of this chapter I wish to discuss Cooper's conception of an action as the form of a novel. Later on, I shall offer a detailed analysis of *The Deerslayer* to illustrate my general statements here. I imply no denigration of his elder contemporary in saying that it is a different conception from Sir Walter Scott's, which has relations with the picaresque eighteenth-century novel and which likes to follow the hair-raising trail of a charming young swashbuckler from adventure to adventure, the whole series of episodes finding its continuity through the characters and the mechanics of plot. Cooper also has his relations with this tradition, and the danger is that as one reads through so much that he should *not* have written, this may seem equally the pattern for him. But at his best, the most flagrant adventures are intrinsic parts of a developing moral theme, the whole of which becomes the form of the completed tale. Neither the characters nor their acts are extraneous to this theme, nor is the theme independent of the physical components of the story. For Cooper at his best, an action is the intensified motion of life in which the spiritual and moral faculties of men are no less engaged than their physical selves. Cooper writes adventure stories; but an adventure is only the conventional boundary of this motion of life, the stylistic or structural limits within which it presents itself to us in fictional form.

The Cooper I propose to discuss in this essay begins with Jane Austen. It has been shown that Cooper's first novel, *Precaution*, is an imitation of *Persuasion*.[1] *Precaution* is not a good novel, and I believe that no one has ever suggested that it was. It is hardly strange that this early, direct imitation of her failed to profit by her real achievement. But when Cooper moved into his own territory, which was not the English drawing room, he instinctively profited by what was best in her example—by her ability to confer a moral dimension on an action, and to make that dimension the bright, bracing air in which the novel lived, and found its form. We must always bear in mind of course that the importance of action for art is not whether it is violent or composed, but whether it is human or merely mechanical. The young Fabrice learns a good deal on the field of Waterloo, but in terms of human experience it is doubtful if he learns much more than Emma Woodhouse in an English village. The scope, the glory, and the danger of an action are only deceptively played out on its external stage. Their significance for art, as for the human being, is enacted on the interior stage of self-awareness and knowledge.

To linger on Cooper's obligations to Jane Austen is to proceed at once to the differences. The nature of these differences may be conveniently suggested here by saying that Cooper also exhibits occasional accidental similarities to a novelist who wrote after him—I mean Dostoevski.[2] In Jane Austen the field of dramatic action tends to be concentrated in the evolving consciousness of her heroines. In Cooper, physical violence is frequently a surgeon's probe that explores a moral question outside the consciousness of any one of the characters. For Cooper, action as a phenomenon of the physical world has a moral significance in its own right. It is this ability to deal with violent action that is both one of his finest marks as a writer, and a recurrent temptation to the simple narrative artist in him to decline from his highest level. Later on, when I deal with *The Deerslayer*, Cooper's skill in weaving a moral pattern from action will become apparent; but at this point, as an indication of the suggestive authority with which he can sketch, in a few bold strokes, the physical extremities of a given action, I should like to quote a passage from *The Water-Witch*. The dialogue, as usual with Cooper, is archaic, but on this score he is no worse than Melville in such novels as *Mardi* and *Pierre*, and at his best, the archaism has the effect of stylistically confining the merely mechanical elements of plot and character. The men in the following passage are stranded on a raft at sea with little hope of rescue:

Until the stern of the French frigate was seen retiring from the raft, those who were on it had not been fully sensible of the extreme danger of their situation. Hope had been strongly excited by the return of dawn; for while the shadows of night lay on the ocean, their situation resembled that of one who strove to pierce the obscurity of the future, in order to obtain a presage of better fortunes. With the light had come the distant sail. As the day advanced, the ship had approached, relinquished her search, and disappeared, without the prospect of return.

The stoutest heart among the group on the raft began to sink at the gloomy fate which now seemed inevitable.

'Here is an evil omen!' whispered Ludlow, directing his companion's eyes to the dark and pointed fins of three or four sharks, that were gliding above the surface of the water, and in so fearful a proximity to their persons as to render their situation on the low spars, over which the water was washing and retiring at each rise and fall of the waves, doubly dangerous.—'The creature's instinct speaks ill for our hopes.'

'There is a belief among seamen, that these animals feel a secret impulse, which directs them to their prey,' returned the Skimmer. 'But fortune may yet balk them. Rogerson!' calling to one of his followers;—'thy pockets are rarely wanting in a fisherman's tackle. Hast thou, haply, line and hook, for these hungry miscreants? The question is getting narrowed to one in which the simplest philosophy is the wisest. When eat or to be eaten, is the mooted point, most men will decide for the former.'

A hook of sufficient size was soon produced, and a line was quietly provided from some of the small cordage that still remained about the masts. A piece of leather, torn from a spar, answered for the bait; and the lure was thrown. Extreme hunger seemed to engross the voracious animals, who darted at the imaginary prey with the rapidity of lightning. The shock was so sudden and violent that the hapless mariner was drawn from his slippery and precarious footing into the sea. The whole passed with frightful and alarming rapidity. A common cry of horror was heard, and the last despairing glance of the falling man witnessed. The mutilated body floated for an instant in its blood, with the look of agony and terror still imprinted on the conscious countenance; at the next moment, it had become food for the monsters of the sea.

All had passed away, but the deep dye on the surface of the ocean. The gorged fish disappeared; but the dark spot remained near the immovable raft, as if placed there to warn the survivors of their fate.

There is an extraordinary quality about this passage that springs from Cooper's sense of the imponderable nature of reality. The effectiveness arises, not only from the electrically vivid economy with which the tragedy is created before us, but in the way the horror is re-absorbed into the inscrutable world of nature. Even within the brief compass of the quotation Cooper suggests that world of nature to us—the darkness of night on the ocean, the return of dawn with its delusive promise of hope. The immensities of ocean, wilderness, prairie, or antarctic waste are always, in Cooper, a means of accenting the human situation. Usually he conceives this in a peculiarly personal way—the natural, impersonal immensity not over-shadowing man, but purifying him and adding a lustre of dignity to his role by the very resistance it compels him to offer. But there is also a vein of something more austere in Cooper, and we glimpse it here. There is classical irony in the way the Skimmer's philosophy, eat or be eaten, vindicates the shark. After the sudden violence, the cry of horror and the despairing glance, peace returns upon the scene; but it is symbolized by the gorged fish sinking, satisfied, into the ocean's depths, and by the spot of blood on the ocean's surface, which, like all memorials of vanished violence, accents the silence into which it survives. The stark conception of fate (it is almost Fate) that momentarily appears in the last line might have pleased Hardy; but while it is an element of Cooper's imagination, its importance lies in the fact that he refused it. I point to the quality here because this stoic mood of resignation and acceptance, common among men whose imaginations dwell, as Cooper's did, among natural vastnesses, generates in the American novelist a rigorous and unyielding resistance. This resistance does much to explain his predilection for great physical violence in his novels; and it helps us to understand how Cooper is able to express through actions that a lesser novelist would only have shaped into another tale of adventure, significant intuitions into the moral nature of reality. But before leaving this passage a word should be said of the superb technical skill with which Cooper catches the excitement of the scene. He leads us to the moment of crisis through a full circumstantial account of the surrounding details, and then, changing his timing with perfect dramatic precision, he seizes the salient points of the tragedy as the unnerved spectator himself might have taken them in, almost instantaneously. And then, the moment after the shock of violence, there is the resurgence of quiet again; an effective orchestration, on a very small stage, of turbulence and calm.

II

This remarkable ability to delineate the local details of action and violence is an important part of Cooper's greatness. But action conceived as the form of the novel—in any meaning that can be taken seriously—requires something more than a bravely sustained sense of derring-do. For Cooper, however deceptively the significance of an action may seem at times to reside in the turmoil and heady adventure, it usually resolves itself into a moral dilemma which the reader, even more than the protagonists, is invited to explore. No one has done justice to this quality in Cooper because the dilemma is frequently presented in terms of a conventional novel of divided loyalties. This is true of his Revolutionary novels, two of which I shall speak of briefly here. But the divided loyalties, so convenient a framework for an adventure plot, are intimately associated with Cooper's awareness of the virtues and deficiencies of America. The drama is deeply rooted in a moral ambiguity which, focused on the Revolutionary stage, has sometimes seemed too simple a matter to merit serious attention. But it is intimately associated with that division in the American experience which I have discussed in my opening chapters.

Cooper's first novel on an American theme was *The Spy*. The pattern of which I am speaking is particularly accessible here. We are presented with a colonial family, the Whartons, who have withrawn from New York at the beginning of the Revolution, and are making their home in Westchester County, the so-called neutral ground. Most of the action occurs in the neutral ground, and while one would not be justified in finding specific symbolic implications here, the fact does carry a certain significance for the imagination. The elder Mr. Wharton, a wealthy and cultivated but somewhat simple-minded colonial, refuses to make a choice between the English and Americans. His son is a Captain in the British army, while of his two daughters, Sarah, the elder, favours the Crown; Frances, the Americans. The following scrap of very pedestrian dialogue not only illustrates the situation out of which the action grows, it is representative of the way in which Cooper keeps the 'tension' in the foreground. Sarah, speaking first, addresses a distinguished stranger who has sought shelter for the night at their home in Westchester:

'I do wish, with my father, that this cruel war was at an end, that we might return to our friends once more.'

'And you, Miss Frances, do you long as ardently for peace as your sister?'

'On many accounts I do . . . but not at the expense of the rights of my countrymen.'

'Rights,' repeated her sister impatiently; 'whose rights can be stronger than those of a sovereign; and what duty is clearer than to obey those who have a natural right to command?' . . .

'I gave you to understand, that my sister and myself differed in our political opinions; but we have an impartial umpire in my father, who loves his own countrymen, and loves the British, so sides with neither.'

Naturally, Cooper is always with the Americans in the final choosing of sides, but in these novels of the Revolution, both the right and the wrong of the matter is in the heart of the actor, whether he be English or American. As the plot unfolds, along the lines suggested, *The Spy* becomes a kind of debate in action between the American and British points of view, but it is not a debate that moves towards any simple solution. The conventional conflict of the plot is intimately associated with a deeper moral ambiguity which Cooper found in American experience, and the infusion of this deeper interest, even though very sporadic in the Revolutionary novels, lends a fitful vitality to what otherwise might have been wholly mechanical. The most important character in *The Spy* is Harvey Birch, who gives the book its name.[3] There is an oddity about his role and character that makes him appear as a kind of emblematic projection of Cooper's own inner conflicts and tensions. Harvey is Washington's favourite spy—an American spy who functions by posing as a British spy among the Americans. Of the Americans, Washington himself is the only one who knows that Harvey Birch, hated by his own countrymen as a traitor worthy of the gallows, is a hero. The true state of the case, for some reason, can never be made known, for in Birch's final interview with the Commander-in-Chief, Washington says to him:

> 'Our situations are different; I am known as the leader of armies—but you must descend into the grave with the reputation of a foe to your native land. Remember that the veil which conceals your true character cannot be raised in years—perhaps never.'

Cooper who, in time, popularly came to be considered a foe of American social institutions, was quite capable of forecasting his own role here. Considering his temperament and the avidity with which he seems to have sought personal unpopularity, very little of the spirit of prophecy would have been required. But the interesting thing about Harvey Birch is that he seems almost wholly composed of ambiguities wrapped around his inner dedication to the cause of America. He is called 'the spy of the neutral ground', and perhaps the term is more apposite than 'American' would be. Cooper has been criticized for not permitting Harvey's true identity to be made known at the close of the Revolution, but the very essence of his identity and meaning consists in the ambiguity of his position. He is a kind of ritual character moving between the American and the British lines, and symbolizing by his own long, dedicated life of suffering and revilement at the hands of his countrymen the fate of those disinterested Americans (or so Cooper seems to be saying) who in other capacities than that of a spy, have also occasionally brought useful information from the British into the United States. In a sense, the benevolent and misunderstood Harvey, who labours as dangerously for the welfare of the good royalist characters in the novel as he does for the good republicans, is a channel of communication between two points of view. I would not contend that this aspect of Harvey Birch is effectively developed in *The Spy*, but it does hover perceptibly in the background, and it is responsible for most of the interest the novel still has.

Moving now to a later and less well known novel, *Wyandotté*, published in 1843, one sees the same pattern of action and conflict evolving, but somewhat more subtly, for *Wyandotté* is a better novel. Replacing Mr. Wharton in this novel is Captain Willoughby, retired from the British army, and living on a

large frontier estate. Like Mr. Wharton, Captain Willoughby has a son who is an officer in the British army in America, and a daughter who marries an American officer. Captain Willoughby himself, while a man of stronger character than Mr. Wharton, is no less given to crucial indecision on the same points. 'The difficulty,' he remarks, in summing up his state of mind, '. . . is to know which *is* one's country. It is a family quarrel, at the best, and it will hardly do to talk about foreigners at all.' Captain Willoughby's closest friend is the Anglican clergyman, Mr. Woods, who tends to favour the American side in the Revolution whereas the Captain, at least in his arguments with the priest, favours the British. The following passage has no distinction from a literary point of view, but it is worth quoting because it indicates, in clearer terms than usual, Cooper's conception of the Revolutionary struggle as a continuing debate between two attitudes to which he was not prepared, except in the specifically political sense, to serve up a facile resolution. The passage occurs at the breakfast table the morning after a particularly protracted argument between Captain Willoughby and the chaplain on the merits of the Revolution:

The parties mentioned entered the room in the order named; the usual salutations followed, and all took their seats at table. Captain Willoughby was silent and thoughtful at first, leaving his son to rattle on in a way that betokened care, in his view of the matter, quite as much as it betokened light-heartedness in those of his mothers and sisters. The chaplain was rather more communicative than his friend; but he, too, seemed restless, and desirous of arriving at some point that was not likely to come uppermost in such a family party. At length the impulses of Mr. Woods got the better of his discretion even, and he could conceal his thoughts no longer.

'Captain Willoughby,' he said, in a sort of apologetic, and yet simple and natural manner, 'I have done little since we parted, seven hours since, but think of the matter under discussion.'

'If you have, my dear Woods, there has been a strong sympathy between us; I have scarcely slept. I may say I have thought of nothing else myself, and am glad you have broached the subject again.'

'I was about to say, my worthy sir, that reflection and my pillow, and your sound and admirable arguments, have produced an entire change in my sentiments. I think now altogether with you.'

'The devil you do, Woods!' cried the 'Captain, looking up from his bit of dry toast in astonishment. 'Why, my dear fellow—this is odd—excessively odd, if the truth must be said. To own the real state of the case, chaplain, you have won *me* over, and I was just about to make proper acknowledgements of your victory.'

This is intended for a touch of comedy; but it does indicate the spirit in which Cooper wrote these novels. They are not only an outward record of the Revolutionary struggle; they are also a dialectic between opposing sides, with the answer held in suspension. Cooper's fine description of the battle of Bunker Hill in *Lionel Lincoln* is written with a sympathetic emphasis on the British point of view, and it is worth remembering that in that novel, as indeed in *Wyandotté*, the principal characters solve their dilemma by returning to the Mother Country in the end, and leading very graceful upper-class lives. The martial conflict in these novels moves inevitably towards a concern with the related cultural conflict, and this Cooper was to make the subject of another series of his novels. But the pressure of this other, and more serious, interest is felt—even if faintly—behind the episodic action of the Revolutionary fiction, and it suggests an interest deeper than we are accustomed to look for in them. It permits an effective infusion of the personal. The Revolutionary novel in the hands of Cooper is an early forerunner of the American international novel, and in it we can study the American sensibility in the process of formulating one of its most characteristic expressions. Although I have been able barely to touch on these novels here, it may be sufficient to suggest the way in which Cooper confers a new formal significance on action by rooting it firmly in a felt moral dilemma or problem. In the Revolutionary novels the moral dilemma gives rise to, and controls, the dramatic action. It is the principle of cohesion among the scattered episodes which, without it, would merely range themselves in long and rambling narratives of random adventure.

III

I have been speaking of a certain moral ambiguity in Cooper's relation with America. It is characteristic—this dual role of simultaneously championing America as the true home of political virtue while shuddering more or less obtrusively at her cultural deficiencies—of the more serious novelists in America in the nineteenth century. This ambiguity of vision and valuation produced a high degree of detachment in these artists, and they used it effectively in their work. In Cooper, to whom the mechanics of plot meant more than to the others, we find this detachment manifesting itself in a curious and recurrent way. Cooper, like so many other writers in the nineteenth century, loved disguises—to superimpose one identity over another. We have already noted the ambiguous double role of Harvey Birch, but it is a rare novel in Cooper's canon in which someone doesn't turn up in masquerade, wearing false hair, a false name, or a false accent. In Cooper, the 'restless analyst' is quite likely to deliver his penetrating social criticisms from behind the protection of an assumed identity. The taste for disguise and the double identity is partly explained by the demands of the kind of plot Cooper favoured—but not entirely so. It helped to maintain that distance between himself and the American matter that is the substance of his novels—a distance that he found psychologically indispensable for the exercise of his critical judgement. Instead of expatriating himself in a foreign country, one might say that Cooper found it almost as satisfactory to dress up like a foreigner on home territory.

In 1828 Cooper published *The Travelling Bachelor: or Notions of the Americans*. It is sometimes a dull book but nevertheless it is a brilliant manual of social criticism on the America of that decade. The book is written in the first person, in the form of letters, and Cooper chooses to speak in the role of an intelligent and sympathetic European seeing the country for the first time. Before visiting the United States, this young man makes a friend of an American whom he meets abroad, and who is named Cadwallader. Cadwallader is Cooper's idea of the *good* American, and the description of him is worth quoting because it shows how near, even at this early date, the ideal was to its definitive expression in the later novels of James:

> On the road between Moscow and Warsaw, I encountered a traveller from the states of North America. He was about to end a long pilgrimage, in Europe, Asia, and Africa, and to return eager as a discharged Swiss, to the haunts of his youth, in the other hemisphere. He appeared like one who was wearied with the selfishness, struggles and factitious distinctions of our eastern regions. Truly, there was something so naïf, and yet so instructed —so much that was intellectual, and withal, so simple—a little that was proud, blended with something philosophical, in the temperament and manner of this western voyager, that he came over my fancy with the freshness of those evening breezes, for which you will shortly be panting, on the shores of the Dardanelles.

Here we have an early portrait of the American's conception of the virtuous, cultivated American that was to be fully rounded out by James. It is characteristic of these fictional Americans that although they always manage to live in Europe, they are always longing to return to the scenes of their youth, and Cooper's Americans are no exception. I have already discussed in the previous chapter some of the political implications of *The Redskins*. Cooper gives us, in this novel, an overblown description of one of these pre-Jamesian expatriates. Mr. Hugh Roger Littlepage, being endowed with a very ample estate, which has increased steadily as property values have risen through several generations in and around New York, has passed twenty of his fifty-nine years off the American continent:

> Mr. Hugh Roger Littlepage, senior, then, had a system of his own, in the way of aiding the scales to fall from American eyes, by means of seeing more clearly than one does, or can, at home, let him belong where he may, and in clearing the specks of provincialism from off the diamond of republican water. He had already seen enough to ascertain that while 'our country' as this blessed nation is very apt on all occasions, appropriate or not, to be called by all who belong to it, as well as by a good many who do not, could teach a great deal to the old world, there was a possibility—just a *possibility*, remark, is my word—that it might also learn a little. . . .

My Uncle Ro was fond of Paris, and he had actually become the owner of a small hotel in the faubourg, in which he retained a handsome furnished apartment for his own use. The remainder of the house was let to personal tenants; but the whole of the first floor, and of the *entresol*, remained in his hands. As a special favour, he would allow some American family to occupy even his own apartments—or rather *appartement*, for the words are not exactly synonymous—when he intended to be absent for a term exceeding six months, using the money thus obtained in keeping the furniture in repair; and his handsome suite of rooms, including a *salon, salle à manger, antichambre cabinet*, several *chambres a coucher*, and a *boudoir*—yes, a male *boudoir*! for so he affected to call it—in a condition to please even his fastidiousness.

This is hard to take, and when Cooper is writing at this level, as he does much too often, we have an example of how a Democrat as well as a Whig can contribute his bit to the genteel tradition. But even those twenty years in Europe and the elegant Parisian boudoir can't prevent Uncle Ro from returning enthusiastically to his native country to confer on the Republic the blessings of his greater refinement. It is typical of the worst in Cooper (although the worst is usually amusing) that he causes Mr. Littlepage, the better to observe American *mores* after so long an absence, to disguise himself as a German pedlar, impressively bewigged and formidably equipped with an immigrant's accent (painstakingly spelled out). We see, not how Cooper faintly adumbrated the international but patriotic American as developed by James, but how he created a caricature that it took all James's art to soften. James did not invent the type represented by his cultivated Americans in Europe. He found them already dusty and badly battered on the work shelves of American fiction when he began to write.

What is important in remarking these resemblances, however, is a fundamental similarity between Cooper's sense of American deficiencies and James's. We are all familiar with James's famous description from his *Hawthorne* of what America lacked in the way of social and cultivated amenities that were at the ready disposal of the European novelists. To return for a moment to *The Travelling Bachelor*, this description of the deprivations facing the American novelist shows a remarkable resemblance to James's list, and an almost identical conception of American cultural poverty, at least as far as the artist is concerned:

> The second obstacle against which American literature has to contend, is in the poverty of the materials. There is scarcely one which contributes to the wealth of the author, that is found, here, in veins as rich as in Europe. There are no annals for the historians; no follies (beyond the most vulgar and commonplace) for the satirist; no manners for the dramatist; no obscure fictions for the writer of romance; no gross and hardy offences against decorum for the moralist; nor any of the rich artificial auxiliaries of poetry. The weakest hand can extract a spark from flint, but it would baffle the strength of a giant to attempt kindling a flame with a pudding stone. I very well know that there are theorists who assume that society and institutions of this country are, or ought to be, particularly favourable to novelties and variety. But the experience of one month, in these states, is sufficient, to show any observant man the falsity of their position. . . . I have never seen a nation so much alike in my life as the people of the United States, and what is more, they are not only like each other, but they are remarkably like that which common sense tells them they ought to resemble. . . . In short, it is not possible to conceive a state of society in which more of the attributes of plain good sense, or fewer of the artificial absurdities of life, are to be found, than here. There is no costume for the peasant (there is scarcely a peasant at all), no wig for the judge, no baton for the general, no diadem for the chief magistrate. The darkest ages of their history are illuminated by the light of truth; the utmost efforts of their chivalry are limited by the laws of God; and even the deeds of their sages and heroes are to be sung in a language that would differ but little from a version of the ten commandments.

In the passages that I have been quoting here we are able to recognize the germs of the international novel. We are confronted by that deeply rooted ambivalence of feeling about American customs and institutions—the ardent patriotism qualified by a persistent restlessness in the presence of republican plainness that sometimes looks a little like radical distaste. And especially there is the international American himself, the American gentleman rampant on a field of mid-Atlantic blue.[4] To revert for a moment to the first part of this chapter, it is perhaps clearer by this time how the drama of divided loyalties in the Revolutionary struggle was associated in Cooper's imagination with this deeper kind of ambiguity. But the Revolutionary novels, while a step in the direction of the international novel, were yet a form to themselves. Cooper, however, wrote several novels that, in formal structure, more nearly approach the characteristic pattern as it was to be developed later. The essential note of the international novel is that it provides a stage on which the American and European cultures dramatically encounter, criticize, and possibly supplement each other. In 1838 Cooper published two long novels, *Homeward Bound* and *Home as Found*.[5] They tell of the return to America, after many years abroad, of Edward Effingham, his daughter Eve, and Edward's caustic brother, John Effingham. Theoretically, the Effingham patriotism is exalted and pure. If, on the evidence of their conduct in the novels, it does not induce them to think well of their country, it enables them to think very well of themselves. Eve Effingham is one of those American princesses of whom we hear more later when Milly Theale goes to Europe; and in Cooper's candid account of Eve's idea of her own birthright as an American we are face to face with that inebriated *sense of himself* that the American still cherishes:

> Eve actually fancied that the position of an American gentleman might really become, nay, that it *ought* to be the highest of all human stations short of that of sovereigns. Such a man had no superior, with the exception of those who actually ruled, in her eyes, and this fact, she conceived rendered him more than noble, as nobility is usually graduated. She had been accustomed to seeing her father and John Effingham moving in the best circles of Europe, respected for their information and independence, undistinguished by their manners, admired for their personal appearance, manly, courteous, and of noble bearing and principles, if not set apart from the rest of mankind by an arbitrary rule connected with rank. Rich, and possessing all the habits that properly mark refinement, of gentle extraction, of liberal attainments, walking abroad in the dignity of manhood, and with none between them and the Deity, Eve had learned to regard the gentlemen of her race as the equals in station of any of their European associates, and as the superiors of most, in everything that is necessary to true distinction.

Certainly John Adams would have included the Effinghams in the natural aristocracy. It should be emphasized that

Cooper is not, even implicitly, critical of Eve's attitude. It is his position as well as hers. When we compare this passage, and, indeed, the whole conception and conduct of the Effingham family, with the pages of bitter social criticism against American manners and institutions (most of it devastatingly correct, but delivered with an unction and a rudeness that amounts to boorishness, or worse) we are squarely confronted with the paradox that has confused so many readers of American writers, and particularly of James. Where so much animus seems to exist against the surfaces of American life, doesn't it, *shouldn't it*, indicate a rooted dislike for America herself? But against the animus we are able to score up the conception of extreme American virtue, and the ludicrous dream of the American gentleman that Eve Effingham gives us, and which may be taken as fairly representative. These contradictions point back to that division in American experience which we have already discussed at some length in the opening chapters. The paradox has great charm because there are a variety of ways in which it can be understood, in the course of examining which we are brought into touch with most of the currents of American thought, and particularly of political thought. Detailed analysis of the Effingham family could show that the reality they stand for in a not overly subtle fashion is a queer combination of Adams's aristocracy, Jefferson's liberal faith in the democratic possibilities of America, with more than a perceptible taint of Hamiltonian snobbishness and financial acuteness. The apparent contradiction of which I have been speaking is not merely the result of a desire for Europe on the part of a few talented or eccentric Americans. It is an historical tension at the deepest level of the American sensibility.

IV

The five Leatherstocking novels are, as a group, Cooper's greatest work. They were composed at long intervals across his active career, *The Pioneers* appearing in 1823, while the last of the series, *The Deerslayer*, was not published until 1841. The continuity in these novels is provided by the character of Leatherstocking himself—the hunter, Natty Bumppo; but the novels do not record a consistent chronological record of

Natty's life. He is an old man in the first; he dies in the third novel, *The Prairie*; while in *The Deerslayer*, in which the conception of Natty's character is fully matured, he is a young man on his first warpath. *The Deerslayer* is probably the best thing Cooper ever wrote, and it is one of the important masterpieces of American literature. We see here his conception of an action as the form of a novel—that conception we have already discussed in relation to the minor novels—perfectly realized here in his art.

The action of *The Deerslayer* takes place at the beginning of the French and Indian War, but the adventures it records are only indirectly associated with that struggle. The novel opens, as so often with Cooper, with a vision of the American forest:

> Whatever may be the changes produced by man, the eternal round of the seasons is unbroken. Summer and winter, seedtime and harvest, return in their stated order with a sublime precision, affording to man one of the noblest of all the occasions he enjoys of proving the high powers of his far-reaching mind, in compassing the laws that control their exact uniformity, and in calculating their never-ending revolutions. Centuries of summer suns had warmed the tops of the same noble oaks and pines, sending their heats even to the tenacious roots, when voices were heard calling to each other, in the depths of a forest, of which the leafy surface lay bathed in the brilliant light of a cloudless day in June, while the trunks of the trees rose in gloomy grandeur in the shades beneath. The calls were in different tones, evidently proceeding from two men who had lost their way, and were searching in different directions for their path.

'. . . two men who had lost their way, and were searching in different directions for their path.' We shall not be portentous if we bring a maximum of meaning to this line. When the two men emerge from the forest into the little clearing we are face to face with the handsome hunter, Hurry Harry, and his companion, Deerslayer, who is Natty Bumppo as a young man in his early twenties. In the long novel that here opens we begin to trace, beyond the pattern of violent physical action, two opposing moral visions of life which are embodied in these two woodsmen. This is the true form and drama of *The Deerslayer*, which is played out against a background of Indian attack and ambuscade—played out on a stage almost classically circumscribed, and over a period of only several days. These severe limits of place and duration impart a unity to the novel that, despite the incidents, which are more than usually densely gathered for Cooper, gives a prominence to the moral theme and its deeper meaning. Deerslayer's values are not only defined through the action, their influence becomes the diffused atmosphere that the others breathe. They do not exist as a separable commentary on the action; they are in the heart of the action itself.

As *The Deerslayer* is no longer inevitably read, even by children, my comments may be more intelligible if I offer a brief résumé of the plot. Reduced to these proportions, it is nothing more than a somewhat exaggerated adventure tale. Deerslayer has lived with, and been educated by, the Delawares, a tribe of Indians for whom Cooper always showed a particular fondness. Among the Delawares his special friend has been the handsome and noble young chief, Chingachgook, betrothed to the Delaware maiden, Wah-ta!-Wah. Before the story opens, Wah-ta!-Wah, coveted for her beauty by many young braves, has been kidnapped by Briarthorne, a traitor to his tribe, and carried into the western wilderness where a hunting expedition of Hurons, or Mingoes, are encamped on the shores of Lake Otsego, which goes under the name of the Glimmerglass. The Hurons, friendly to the French, have travelled this far from the Canadas, and, in their present encampment, are trespassing on English territory, although the remoteness of the spot enables them to do so with impunity. Chingachgook, learning that Wah-ta!-Wah has been carried here, makes an engagement with his friend, Deerslayer, to undertake the rescue of his betrothed—and the two are to meet, at a certain time, by a certain rock, on the shores of the Glimmerglass. It is while travelling to keep this meeting that Deerslayer meets Hurry Harry in the wilderness. They two have known each other before, and as Hurry is also headed for the Glimmerglass, the two join forces. The purpose of Hurry's expedition is to visit a family that lives in this isolated spot, Tom Hutter and his daughters, the beautiful Judith and her feeble-minded sister, Hetty. Despite Judith's reputed indiscretions with the officers of an English garrison a day's march away in the wilderness, Hurry is infatuated with Judith's beauty and wishes to marry her. The Hutter family (with the exception of poor Hetty, who becomes a bore) is very well done. Cooper was always at his best when creating rather sinister old men; and Tom Hutter, who has withdrawn into the wilderness because of a price on his head for piracy, compares favourably with Aaron Thousandacres in *The Chainbearer*, and with Ishmael Bush in *The Prairie*. For the sake of security against Indian attacks Tom Hutter has built a log house, referred to as the Castle, on piles near the middle of the lake; and for additional security and convenience, he has constructed a large flat-bottomed boat, called the *ark*, in which he and his daughters live during the summer. The ark and the castle, with occasional sojourns on the lake shore, become the scene of the crowded action that follows.

The Hurons have just learned of the outbreak of hostilities between the French and the English, and as adherents of the former, they are reluctant to break up their summer encampment without bearing away, as trophies of their trip into enemy country, the scalps of the whites on the Glimmerglass. They are met half-way in their desire by Hutter and Hurry, who desire Indian scalps to collect the bounty the British colonial government has placed on that commodity. The action is complicated by the arrival of Chingachgook, who, from more honourable motives, joins in the scalping expeditions of the white men. It is not necessary to detail the incidents that follow in quick succession. Reduced to a synopsis most plots sound exaggerated or silly, and this is particularly true of Cooper. Much of the persuasiveness of his actions comes from a perfect sense of dramatic timing, and this quality is especially strong in *The Deerslayer*. As the novel progresses towards the later chapters, it comes to resemble a complicated choreography whose intricate measures resolve themselves into several lucid basic movements. There is, first of all, the opposition of two basic points of view represented in action by Deerslayer and Hurry Harry; there is also the opposition of two racial viewpoints for which identical acts may mean honour or dishonour; and, finally, there is the essential theme of Deerslayer's dedication to his own vision of truth. Cooper had never been able to resolve the division in American experience that divided, for example, his European political novels from the Littlepage trilogy, and which made the Effinghams such grotesque failures; but here the conflict is completely transmuted into other terms that are amenable to artistic resolution, and Natty, even though he cannot read, is more of a gentleman in the wilderness than the Effinghams were in their drawing-rooms. But I shall be more explicit about this in the next chapter when I discuss Natty Bumppo as a critical symbol of American experience.

A great part of the effectiveness of *The Deerslayer* arises from Cooper's control of the natural moods of sky, light, and darkness on the Glimmerglass to intensify the emotional movement of the action. The Glimmerglass, which is the confined and the confining scene of all that happens, in its variety of natural moods between midnight, noon, and midnight, constantly suggests that equilibrium in nature which is the serene and indifferent resolution of all violence and blood. But if, after violence, Cooper describes it again and again in some tranquil dusk of early morning or burst of cheerful sunlight to suggest the returning dominance of nature after an interval of human strife, he uses it also to enforce the dramatic necessities of the action at any given time. The following description of night on the Glimmerglass is long, but I quote it because it illustrates the quality of Cooper's writing, which is better in this novel than usual. Because of the threatened hostilities of the Hurons against the Castle during the night, Hutter and Deerslayer decide to embark their whole party in the ark, which is more expedient, both for defence and escape. It is already night when they embark in the large slow-moving boat, whose biblical name is itself something of a portent:

> The vicinity of the hills, with their drapery of pines, had the effect to render nights that were obscure, darker than common on the lake. As usual, however, a belt of comparative light was stretched through the centre of the sheet, while it was within the shadow of the mountains, that the gloom rested most heavily on the water. The island, or castle, stood in this belt of comparative light, but still the night was so dark, as to cover the departure of the ark. At the distance of an observer on the shore, her movements could not be seen at all, more particularly as a background of dark hillside filled up the perspective of every view that was taken diagonally or directly across the water. The prevalent wind on the lakes of that region is west, but owing to the avenues

formed by the mountains, it is frequently impossible to tell the
true direction of the currents as they often vary within short
distances, and brief differences of time. This is truer in light fluc-
tuating puffs of air, than in steady breezes; though the squalls of
even the latter are familiarly known to be uncertain and baffling
in all mountainous regions and narrow waters. On the present
occasion, Hutter himself (as he shoved the ark from her berth at
the side of the platform) was at a loss to pronounce which way
the wind blew. In common, this difficulty was solved by the
clouds, which, floating over the hill tops, as a matter of course,
obeyed the currents; but now the whole vault of heaven seemed a
gloomy wall. Not an opening of any sort was visible. . . .

The action of *The Deerslayer* is convincing because the world
in which it occurs is created with vividly realized circumstantial
detail. It is less mere description than it is the evocation of the
tangible reality of *things*. The passage just quoted loses a good
deal by being torn from context. Its pressure on the nerves
depends on the way it focuses, in the appalling, empty atmosphere of surrounding black, the suspense that has been built
up through pages. It bears an interesting similarity with a
passage from Cooper's great admirer, Joseph Conrad ('F.
Cooper is a rare artist. He has been one of my masters. He is
my constant companion,' letter to Arthur Symonds, 1908).
The passage I am referring to is that famous description of
the night Nostromo and Martin Decoud spend in a lighter on
the Gulf with the silver shipment to the Gould mine:

A great recrudescence of obscurity embraced the boat. The sea
in the gulf was as black as the clouds above. Nostromo, after
striking a couple of matches to get glimpses of the boat compass
he had with him in the lighter, steered by the feel of the wind on
his cheek.

It was a new experience for Decoud, this mysteriousness of the
great waters spread out strangely smooth, as if their restlessness
had been crushed by the weight of that dense night. The Placido
was sleeping soundly under its black poncho.

The main thing now was to get away from the coast and gain
the middle of the gulf before day broke. The Isabels were somewhere at hand. 'On your left as you look forward, señor,' said
Nostromo suddenly. When his voice ceased, the enormous stillness, without light or sound, seemed to affect Decoud's senses
like a powerful drug. He didn't even know at times whether he

were asleep or awake. Like a man lost in slumber, he heard nothing, he saw nothing.

In both passages the blackness is so palpable that it is more concrete than the reality it conceals. And it provides a medium that confers a startling intensity on the actions that it feigns to smother. Both Cooper and Conrad share this extraordinary ability of rendering transient sensations and evocations of atmosphere with a psychological immediacy that can be terrifying. Although it is too long to quote here, an admirable instance of this quality in Cooper occurs in Chapter VI. Tom Hutter and Hurry Harry, impelled by the desire to secure the bounty on Indian scalps, have made an expedition to shore under cover of the darkness to visit the Huron encampment which, they believe, is on this occasion inhabited solely by squaws and children, the warriors having withdrawn for the night to another part of the lake shore. Deerslayer, unable to prevent this excursion, is drawn up in a canoe among the rushes. Cooper evokes the atmosphere of the darkness brooding on the Glimmerglass with great effectiveness—'a gloom of night which threw its shadowy and fantastic forms around the lake, the forest, and the hills. . . . The size of the lake brought all within the reach of the human senses. . . .' Suddenly, through this solitude comes the quavering call of a loon from the opposite shore of the lake: 'Shrill, tremulous, loud, and sufficiently prolonged, it seems the very cry of warning.' And then, as the cry of the loon subsides a second time, 'the profound stillness of night and solitude was broken by a cry so startling as to drive all recollection of the more melancholy call of the loon from the speaker's mind. It was a shriek of agony that came either from one of the female sex, or from a boy so young as not yet to have attained a manly voice. . . . Heart-rending terror —if not writhing agony—was in the sounds, and the anguish that had awakened them was as sudden as it was fearful.'

Tom Hutter and Hurry Harry are not simple cases of moral depravity. Their villainy, which, as we see it, is confined to a habit of scalping Indians, is strictly legal, and encouraged by the government, and Cooper is fully aware of all their implications for American society. For if Hurry and Tom Hutter are not the Americans of the new age, they seem to have their relations with them. Their impressiveness in the book, however, springs from the concrete richness with which they are realized. They are before us, not only as superbly solid physical embodiments of the American wilderness-man, but the nature of the violent, if narrow, action is exactly calculated to illuminate the restricted stage of their moral consciousness. In an early dialogue between Deerslayer and Hurry on the subject of Indians, we have a finely drawn picture of Hurry's mental processes—a picture so typical of a pattern that was to become representative of one line of American rationalizing that in Hurry we almost feel we have the artistic progenitor of Senator McCarran's racial ideal:

'I look upon the red-men to be quite as human as we are ourselves, Hurry. They have their gifts, and their religion, it's true; but that makes no difference in the end, when each will be judged according to his deeds, and not according to his skin.'

'That's downright missionary, and will find little favour up in this part of the country, where the Moravians don't congregate. Now, skin makes the man. This is reason; else how are people to judge of each other. The skin is put on, over all, in order that when a creatur', or a mortal, is fairly seen, you may know at once what to make of him. You know a bear from a hog, by his skin, and a grey squirrel from a black.'

'True, Hurry,' said the other looking back and smiling; 'nevertheless, they are both squirrels.'

'Who denies it? But you'll not say that a red man and a white man are both Injins?'

'No; but I *do* say they are both men. Men of different races and colours, and having different gifts and traditions, but, in the main, with the same natur'. Both have souls; and both will be held accountable for their deeds in this life.'

Hurry was one of those theorists who believed in the inferiority of all the human race who were not white. His notions on the subject were not very clear, nor were his definitions at all well settled; but his opinions were none the less dogmatical or fierce. His conscience accused him of sundry lawless acts against the Indians, and he had found it an exceedingly easy mode of quieting it, by putting the whole family of red men, incontinently, without the category of human rights. Nothing angered him sooner than to deny his proposition, more especially if the denial were accompanied by a show of plausible argument; and he did not listen to his companion's remarks with much composure of either manner or feeling.

Hurry as a moralist is a type we have with us still in American literature. This passage might be compared with the long argument on Indian-killing in Melville's *The Confidence Man*. But Cooper is more successful because Hurry is a thoroughly realistic figure, whereas Melville's Indian-killer, Colonel Moredock, although an actual historical person, exists in the medium of Melville's irony with an unsatisfactory (that is to say, a muddy) ambiguity. Melville would have rejected the clear-cut 'placing' of values which the presence of Deerslayer achieves. And moving up from Melville, we can find Hurry's mental type persisting in the wealthy and socially secure Tom Buchanan of Scott Fitzgerald's *The Great Gatsby*:

> 'Civilization's going to pieces,' broke out Tom violently. 'I've gotten to be a terrible pessimist about things. Have you read *The Rise of the Coloured Races* by this man Goddard? . . . Well, it's a fine book, and everybody ought to read it. The idea is if we don't look out the white race will be—will be utterly submerged. It's all scientific stuff; it's been proved.'

Or, going on from fiction to more 'responsible' utterances, we have this from Teddy Roosevelt in his pre-Presidential years:

> I don't go so far as to think that the only good Indians are the dead Indians, but I believe that nine out of every ten are, and I shouldn't like to enquire too closely into the case of the tenth. The most vicious cowboy has more moral principle than the average Indian.[6]

In Hurry Harry and his moral vision of life we have an early representative of a type that was to become a dominant element in American civilization as it moved along towards the Gilded Age—a type that could supplant moral motives by motives of commercial expediency, and pretend, even to itself, that the substitution had never been made. Cooper's perceptions in creating Hurry Harry are profound and accurate. Although he does not perceptibly wince at the idea of scalping Indian children for the bounty, he is a pattern of the forthright, impulsive, attractive young American. Much of Cooper's genius is shown in the way he effectively suggests the squalid reality behind the romantic figure of the woods. And it is well to bear in mind that this brand of American romanticism was partly cultivated in Cooper's day for the sake of putting some colour of attractive decorum on the crimes of the American wilderness, without which the expansion of the frontier would have notably lagged, or so it seemed.[7] The delicacy of Cooper's distinctions is poised and precise. If he gives the dark side of Hurry, he never identifies him with the overt criminality of old Tom Hutter, the ex-pirate:

> But neither of these two rude beings, so ruthless in all that touches the rights and interests of the red man, though possessing veins of human feeling on other matters, was much actuated by any other desire than a heartless longing for profit. Hurry had felt angered at his sufferings, when first liberated, it is true, but that emotion had soon disappeared in a habitual love of gold, which he sought with the reckless avidity of a needy spendthrift, rather than with the ceaseless longings of a miser. In short, the motive that urged them both so soon to go against the Hurons, was an habitual contempt of their enemy, acting on the unceasing cupidity of prodigality. The additional chances of success, however, had their place in the formation of the second enterprise. It was known that a large portion of the warriors—perhaps all— were encamped for the night, abreast of the castle, and it was hoped that the scalps of helpless victims would be the consequence. To confess the truth, Hutter in particular—he who had just left two daughters behind him, expected to find few but women and children in the camp. This fact had been but slightly alluded to in his communications with Hurry, and with Chingachgook it had been kept entirely out of view.

Hurry Harry is the portent of how things were to go in America. Hurry is a woodsman, but his relation with the wilderness is opposed to Deerslayer's. His true roots are in the settlements, and the wilderness exists for him essentially as a business that he may make periodic visits to 'civilization' with his pockets jingling. Hurry is an indication of how things *will* be, Deerslayer of how they *might* have been. Deerslayer exists on a different level of the imagination than Hurry. He is essentially a poetic evocation, and his conception inevitably incorporates an element of myth in so far as myth may be defined as the incarnation of racial aspiration and memory.

His vision of life is best summed up in this speech from Chapter XV:

> As for farms, they have their uses, and there's them that like to pass their lives on 'em; but, what comfort can a man look for in a clearin' that he can't find in double quantities in the forest? If air, and room, and light, are a little craved, the wind-rows and the streams will furnish 'em, or here are the lakes for such as have bigger longings in that way; but where are you to find your shades, and laughing springs, and leaping brooks, and venerable trees, a thousand years old, in a clearin'? You don't find *them*, but you find their disabled trunks, marking the 'arth like head-stones in a graveyard? It seems to me that the people who live in such places, must be always thinkin' of their own ends, and of natural decay; and that, too, not of the decay that is brought about by time and natur', but the decay that follows waste and violence. Then as to churches, they are good, I suppose, else wouldn't good men uphold 'em. But they are not altogether necessary. They call 'em the temples of the Lord; but Judith, the whole 'arth is a temple of the Lord to such as have right minds. Moreover, all is contradiction in the settlements, while all is concord in the woods. Forts and churches almost always go together, and yet they're downright contradictions; churches being for peace, and forts for war.

Tolerance is a somewhat imprecise word to use in a discussion such as the present one, but tolerance is nothing more than intelligence and sensitive understanding—perception deep enough to find the substantial likeness under the shadows of division. If there is a poetry of tolerance, Deerslayer is its expression. It is what radically distinguishes him from the more characteristically American Hurry Harry. The following exchange between them may seem to add but little to a quotation I have already given, but so important in this quality for understanding Deerslayer and his role that some repetition is justified:

> 'God made us all, white, black, and red; and, no doubt, had his own wise intentions in colouring us differently. Still, he made us, in the main, much the same in feelin's; though I'll not deny he gave each race its gifts. A white man's gifts are christianized, while a red-skin's are more for the wilderness. Thus, it would be a great offence for the white man to scalp the dead; whereas it's a signal vartue in an Indian. Then ag'in a white man can't

D

amboosh women and children in war, while a red-skin may. 'Tis a
cruel work, I'll allow; but for them it's *lawful* work, while for us it
would be grievous work.'

'That depends on your inimy. As for scalping, or even skinning
a savage, I look upon them pretty much the same as cutting off
the ears of wolves, for the bounty, or stripping a bear of its hide.
And then you're out significantly, as to taking the poll of a red-
skin in hand, seeing that the very Colony has offered a bounty for
the job; all the same as it pays for wolves' ears, and crows' heads.'

Cooper never forgets that Hurry's scalping practices are
legally sanctioned and encouraged by the government under
which Deerslayer also lives. Perversely, it is Hurry, not Deerslayer, who follows the pattern set down by the Colony for the
preservation of law, order, and the more doubtful decencies.
This obviously relates to the dilemma that confronted Cooper
in his other novels, and which is at the base of much of his
social criticism. In some ways Deerslayer is as much of an
outsider in the American wilderness as the Effinghams were in
the American drawing-rooms that shattered their sensibilities.
But as a positive norm, Deerslayer is both a moral and an artistic
triumph.

But the mere statement of Deerslayer's tolerance, as it comes
out in such passages of dialogue as the one here quoted, does
an injustice to the living figure of Deerslayer as it exists in the
novel. The whole action is animated by Deerslayer's vision.
It takes firm control of the action, elevating it above plot
mechanics into the realm of life and moral form. Closely
related to, and growing out of this tolerant understanding of
life is a reverence for life itself. One of the most moving passages
in *The Deerslayer* occurs in Chapter VII when Deerslayer kills
his first Indian in self-defence. Mr. Yvor Winters in *Maule's
Curse* has quoted lengthily from this passage, which he refers
to as 'probably the best single passage of prose in Cooper'. I
have not the space to deal with it here, but its importance lies,
not only as Mr. Winters maintains, in powerfully communicating 'the tremendous impersonal quiet of the American
wilderness' (though it certainly does that), but in registering,
both with tenderness and surgical realism, the tensions of a
highly developed and refined moral consciousness under the
shock of a brutal necessity.

Dramatically, the central episode of *The Deerslayer* is that in which Natty, a captive of the Hurons, is released on his honour for a period of twenty-four hours, but at the end of that time is obligated to return to captivity with the almost certain knowledge that he will be put to torture and death. Natty keeps the terms of his promise to the letter, although to do so appears madness to his companions, and probably seems ludicrous heroics to most readers. Nevertheless, this episode is the key to the significance of Deerslayer's life, which is moulded in the imagination with the firm spiritual contours of the saint. It reveals Natty's vision of life to us as a passionate dedication to truth—and truth, not as the pragmatical nothingness it was to become in American life, but as a religious conception. To Hurry Harry's argument against his returning to the Hurons ('What's an Injin or a word passed, or a furlough taken from creaturs like them, that have neither souls nor names?'), Deerslayer replies:

'If they've got neither souls nor names, you and I have both, Harry March, and one is accountable for the other. This fur-lough is not, as you seem to think, altogether a matter atween me and the Mingoes, seeing it is a solemn bargain atween me and God. He who thinks that he can say what he pleases, in his distress, and that 'twill all pass for nothing, because 'tis uttered in the forest, and into red men's ears, knows little of his situation, and hopes, and wants. The words are said to the ears of the Almighty. The air is his breath, and the light of the sun is little more than a glance of his eye.'

What I have said here about *The Deerslayer* I hope will illus-trate my remark at the opening of this chapter that 'for Cooper at his best, an action is the intensified motion of life in which the spiritual and moral faculties of men are no less engaged than their physical selves. Cooper writes adventure stories; but an adventure is only the conventional boundary of this motion of life. . . .' In *The Deerslayer* the moral and the physical action are intrinsically dependent on each other, and this was some-thing new in the English novel since Jane Austen. It is highly probable that Cooper himself was not aware of his achievement along these lines, but it was possible because Cooper's motives in writing were deeply embedded in the new American experi-ence he was trying to express. He may have wished to entertain his readers, but whether consciously or not there was a deeper creative urge at work which made him strive to clarify his own experience as an American. I shall have more to say of the way in which Leatherstocking represents an artistic resolution of that troubled experience. But the mere act of imposing such a responsibility on a fictional symbol itself constitutes an important innovation in form.[8]

Symbolism and Subject Matter

I

SOME years ago Mr. Edmund Wilson wrote in *Axel's Castle* that by the middle of the nineteenth century in the United States, the Romantic writers, Poe, Hawthorne, Melville, and Emerson, were developing in the direction of symbolism.[1] Since that relatively innocent day the application of symbolist theory to American literature has threatened to Cassirerize several major American masterpieces out of existence as significant works of art. A recent book, taking up the same authors mentioned by Mr. Wilson, treats them under this rubric: 'To consider the literary work as a piece of language is to regard it as a symbol, autonomous in the sense that it brings into existence its own meaning.' [2] And Mr. Charles Feidelson, from whose *Symbolism and American Literature* this passage is taken, begins his book by saying: 'The unified phase of American literature which began with the tales of Hawthorne and Poe and ended with Melville and Whitman was not recognized as such by the men who made it.' [3]

My purpose in quoting Mr. Feidelson here is to suggest that the current emphasis on symbolism, and on symbolism of a particular kind, is unfortunate in two respects. It tends to draw an unnatural division in the American literary tradition, to place an important group of writers on the wrong side of sadly misplaced tracks; and, secondly, it minimizes or even denies the importance of subject matter to the symbolist artist. He is left with only the symbolizing process of his own mind for subject-matter.

This is clearly not the symbolism of, say, Whitehead, for whom symbols did not create their own meanings, but represented and explored objective reality.[4] And although Mr. Feidelson groups Henry James among those American writers whose work 'lay in a realm of meaning equally distinct from his own ego and from the world of objective experience',[5] neither does it seem to be the symbolism of James. 'I ... guard myself against the accusation of intimating that the idea, the subject of a novel or a picture, does not matter. It matters, to my sense, in the highest degree.[6] And we recall James's mature dissatisfaction with *The American* precisely because he believed it to be deficient in that quality of relatedness to object experience. 'The balloon of experience,' he wrote in the 'Preface', 'is in fact of course tied to the earth, and under that necessity we swing, thanks to a rope of remarkable length, in a more or less commodious car of the imagination; but it is by the rope we know where we are, and from the moment that cable is cut we are at large and unrelated.' [7]

In effect, the extreme theory of symbolism I have been discussing denies to the artist the role of interpreting in his art the world in which he lives: or, at any rate, the world of his religious, political, and social experience and belief. It is a hopeless theory to argue with, for in a world where the ground of the symbol is only itself, and language is autonomous, the credentials of any opposing argument are automatically open to question. It is obvious that the present argument, which attempts to ground the form of the American novel in its relation to a 'new American experience' would be absurd if such a view of symbolism were true. In this chapter I have no intention of discussing symbolist theory at all. But I wish to examine passages from the works of two writers who are excluded from Mr. Feidelson's 'unified phase of American literature' with the intention of showing that, although they have never been called symbolists, the vitality of these passages exists in their symbolic enactments. The symbolism we shall find in them is related to the objective world in which the authors lived, and its final effect is one of moral judgement on that world. The second passage I shall examine is from Cooper, and it will, I hope, help to relate him to that 'unified phase of American literature' from which he has been excluded.

II

The first passage I wish to analyse is one from eighteenth-century prose. Hector St. John Crèvecoeur's *Letters from an American Farmer* was first published in London in 1782. I should like to take a passage from his expository prose, having no symbolic ambitions, and coming from a period to which

symbolism in our sense meant little or nothing, and show how a
recorded factual situation can slip the leash of the external
limitations imposed by the objective data it describes, and,
rising to a high imaginative level, live in the mind with essentially symbolic life which is intrinsically related to the facts it
records:

I was not long since invited to dine with a planter who lived
three miles from ——, where he then resided. In order to avoid
the heat of the sun, I resolved to go on foot, sheltered in a small
path, leading through a pleasant wood. I was leisurely travelling
along, attentively examining some peculiar plants which I had
collected, when all at once I felt the air strongly agitated, though
the day was perfectly calm and sultry. I immediately cast my eyes
toward the cleared ground, from which I was but a small distance, in order to see whether it was not occasioned by a sudden
shower; when at that instant a sound resembling a deep rough
voice, uttered, as I thought, a few inarticulate monosyllables.
Alarmed and surprised, I precipitately looked all round, when I
perceived at some six rods distance something resembling a cage,
suspended to the limbs of a tree; all the branches of which appeared
covered with large birds of prey, fluttering about, and anxiously
endeavouring to perch on the cage. Actuated by an involuntary
motion of my hands, more than by any design of my mind, I
fired at them; they all flew to a short distance, with a most
hideous noise; when, horrid to think and painful to repeat, I perceived a negro, suspended in the cage, and left there to expire!
I shudder when I recollect that the birds had already picked out
his eyes, his cheek bones were bare; his arms had been attacked
in several places, and his body seemed covered with a multitude
of wounds. From the edges of the hollow sockets and from the
lacerations with which he was disfigured, the blood slowly
dropped, and tinged the ground beneath. No sooner were the
birds flown, than swarms of insects covered the whole body of
this unfortunate wretch, eager to feed on his mangled flesh and
to drink his blood. I found myself suddenly arrested by the power
of affright and terror; my nerves were convulsed; I trembled, I
stood motionless, involuntarily contemplating the fate of this
negro, in all its dismal latitude. The living spectre, though
deprived of his eyes, could still distinctly hear, and in his uncouth
dialect begged me to give him some water to allay his thirst.
Humanity herself would have recoiled back with horror; she
would have balanced whether to lessen such reliefless distress, or

mercifully with one blow to end this dreadful scene of agonizing torture! Had I had a ball in my gun, I certainly should have despatched him; but finding myself unable to perform so kind an office, I sought, though trembling, to relieve him as well as I could. A shell ready fixed to a pole, which had been used by some negroes, presented itself to me; filled it with water, and with trembling hands I guided it to the quivering lips of the wretched sufferer. Urged by the irresistible power of thirst, he endeavoured to meet it, as he instinctively guessed its approach by the noise it made in passing through the bars of the cage. Tankè, you whitè man, tankè you, putè some poison and givè me.' 'How long have you been hanging there?' I asked him! 'Two days, and me no die; the birds, the birds, aaah me!' Oppressed with the reflections which this shocking spectacle afforded me, I mustered strength enough to walk away, and soon reached the house at which I intended to dine. There I heard that the reason for this slave being thus punished, was on account of his having killed the overseer of the plantation. They told me that the laws of self-preservation rendered such executions necessary; and supported the doctrine of slavery with the arguments generally made use of to justify the practice; with the repetition of which I shall not trouble you at present.—Adieu.[8]

It is not the shock value of this passage that makes it so intensely a fact in the imagination of the reader. Horrible facts are self-purging. The mind casts them out for her better health. But here the caged negro acquires a symbolic status and will not be exorcized. The image of a caged man is not in itself capable of assaulting the imagination in this way, as Marlowe's Bajazet can prove. Certain basic elements combine in Crèvecoeur's passage—quite apart from his explicit intention—to form the dominant symbol, and if any of these were absent the passage would lose its mysterious power.

To begin with, the vision bursts on one in the midst of the so-called best possible of worlds—a world adequately held before the mind, not only in the full context of Crèvecoeur's book, but by the measured periods and the decorous eighteenth-century vocabulary in which he writes. Transfer this episode to any other century—it will have its own quality of nightmare perhaps, but it will be very different from what we have here. Profound as his shock is, Crèvecoeur measures it by the restrained code of an eighteenth-century gentleman; but still his sickening sense of horror comes through like a hideous dye, obscuring the pastoral brightness of the rural scene. This contrast between his true feelings and the restrained, almost artificial expression of them illuminates the picture more vividly than anything else could; and it underscores the distorted reality of the world he lives in that he encounters the ghastly sight while walking through a pleasant wood to fulfil a genial social obligation.

In the sense the passage gives of an eighteenth century filled with neatly plotted categories, and socially with conceptions of regulation and caste, the cage suddenly becomes a symbol of metaphysical nightmare, and the negro himself a symbol of the terrible cost of merely man-made order. The whole passage is filled with effective touches that contribute to the life of the symbol. The agitation of the air, for example, which Crèvecoeur says was caused by the moving wings of the birds of prey, he mistakes at first for the sound of a sudden shower of rain. As so often in art, rain is like the promise of mercy or gentleness. But here the promise ends in a mockery by nature herself. It signifies the return of the tormentors. And there is the figure of the negro: we see him—all that is left of his human personality —concentrated in a supplication for death. And there is the faint but terrible sacramental echo (Crèvecoeur had been a student of the Jesuits in France) of the insects, 'eager to feed on his mangled flesh and to drink his blood'. Then, after the shocking irony of, 'with the repetition of which I shall not trouble you at present', the passage in the letter ends, as Crèvecoeur takes leave of his correspondent, with the gentlest, the softest of all farewells—Adieu.

This 'melancholy scene', as he calls it, which Crèvecoeur encountered in the Carolina woods one afternoon nearly two centuries ago cannot matter very much now merely as historical fact. But Crèvecoeur was creating a symbol without knowing it. It is not the fact that arrests us, but the way he recreated it in language. The language is not merely in touch with the immediate tragedy; it has its roots in a reality that was vaster than Crèvecoeur was consciously aware of. From the implicitly ironic interplay beween his polite and measured prose reflecting the illusion of external order in the universe, and the hideous, torturing fact of the caged negro, there open the richest symbolic perspectives. This kind of symbolism, so deeply immersed in the reality of human experience, is worth more, it seems to me, than a symbolism which is only interested in intellectual method, and whose roots are cut off from life.

III

Cooper, as I have said, is not allowed to stand with the symbolist writers. This is partly because the excessive claims made for symbolism today have a tendency to blind us to those subtle, but more modest, achievements of symbolic technique where the method itself is working quietly hand in hand with the materials and pressures of external reality, and where the symbolic process is not defined by the operation of some one overwhelming symbol such as Moby Dick, but is a quality of imagery and organization in the texture of the prose, gradually gathering towards a concentration of effect that is, in fact, a symbol although it may not overtly present itself as one. No one would wish to pass Cooper off primarily as a symbolist writer, and yet because all successful art contains a strong symbolic element, the best parts of Cooper are open to a symbolic interpretation if we assume a real connection between symbolic technique and objective reality. In the following several pages I shall consider the nature of this symbolist element in Cooper. The assumption is that Cooper was not interested in symbols and that the writers who came later were not interested in anything else. Perhaps no American writer was less curious about form or method as such than Cooper, but his work is evidence that he was passionately concerned with American experience. This experience demanded a symbol, and Cooper resorted to it almost spontaneously, even without knowing it.

Natty Bumppo has often been called the greatest figure in American fiction, but his final reality for our imagination is not, I think, the reality of a fictional character with a certain history and with a set of human relationships. Rather, he embodies a meaning for us that his recorded acts do not adequately explain. Natty Bumppo is no more a mere frontiersman for us than Moby Dick is a mere whale. In the final analysis, Natty is not a 'character' in the nineteenth-century sense at

all, but a symbol. This is not to say that Natty Bumppo claims
an autonomous existence as a symbol out of relation to everything but himself. The *idea* of Natty grows out of the complex
tensions of the American experience, and as he progressively
takes form in the novels as a symbol he activates stores of energy
which are latent in the American experience he is expressing.
And this is a radically different process from the one by which
Taji in *Mardi* becomes, in his voyaging, a symbol of a symbol.

Natty Bumppo's role has been consistently misunderstood.
Mr. James Grossman writes of him:

> Natty in keeping clear of civilization's responsibilities had held
> on to its higher and also to its pleasanter values. The primitive
> forest in which he lives his youth and the naked plains on which
> he dies are scenes of horror and violence because of the deeds of
> the other white characters in the story, but for Natty they are
> always the great good place, an inviolable retreat from the pres-
> sure of reality. His life there is a kind of ideal bachelor existence,
> fastidious and untouched by the lives of others. He can afford to
> be helpful to every stranger, loyal for the duration of the adven-
> ture but without risk of committing himself too far. His one per-
> manent friend, Chingachgook, is a member of another race, and
> strong though their feeling for each other is, a correctness of tone
> pervades their relation and saves it from intimacy. Natty turns
> the wilderness into a salon and indulges with every newcomer the
> passion for endless talk that is characteristic of so many lovers
> of solitude.[9]

This passage proceeds on the assumption that Natty is an
ordinary fictional character who can be judged, in some
degree, by criteria of social reality. But to accuse Natty Bumppo
of shirking his social obligations is as far fetched as to accuse
Huckleberry Finn of juvenile delinquency. By the time Natty
dies as a very old man in *The Prairie* we are not at the death
scene of a man as much as we are at the apotheosis of an intellectual and spiritual attitude—an attitude that cannot be
abstracted or paraphrased successfully because it has been
developed with the concrete particularity of realized art. Just
as Yeats's complex symbol of Byzantium is the heaven of the
creative imagination, so Natty Bumppo remains a perpetual
possibility of perfection to the American imagination—and a
perpetual reproach.

The final sentence of the Leatherstocking series sums up the meaning of Natty: 'We live in a world of transgressions and selfishness, and no pictures that present us otherwise can be true; though happily for human nature, gleamings of that pure Spirit in whose likeness man has been fashioned are to be seen relieving its deformities and mitigating, if not excusing, its crimes.'   It is not a distinguished sentence, but it suggests the role that Natty plays. It is a ritual role in that he enacts the conscience of America in so far as it has a traditional continuity. He does not flee from the responsibilities of civilization as much as he is driven from the settlements by his refusal to compromise with what appears a failure of integrity in his eyes. The success of Cooper's treatment comes from the way he was able to endow the figure symbolizing such a meaning with the ability to live and grow in the imagination. *The Prairie*, it may be agreed, is the second best of the Leatherstocking tales, and I should like to consider one or two passages from it here as an illustration of that symbolist element which I have said is present in Cooper.

In the opening chapter, our first encounter with Natty Bumppo elevates him to a giant dimension in the imagination— and this first glimpse we have of him, like the last, is a measure of the symbolic content he claims. It is possibly the finest example of American baroque art that we have. There is a super-human and flame-like quality about it, an arrested violence. It will be necessary to incorporate a somewhat lengthy quotation here to make my point. It begins with a description of Ishmael Bush and his family as, towards nightfall, their small wagon train makes its way across the prairie:

> Still, the leader of the emigrants steadily pursued his way with no other guide than the sun, turning his back resolutely on the abodes of civilization, and plunging, at each step, more deeply if not irretrievably, into the haunts of the barbarous and savage occupants of the country. As the day drew nigher to a close, how-ever, his mind, which was, perhaps, incapable of maturing any connected system of fore-thought, beyond that which related to the interests of the present moment, became, in some slight degree, troubled with the care of providing for the wants of the hours of darkness.
> On reaching the crest of a swell that was a little higher than

the usual elevations, he lingered a minute, and cast a half-curious eye, on either hand, in quest of those well-known signs, which might indicate a place where the three grand requisites of water, fuel, and fodder were to be obtained in conjunction.

It would seem that his search was fruitless; for after a few moments of indolent and listless examination, he suffered his huge frame to descend the gentle declivity, in the same sluggish manner that an over-fatted beast would have yielded to the downward pressure.

His example was silently followed by those who succeeded him, though not until the young man had manifested much more of interest, if not of concern, in the brief inquiry, which each, in his turn, made on gaining the same lookout. It was now evident, by the tardy movement both of beasts and men, that the time of necessary rest was not far distant. The matted grass of the lower land presented obstacles which fatigue began to render formidable, and the whip was becoming necessary to urge the lingering teams to their labour. At this moment, when, with the exception of the principal individual, a general lassitude was getting the mastery of the travellers, and every eye was cast, by a sort of common impulse, wistfully forward, the whole party was brought to a halt, by a spectacle, as sudden as it was unexpected.

The sun had fallen below the crest of the nearest wave of the prairie, leaving the usual rich and glowing train on its track. In the centre of this flood of fiery light, a human form appeared, drawn against the gilded background, as distinctly, and, seemingly as palpable, as though it would come within the grasp of any extended hand. The figure was colossal; the attitude musing and melancholy, and the situation directly in the route of the travellers. But embedded, as it was, in its setting of garish light, it was impossible to distinguish its just proportions or true character.

The effect of such a spectacle was instantaneous and powerful. The man in front of the emigrants came to a stand, and remained gazing at the mysterious object, with a dull interest, that soon quickened into superstitious awe. His sons, so soon as the first emotion of surprise had a little abated, drew slowly around him, and, as they who governed the teams gradually followed their example, the whole party was soon condensed in one, silent, wondering group. Notwithstanding, the impression of a supernatural agency was very general among the travellers, the ticking of gunlocks was heard, and one or two of the bolder youths cast their rifles forward, in readiness for service.

Probably no other novel in the language has first presented its principal character to us in so heroic a way. It is remarkable that Leatherstocking manages to sustain the implications of this introduction, which would be impossible were he to be considered a naturalistic character in Mr. Grossman's sense. In this scene Cooper gives him to us almost as a natural evocation of the land itself—a kind of guardian spirit of the wilderness and the prairies who stands directly across the path of the spoilers. The Bush family regards the figure with supernatural awe, and to the reader, for whom the figure as its stands magnified in fiery light remains unidentified until the end of the chapter—to the reader also it is not a *human* form. The unusual power of the passage flows, as nearly always with Cooper, from a perfect sense of timing, and from a remarkable plastic vision that enables him to group details into palpable and contrasting masses. The Bush family, themselves a remarkable achievement in the creation of character, are the perfect spectators for this vision of Natty Bumppo. Their brooding heaviness, their sinister quality, the torpid but sure movement of their imaginations under powerful stimulus, provide exactly the right preparation for Cooper's baroque description of the colossal fiery figure in the sky. For several pages Cooper leads us towards the vision with the slow-moving wagon train, the teams growing tired as daylight fades, the prairie grass longer and more matted. The reader himself begins to participate in that general fatigue which will permit the vision to react on him with maximum effect. This is not simply a dramatic entrance made by the chief character. Cooper never allows Natty to lose entirely that aura of almost supernatural power that he acquires here.

With the exception of *The Pioneers* all the Leatherstocking tales are stories of flight and pursuit; yet the chase, as it occurs in the individual novels, is merely a matter of plot mechanics. But on the other hand, the flight of Natty Bumppo before the woodchoppers as they move steadily into the West, clearing the forest before them, is a flight charged with deeper significance, and despite the futility of paraphrase here, I wish to consider a little more fully what this flight means when we consider it as a symbol. Perhaps one of the characters in *The Prairie* gives as adequate a description of Natty's meaning as anyone is ever likely to:

The man I speak of was of great simplicity of mind, but of sterling worth. Unlike most of those who live a border life, he united the better instead of the worse qualities of the two people. He was a man endowed with the choicest—and perhaps the rarest —gift of nature—that of distinguishing good from evil. His virtues were those of simplicity. In courage he was the equal of his red associates. In short, he was a noble shoot from the stock of human nature, which could never attain its proper elevation and importance, for no other reason than because it grew in the forest.

This ability to distinguish good from evil is the ultimate note of Natty Bumppo's character, and it provides the moral passion of his flight. This flight before the advance of American civilization is virtually a moral judgement on it. Cooper presents it most often in terms of Natty's hatred of the destructive waste and selfishness of the settlements, and yet it is much more complex than that. We have glanced briefly at Cooper's indignant social criticisms of America in the Effingham novels; we have looked more carefully at his astute political criticisms, and have considered his despair in the face of agrarian reforms that he thought spelled the downfall of aristocratic thought and feeling in his country. Certainly, the medium of Cooper's mind was subtle enough to permit an attitude of great complexity to take shape. In his political and agrarian novels he enlarged the scope of the novel itself by introducing ideas in a functional and structural way. These ideas became the very substance of the novels. Important as this was technically in the development of fictional form, the novels remain very incomplete successes because Cooper's personal feelings and imagination never seem wholly involved. In the Leatherstocking tales the reverse is true. The ideas are not present as such, although they may make their presence felt indirectly. Instead, the imagination takes over. Natty Bumppo is not a 'character' in the sense Mr. Grossman implies, but a symbol thrown up from the depths of Cooper's own response to America, a response that involved both love and revulsion. Natty's love for the land of America is mystical in its proportions, and yet the civilization she was producing seemed a violation of that land itself. Natty's flight across the continent is an unconscious but profoundly realized symbol of Cooper's own recoil. But whereas in the Effingham novels we are mainly conscious of the hatred Cooper felt for the national manners and ideas that he believed had betrayed American's spiritual obligations and possibilities, in the Leatherstocking tales we are aware of that tolerance and charity that was, after all, the prime mover in his complicated attitude.

In *The Prairie*, then, Cooper endows Natty Bumppo in his symbolic role with heroic grandeur. In the opening chapter he steps into our vision from a heaven on fire, and in his magnificent death scene, which is the finest thing in the book, the old man sits facing the setting sun with his old hunting dog dead at his feet. It is not accidental that Cooper has managed to suggest that Natty Bumppo steps back into the flaming heavens from which he seemed to come. The scene has a largeness and simplicity that carries the mind back to some remote heroic age, and it places a seal of consecration on Cooper's response to American society and reality. And at the same time it carries intimations of impending tragedy that look forward to Gatsby's death some eighty years later in Scott Fitzgerald's novel.

VI

Hawthorne's Short Stories

IN his essay, 'Society and Solitude', Emerson has a fine passage through which we can enter into a consideration of one of the central problems in Hawthorne's art, his concern with solitude in a democratic society.   Emerson writes :

> Though the stuff of tragedy and romance is in a moral union of two superior persons whose confidence in each other for long years, out of sight and in sight, and against all appearances, is at last justified by victorious proof of probity to gods and men, causing joyful emotion, tears and glory,—though there be for heroes this *moral union*, yet they too are as far off as ever from an intellectual union, and the moral union is for comparatively low and external purposes, like the co-operation of a ship's company or of a fire-club. But how insular and pathetically solitary are all the people we know! Nor dare they tell what they think of each other when they meet in the street. . . .
>
> Such is the tragic necessity which strict science finds underneath our domestic and neighbourly life, irresistibly driving each adult soul with whips into the desert, and making our warm covenants sentimental and momentary. We must infer that the ends of thought were peremptory, if they were to be secured at such ruinous cost. They are deeper than can be told, and belong to the immensities and eternities. They reach down to that depth where society itself originates and disappears; where the question is, which is first, man or men? where the individual is lost in his source.

And he goes on to emphasize the isolation of men of genius: 'We pray to be conventional. But the wary heaven takes care you shall not be if there is anything good in you. Dante was very bad company . . .' and so on. In these quotations we have the problem of the artist, the exceptional spirit, in a democratic society. It was a problem that preyed on the nineteenth-century American conscience. Was the man of genius worth the special privileges and indulgences he required from society, or was the first duty of all men to sacrifice themselves in the interests of a levelling social fabric to which American political theory had already attached a mystique?

To the nineteenth-century American, such a society as he believed was developing in his own country was indeed one of the preemptory ends of thought, but at the same time the writers whom we are considering were aware, like Emerson, of the ruinous cost; and they were aware of it because it was principally they, as artists, who were called upon to pay. The penalty of genius was isolation, exclusion from the democratic community whose tendency, as Cooper had said, was 'in all things towards mediocrity'. The problem of the artist was, at one level, a political one. We can come at this aspect of it most directly in the early Federalist writers of the Republic such as Joseph Dennie or Fisher Ames. In 1807 an anonymous writer in the *Boston Anthology* had written:

> We know that in this land, where the spirit of democracy is everywhere diffused, we are exposed, as it were, to a poisonous atmosphere, which blasts everything beautiful in nature, and corrodes everything elegant in art; we know that with us 'the rose petals fall ungathered' and we believe that there is little to praise and nothing to admire in most of the objects which first present themselves to the view of the stranger.[1]

While something of this attitude was to be preserved later in the genteel tradition, the development of a democratic philosophy in Jeffersonianism, and later in Jacksonianism, attracted the best intelligences away from a programme of mere reaction and finance. Here, then, is a clearly defined split in the consciousness of the American artist of the time. Wasn't it possible that the practice of his art, which by its very nature set him apart from society as an observer and an analyst—wasn't it possible that it somehow constituted a betrayal of his own nature as an American? It often seemed so to Hawthorne's New England conscience. But, with a shift of mood, wasn't it perhaps the artist after all who was betrayed by his political and social traditions? The problem could cut both ways and did. We have already considered the debate, finally un-resolved, between Cooper's European political novels and his Littlepage trilogy. The tension between solitude and democratic community is not identical with that, but it is related.

Had Hawthorne been able to regard the matter from the point of view of the anonymous writer in the *Boston Anthology* it would have been a simple matter to put the case in terms of a black and white contrast in favour of the artist. In stories like *The Devil in Manuscript* Hawthorne's rage at society sometimes broke through, but ultimately he saw the role of the artist as involved in the greater question of his human relationship with his fellow men. And on this score Hawthorne was never secure. One of the most personal passages in Hawthorne's writings occurs in his introduction to *The Scarlet Letter*, 'The Custom House':

> Either of these stern and black-browed Puritans would have thought it quite a sufficient retribution for his sins that after so long a lapse of years the old trunk of the family tree, with so much venerable moss upon it, should have borne, at its topmost bough, an idler like myself. No aim that I have ever cherished would they recognize as laudable; no success of mine, if my life, beyond its domestic scope, had ever been brightened by success, would they deem otherwise than worthless, if not positively disgraceful. 'What is he?' murmurs one grey shadow of my forefathers to the other. 'A writer of story books! What kind of business in life, what manner of glorifying God, or being serviceable to mankind in his day and generation may that be? Why, the degenerate fellow might as well have been a fiddler!' Such are the compliments bandied between my great grandsires and myself across the gulf of time! And yet, let them scorn me as they will, strong traits of their nature have intertwined themselves with mine.'

There is evidence that throughout his life he suffered an incapacity to adjust himself practically to the society that, as an American, he wished to believe in. He wished to express his solidarity with it, and this became a nervous necessity in that degree in which he found it difficult to cast aside his dissatisfactions with it. To state the case succinctly: Hawthorne's compulsive affirmation of American positives, particularly in the political sense, led to a rejection of the idea of solitude; and solitude as an expression of aristocratic withdrawal seemed to side with Europe rather than with America when the two traditions stated their respective claims. But unfortunately it also seemed to side with the practice of his art.

This ambiguity, which is a very complex one, lies near the centre of all of Hawthorne's art, and it reflects that 'tragic necessity' Emerson described in the passage quoted above. The 'moral union' envisaged by democracy—especially Jacksonian democracy—is for comparatively low and external purposes, and practically speaking it often seems to preclude anything better. Emerson's native optimism achieved a rather too facile resolution of the tension in his short 'Society and Solitude' essay (which reads like a footnote on Hawthorne), but for Hawthorne himself no easy resolution was possible. The tension between solitude and society, particularly as it is focused in the role of the artist, may be examined to advantage in 'Ethan Brand'. Written about 1848, it is not one of his best stories, but it is one of his most famous and most praised ones. The story is ostensibly concerned, as Mr. Mark Van Doren has pointed out, with 'the idea of a man whom an obsessive desire for perfection in knowledge or virtue or art has driven beyond nature, making him an accomplished but cold-hearted monster'.[2] More fundamentally it is concerned with the problem of the creative artist, and particularly the writer. Hawthorne analyses the problem—or tries to—not in terms of the relation of the artist to his art, but in terms of his relation to society.

Before considering 'Ethan Brand' here, I should like to lead into that story by pausing for a moment on the character of Holgrave in *The House of the Seven Gables*. Holgrave is presented as a type of the artist, and although a daguerreotypist may seem a somewhat limited kind of artist to us, Hawthorne's choice of this particular art is significant. Holgrave takes likenesses. That is to say, he freezes personalities, arrests their vital movement in a static posture. His relation to them is not vital and reciprocal, but rather he stands in relation to them as a collector. His art becomes a symbol of his participation in life. A lodger in the house of Hepzibah Pyncheon and her brother Clifford, he has a tendency to stand aside from their human tragedy and merely observe—to take their likenesses, as it were. He speaks of his own role in these terms:

> 'But you have no conception of what a different kind of heart mine is from your own. It is not my impulse, as regards these two individuals, either to help or hinder; but to look on, to analyse, to explain matters to myself, and to comprehend the drama which, for almost two hundred years has been dragging its slow length

over the ground where you and I now tread. If permitted to witness the close, I doubt not to derive a moral satisfaction from it, go matters how they may.'

Obviously young Holgrave, like Henry James, was a 'restless analyst' and Hawthorne's implication clearly is that Holgrave is a type of the novelist or writer. The reader of *The House of the Seven Gables* can scarcely refrain from concluding that Holgrave is meant to be Hawthorne's comment on himself as artist. Holgrave is certainly not presented as a villain in the novel. He is, indeed, the hero. But his description of his own heart in the passage I have quoted cannot be distinguished from the nature of Ethan Brand's 'crime'. When we compare Holgrave and Ethan Brand—one a hero and the other a monster—and when we consider that, despite Hawthorne's conflicting attitudes towards them, their moral reality is almost identical, we see that Hawthorne is faced here with the seeds of an impossible dilemma. This is the consequence of his trying to treat two problems—the problem of art and the problem of social morality—as if they were one and identical. Hawthorne's art is frequently the point at which two conflicting tendencies in him cross. The conditions of American society repel him, just as they had repelled Cooper, and drive him to retreat from society; but his democratic social conscience urges him, on the contrary, to take a role in society. Naturally enough, he finds that his creative and critical impulses inevitably side with the tendency to withdraw that he feels so strongly. This arouses his sense of guilt, and leads him to entertain confused feelings about art itself. And it would be wrong to underestimate Hawthorne's confusion on the subject of his own art. A greater artist than Cooper, and a finer critic of his own production, he lacked Cooper's clarity of vision concerning his own motives and the function he wished to perform as an artist.

I said that 'Ethan Brand' gives us the artist in his social relations. This identification of Ethan Brand as an artist depends in some measure on seeing him in the full context of Hawthorne's work, but even so, Hawthorne's meaning is sufficiently contained in the story to make it possible to come at it without outside references.

Ethan Brand the watcher of the lime kiln, who has started out many years before the opening of the story on a quest to find the Unpardonable Sin, returns to the scene which had been his starting point. Approaching the lime kiln at night, he finds Bartram, his stupid and vulgar successor, keeping the blaze alight with the help of his little son Joe. The news is spread that the legendary wanderer has returned, and the villagers gather at the kiln to see and question Ethan Brand. Confronted with the villagers themselves, a crew of unattractive and more or less decayed human beings, Ethan Brand seems to have all the advantages on his side, and yet the 'monstrous' element in his nature is revealed by his human remoteness from his former neighbours:

> The idea that possessed his life had operated as a means of education; it had gone on cultivating his powers to the highest point of which they were susceptible; it had raised him from the level of an unlettered labourer to stand on a star-lit eminence, whither the philosophers of the earth, laden with the lore of universities, might vainly strive to clamber after him. So much for the intellect! But where was the heart? That, indeed, had withered,—had contracted,—had hardened,—had perished! It had ceased to partake of the universal throb. He had lost his hold on the magnetic chain of humanity. He was no longer a brother-man, opening the chambers or the dungeons of our common nature by the key of holy sympathy, which gave him a right to share in all its secrets; he was now a cold observer, looking on mankind as the subject of his experiment, and, at length, converting man and woman to be his puppets, and pulling the wires that moved them to such degrees of crime as were demanded for his study.

Ethan Brand was clearly no Jacksonian democrat, and as the story proceeds we gather that Hawthorne means to present him as a symbol of the artist:

> An old German Jew travelling with a diorama on his back, was passing down the mountain-road towards the village just as the party turned aside from it, and, in hopes of eking out the profits of the day, the showman had kept them company to the lime kiln.
> 'Come, old Dutchman,' cried one of the young men, let me see your pictures, if you can swear they are worth looking at!'
> 'Oh yes, Captain,' answered the Jew,—whether as a matter of courtesy or craft, he styled everybody Captain,—'I shall show you, indeed, some very superb pictures!'
> So placing his box in a proper position, he invited the young

men and girls to look through the glass orifices of the machine,
and proceeded to exhibit a series of the most outrageous scratch-
ings and daubings, as specimens of the fine arts, that ever an
itinerant showman had the face to impose on his circle of spectators. The pictures were worn out, moreover, tattered, full of
cracks and wrinkles, dingy with tobacco smoke, and otherwise in
a most pitiable condition. Some purported to be cities, public
edifices, and ruined castles in Europe; others represented Napo-
leon's battles and Nelson's sea-fights; and in the midst of these
would be seen a gigantic, brown, hairy hand,—which might have
been mistaken for the Hand of Destiny, though, in truth, it was
only the showman's,—pointing its forefinger to various scenes of
the conflict, while its owner gave historical illustrations. When,
with much merriment at its abominable deficiency of merit, the
exhibition was concluded, the German bade little Joe put his
head into the box. Viewed through the magnifying glasses, the
boy's round, rosy visage assumed the strangest imaginable aspect
of an immense Titanic child, the mouth grinning broadly, and the
eyes and every other feature overflowing with fun at the joke.
Suddenly, however, that merry face turned pale, and its expression changed to horror, for this easily impressed and excitable
child had become sensible that the eye of Ethan Brand was fixed
upon him through the glass.

'You make the little man to be afraid, Captain,' said the
German Jew, turning up the dark and strong outline of his visage
from his stooping posture. 'But look again, and, by chance, I shall
cause you to see something that is very fine, upon my word!'

Ethan Brand gazed into the box for an instant, and then starting back, looked fixedly at the German. What had he seen?
Nothing, apparently; for a curious youth, who had peeped in
almost at the same moment, beheld only a vacant space of canvas.

'I remember you now,' muttered Ethan Brand to the showman.

'Ah, Captain,' whispered the Jew of Nuremberg, with a dark
smile, 'I find it to be a heavy matter in my show-box—this
Unpardonable Sin!'

The diorama, like Holgrave's camera in *The House of the
Seven Gables*, is a symbol of the way external reality is imprisoned
in art, and of the way human beings can be exploited for the
purpose of artistic effect by the artist. It will be recalled that
before his departure on his quest for the Unpardonable Sin,
Ethan Brand had in some way betrayed a young girl, Esther.
In the paragraph immediately preceding the diorama passage

above, Hawthorne says that Ethan Brand, with cold and remorseless purpose, had made Esther 'the subject of a psychological experiment, and wasted, absorbed, and perhaps annihilated her soul, in the process'. Hawthorne is not explicit about
the nature of this betrayal, but the reader is sure that it was
nothing along the lines of the usual fictional seduction. It was
a matter of the spirit, some kind of violation of the soul. The
diorama passage, following immediately on this reference to
Esther, is meant to make the nature of the crime explicit, and
it associates the crime with the creative process as Hawthorne
frequently, if not always, conceived it.

The pictures in the diorama are the usual subject-matter
of fiction, as subject-matter was thought of by the nineteenth-
century novelist. They remind one of Henry James's famous
list of all the American novelist did *not* possess in the way of
subjects: cities, public edifices, ruined castles, heroic battles
and sea-fights. But here they are all reduced to dioramic scale,
looking a little like reality, and yet not reality. Into this box,
which inevitably reminds the reader of the framework of an
art form, one sees the manipulating hand of the showman,
which might be mistaken for the Hand of Destiny. Obviously
Hawthorne means to suggest the manipulating intelligence of
the artist who exploits reality for the sake of his art. The action
suddenly takes on a more sinister tone in the next incident. The
German Jew asks little Joe to put his head into the box, which
he does with childish joy:

> Viewed through the magnifying glasses, the boy's round, rosy
> visage assumed the strangest imaginable aspect of an immense
> Titanic child. . . . Suddenly, however, the merry face turned pale
> and its expression changed to horror, for this easily impressed and
> excitable child had become sensible that the eye of Ethan Brand
> was fixed on him through the glass.

At best this is an enigmatic passage, and its interpretation
at any level must be a little forced. But it seems most obviously
to mean that Joe has been transported from his natural
habitat in the world into another and illusory world which
possesses only a fake reality. The implication is that in this
strange little world of dioramic illusion he is at Ethan Brand's
mercy, and the passage is clearly intended as an implicit

commentary on the relationship between Brand and Esther in which she had been made the subject of psychological experiment.

After little Joe has withdrawn his head from the box, the Jew says to Brand, apparently with irony:

'But look again, and, by chance I shall cause you to see something that is very fine, upon my word.'

'Ethan Brand gazed into the box for an instant, and then starting back, looked fixedly at the German. What had he seen? Nothing . . . only a vacant space of canvas.'

'I remember you now,' muttered Ethan Brand to the showman.

'Ah, Captain,' whispered the Jew of Nuremberg with a dark smile, 'I find it to be a heavy matter in my show-box,—this Unpardonable Sin!'

What Hawthorne is saying here, somewhat obscurely, is that the reality of art, being a false reality, ends in nothing—only an empty space on canvas. And then the German Jew identifies the diorama with the Unpardonable Sin itself—all of which adds up to no very flattering conception of Hawthorne's own art. The role of the German Jew is not as puzzling as it first appears. Mr. Richard Harter Fogle, with a point that escapes me, says that he is the Wandering Jew who brings with him the fascination of myth and legend.[3] Actually, he represents a daemonic extension of Ethan Brand's personality so that the showman, manipulating the diorama, stands essentially for Ethan Brand as artist.

I do not think that 'Ethan Brand' is a successful story. It is ambiguous in an unsatisfactory way, and at times it seems to totter on the brink of ultimate incoherence. At no time does the imagery and symbolism take over in the way the symbolism of 'My Kinsman, Major Molineux' compels the imagination to unfold, leaving one like its hero Robin, almost trembling with pity and terror. Nevertheless, 'Ethan Brand' does tell us a good deal about Hawthorne's relation to American society, and his inability to conceive an adequate function for the artist in such a society. The conception of art which is developed in this story is unsatisfactory. It sees art, not as a channel of communication and understanding between individuals, but as a field of conflict upon which the artist conducts his nefarious trade of human exploitation. If Emerson's resolution in 'Society and Solitude' seems a little easy to be wholly convincing, Hawthorne as democrat achieves no resolution at all in such a story as this. In effect, he rejects the creatively gifted who cannot or will not be levelled down. But I wish to add at once that when Hawthorne appears in this role it is almost by inadvertence, and because his society offers him no help at all in resolving the tension between the individual and itself.

This tension can be recast in many different forms. In 'Ethan Brand' it is presented in a distorted fashion as the problem of the artist in a democratic society. It is even more obviously capable of a political interpretation, and the psychological variations that can be played on the theme are, of course, nearly unlimited. In any attempt to assess the respective values of the individual and the community when they are deemed to be in conflict, one is, in fact, concerned with the ultimate problem of determining and evaluating the nature of reality itself. 'All literature', Mr. Trilling writes, 'tends to be concerned with the nature of reality—I mean quite simply the old opposition between what really is and what merely seems.' [4] In a society where neither traditional manners nor an orthodoxy exists, the problem is nearly overwhelming, and the serious artist becomes a metaphysician in spite of himself. The sense of intolerable spiritual isolation which is characteristic of so much of Hawthorne's writing, and is perfectly embodied in a figure like Melville's Ahab, would have been impossible had the social and religious traditions of Europe been at Hawthorne's disposal—either for acceptance or rejection. Under the impact of Unitarianism and Transcendentalism, Calvinism had ceased to exist in Hawthorne's New England except as the mantle of respectability worn by Boston merchants, or a nostalgic shadow stripped of sanctions. Without either a mystical Christian community or the living, fluid framework of a traditional social mode, the nineteenth-century American was forced back on the democratic abstraction as the only possible escape for his imprisoned identity.

If Hawthorne felt called upon to press the claims of democracy against the individual and the artist, even to the point of appearing to give the stupid and vulgar Bartram a practical and repulsive triumph over Ethan Brand, it was necessary for him to justify his choice, at least implicitly, by attempting to distinguish between illusion and reality. He had to be able to say that the democratic values were reflections of genuine reality and that aristocratic and artistic values (associated under the rubric of solitude), whenever they conflicted with the claims of the former, were sham. But what traditional criteria did Hawthorne's New England provide him with for making a valid distinction?

We can, I think, uncover a metaphysic concerning the nature of reality that is implicit in Hawthorne's body of fictions. It enters into his stories on two levels. It enters most unpleasantly and unsuccessfully in those stories which reflect Hawthorne's suspicion of the artist, the gifted, creative individual, whom he instinctively sees as the anti-democrat. But on a higher level it becomes the inspiriting life of his art and constitutes the essential form of his stories. On this level it does not reflect the negative conflict between society and solitude, the democrat and the artist, but positively it reflects the community that is sometimes possible between exceptional souls—that 'intellectual' as opposed to 'moral' union which Emerson desired but almost despaired of. Hawthorne is always called a Puritan writer, and before attempting to describe the conception of reality out of which he created his art it will perhaps be advisable to consider very briefly the nature of his religious belief.

Dogmatically speaking, Hawthorne was neither a Calvinist nor a Transcendentalist. Despite his brief association with Brook Farm, his scepticism in regard to the latter is well known. As for the Church, he seems always to have maintained a friendly but unyielding distance. During the years when he was American Consul in Liverpool he took a pew in the American Unitarian church there and sent his son Julian every Sunday, but he himself never appeared. There is a frequently quoted letter of Hawthorne's in which he describes a visit that Melville had made to him during which they went on a long walk together. This letter is always cited as revealing a great deal about Melville, but in fact it reveals as much about Hawthorne himself. Hawthorne says that they

. . . sat down in a hollow among the sand hills (sheltering ourselves from the high, cool wind) and smoked a cigar. Melville, as he always does, began to reason of Providence and futurity, and of everything that lies beyond human ken, and informed me that he had pretty much made up his mind to be annihilated; but still he does not seem to rest in that anticipation; and, I think, will never rest until he gets hold of a definite belief. It is strange how he persists—and has persisted ever since I knew him, and probably long before—in wandering to and fro over these deserts, as dismal and monotonous as the sand hills amid which we were sitting. He can neither believe nor be comfortable in his disbelief; and he is too honest and courageous not to try and do one or the other. If he were a religious man, he would be one of the most truly religious and reverential; he has a very high and noble nature, and better worth immortality than most of us.[5]

The longer one considers the two men the harder it is to resist the conclusion that Melville's was indeed a more religious nature than Hawthorne's. He was tormented by the absence of an acceptable or usable orthodoxy in a way that Hawthorne was not, and at bottom *Moby Dick* is the story of a theological quest which issues, after many years, in the tired disillusionment of *Clarel*. But no better phrase can be devised to describe Hawthorne's temperament than to say that he was a Puritan agnostic. Hawthorne appears to be concerned with religious problems in his art, but on analysis we find that the kind of truth Hawthorne is concerned with is radically different from the kind that Melville seeks, and is, ontologically speaking, on a lower level. Melville's quest is for God, however much he may despair of achieving his end; Hawthorne's, for the fulfilment of the human heart. Despite the frequent suggestion of theological implications in Hawthorne's art, they turn out to be largely illusory. His stories only *seem* religious in their point of view. A representative instance occurs in one of his greatest stories, 'Young Goodman Brown'. Despite its air of Christian propriety, this is one of the most deeply agnostic works of art in existence. The burden of the story is young Goodman Brown's, and hence Hawthorne's, inability to understand either the nature or the *locus* of spiritual reality. If Hawthorne and Melville may ever be said to resemble each other it is on their blackest levels of despair. The ending of 'Young Goodman Brown' reminds one of the last page of *The Confidence Man*:

Often, waking suddenly at midnight, he shrank from the bosom of Faith; and at morning or eventide, when the family knelt

down at prayer, he scowled and muttered to himself, and gazed
sternly at his wife, and turned away. And when he had lived long,
and was borne to his grave a hoary corpse, followed by Faith,
an aged woman, and children and grandchildren, a goodly procession, besides neighbours, not a few, they carved no hopeful
verse upon his tombstone, for his dying hour was gloom.

But even here the interests of the two men diverge. Melville
has not focused his tragic comedy in terms of the human being
at all. The final figure who is betrayed by the masks of illusion
in *The Confidence Man* is the old patriarch, symbolizing God, who
is led away into darkness on the final page. Melville's darkest
book is God's tragedy more than man's. But in 'Young Goodman Brown' the tragedy is fixed squarely in the human heart.
'Young Goodman Brown' can no doubt be read in different
ways, but it can hardly be argued in any interpretation that
Hawthorne is much concerned with Goodman Brown's theology
as such, or with what is likely to happen to him after his burial.
The tragedy occurs on the nearer side of the grave, and in man's
tormented heart.

Hawthorne tortures moral questions into forms of attenu-
ated subtlety because he cannot bring them to a focus in any
perspective of belief. The heir of the Puritan tradition, he
inherited the rigid forms of Calvinism, but it was a Calvinism
that had already collapsed, and he lived among the remnants
of a dead faith while breathing the libertarian air of a New
England Transcendentalism that he could not accept. There
is, then, a tension in Hawthorne's mind that is peculiarly his.
He often seems to pose questions in the old perspective of
Calvinist faith, but he approaches the answers to them with
an inquisitiveness and curiosity—even with an infidelity—that
is the result of the new intellectual freedom of New England.
As a result, there sometimes seems to be a discrepancy between
Hawthorne's questions and answers if we ponder them for
long; or rather let us say that the answers Hawthorne gives
often exist in a carefully maintained margin of doubt.

The opening paragraph of Hawthorne's story, 'The New
Adam and Eve', is his most complete statement of agnosticism:

We who are born into the world's artificial system can never
adequately know how little in our present state and circumstance
is natural, and how much is merely the interpolation of the

perverted heart and mind of man. Art has become a second and
stronger nature; she is a stepmother, whose crafty tenderness has
taught us to despise the bountiful and wholesome ministrations of
our true parent. It is only through the medium of the imagination
that we can lessen those iron fetters which we call truth and
reality, and make ourselves even partially sensible of what
prisoners we are.

It is interesting to note that this passage is in itself ambiguous.
By 'art' does Hawthorne mean the craft of men who have
evolved systems of thought that distort reality, or does he
mean the art of the creative mind? If the latter, he makes an
odd distinction between the art which enslaves and the imagination which frees. Probably Hawthorne was not quite sure
what he did mean here, for the ambiguity is typical of Hawthorne whenever he is on the subject of art. What is important
in this passage is its complete rejection of any philosophic or
theological perspective in which to pose moral questions. All
our thought, all our faith, have become an expression of the
world's artificial system, and our minds and hearts are so
perverted that even our most fundamental concepts of truth
and reality are lies. He almost puts the human mind beyond
the possibility of knowing truth at all. But Hawthorne does
believe in a truth. It is never forthrightly stated in the form
of an explicit credo, but when its scattered parts are gathered
together it becomes the only confession of faith that we ever
really get from him. A suggestive statement occurs in this
same story, 'The New Adam and Eve'. In this story, which is
not among Hawthorne's best ones, he imagines that all the
people in the world have suddenly died, and life begins anew
with the creation of a second Adam and Eve, who awaken to
find themselves in the midst of a modern but completely empty
city:

> Just when the earliest sunshine gilds the mountain tops, two
> beings have come into life, not in such an Eden as bloomed to
> welcome our first parents, but in the heart of a modern city. They
> find themselves in existence, and gazing into one another's eyes.
> Their emotion is not astonishment. Nor do they perplex them-
> selves with efforts to discover what, and whence, and why they
> are. Each is satisfied to be, because the other exists likewise; and
> their first consciousness is of calm and mutual enjoyment, which

seems not to have been the birth of that very moment, but prolonged from a past eternity. Thus content with an inner sphere
which they inhabit together, it is not immediately that the outward world can obtrude itself upon their notice.

Hawthorne's reality is not concerned with the great metaphysical questions that became a creative motive in Melville's
art—questions of what, and whence, and why. The domain of
Hawthorne's reality is the inner sphere of reciprocal love and
affection which he describes here. It is not the sphere only
of love between the sexes. The magnetic chain of humanity
which poor Ethan Brand is supposed to have violated is a
current of sympathy among these inner spheres. It is this inner
sphere of feeling and sympathy which is the psychological and
moral world that Hawthorne as an artist regularly inhabits,
but it is an extremely rarefied country, and Hawthorne has
created some of his best art through his uncertainties as to
what the right relationship is between this inner sphere and
external reality, which he describes as the world's artificial
system. He has created some of his best art on this theme, and,
in quantity, a good deal more of his inferior art, art that leaves
one with a sense of confusion and frustration.

At times Hawthorne seems to conceive this inner sphere of
reality almost as if it were a strip of unexplored country. There
is, of course, danger of appearing too schematic here, but as one
reads and rereads all of Hawthorne's stories, the degree to which
he himself was willing to run that risk seems astonishing.
Roughly speaking, three relationships seem possible with this
territory. First, there is the villainous relationship of the person
who penetrates the country merely for the sake of curiosity,
or to exploit the natural resources. The artist falls under this
head very often. Then there is the tragic relationship of the
person who, because of some native defect of heart, cannot
enter it at all, but remains outside longing for the Promised
Land. Finally, there is the successful relationship exemplified
in 'The New Adam and Eve'. Taking these three possible
relationships in reverse order, we find the successful relationship
developed at some length in a rather tedious story like 'The
Great Carbuncle'.

This story provides an excellent commentary on what Hawthorne means when he says that the mind and heart of man

interpolate false images between us and reality. The great carbuncle itself is a mysterious or supernatural jewel which (Hawthorne hints but never openly states) may never have existed at all. Rather, it seems to be a visible projection of the desires and aspirations of the human beings who seek it. Each of the seekers whom Hawthorne gathers together sees in it an emblem of his own heart. Thus, the man who is called the Seeker, seeks it only for the pursuit itself: 'The pursuit alone is my strength—the energy of my soul—the warmth of my blood —and the pith and marrow of my bones. . . . Having found it I shall bear it to a certain cavern and there grasping it in my arms, lie down and die, and keep it buried with me forever.' Dr. Cacaphodel, the scientist, if he finds it, wishes to reduce it to its first elements in his laboratory and write a folio volume on the results of the analysis. Master Ichabod Pigsnort, the merchant, wants to auction it off to the highest bidder; the Cynic has come on the search simply to establish that such a jewel does not exist, and so on. The story is thoroughly conventional Hawthorne, and is saved from being a slick concoction only because it is in touch with some of his deepest interests. The last pair of seekers is a young married couple named Matthew and Hannah. When the seekers huddle around a fire at night on the mountainside, they tell each other why they are seeking the jewel. When Matthew's turn comes, he says:

'Ye must know, friends, that Hannah and I, being wedded the last week, have taken up the search of the Great Carbuncle, because we shall need its light in the long winter evenings; and it will be such a pretty thing to show the neighbours when they visit us. It will shine through the house so that we may pick up a pin in any corner, and will set all the windows aglow as if there were a great fire of pine knots in the chimney. And then how pleasant, when we awake in the night, to be able to see one another's faces.'

Even to its first readers it must have been obvious at this point that it would be Matthew and Hannah who would see the Great Carbuncle first. Nor could it have come as much of a surprise when they reject it. Matthew says to Hannah:

'Let us go hence, and return to our humble cottage. The blessed sunshine and the quiet moonlight shall come through our

window. We will kindle the cheerful glow of our hearth, at eventide, and be happy in its light. But never again will we desire more
light than all the world can share with us.'

'No,' said his bride, 'for how could we live by day and sleep
by night in this awful blaze of the Great Carbuncle.'

Like the new Adam and Eve, Matthew and Hannah inhabit
an inner sphere together—a sphere of mutual love into which
the outside world obtrudes with difficulty. This inner sphere
alone constitutes significant reality. On the other hand, the
Great Carbuncle represents the world's artifical system, but it
seems to have no existential being of its own. It is only the shifting, impalpable reflection of the perverted points of view of
men whose hearts have no inner reality. For Matthew and
Hannah the vision of the Jewel has the effect of revealing to
them that nothing in the world can increase the reality they
already possess in themselves.

Perhaps it is questionable if the attitude I am analysing here
as the principal framework of Hawthorne's art can properly
be called a metaphysic at all. But it is certain that Hawthorne
had no other and was interested in the possibility of no other.
What man is, or whence he came, or why, did not trouble him,
and he could be, as we have seen, quite explicit about his
complacency on these points. His final perplexity concerning
the nature of reality lacks the density and the ultimate character
of Melville's questionings and doubts, and certainly, on this
level, he lacks Melville's anguish, though he possesses in rich
measure an anguish of his own. His real interest is centred in
the psychological disturbance of the human mind and moral
nature when it is at odds with society: when the proper relationship of the individual with the inner sphere of reality has
somehow been violated. For this reason, those stories which
deal with the fulfilled individual, as 'The Great Carbuncle'
does, are not his best. They are a little insipid; they are not
concerned with those distresses which provoke knowledge as
much as they reflect the spiritual ease of those who have found
their answers in the rather tiresome company of Matthew and
Hannah.

The second relationship, that of the man who is excluded
from the inner sphere of reality because of some native defect
of heart, is programmatically developed in a straightforward

E

story like 'The Christmas Banquet'. Gervayse Hastings, the unhappy hero of that story, describes the misery of his excluded heart in terms that illuminate negatively the meaning of reality for Hawthorne:

> 'You will not understand it,' replied Gervayse Hastings. 'None have understood it—not even those who experience the like. It is a chillness—a want of earnestness—a feeling as if what should be my heart were a thing of vapour—a haunting perception of un-reality! Thus seeming to possess all that other men have—all that men aim at—I have really possessed nothing—neither joy nor griefs. All things—all persons—as was truly said to me at this table long and long ago—have been like shadows flickering on the wall. It was so with my wife and children—with those who seemed my friends: it is so with yourselves whom I now see before me. Neither have I myself any real existence, but am a shadow like the rest.'
>
> 'And how is it with your views to a future life?' inquired the clergyman.
>
> 'Worse than with you,' said the old man, in a hollow and feeble tone; 'for I cannot conceive it earnestly enough to feel either hope or fear.'

However, I prefer to consider here a second story, 'The Minister's Black Veil', which is more complex in its symbolism, and, although not entirely successful, a much better work of art. Its principal defect, as critics have noted before, is its obscurity. It will be recalled that the story tells of Mr. Hooper, the young parson of Milford, who startles his parishioners one Sunday morning by appearing in a pulpit wearing a black veil over his face. The veil becomes a mysteriously evocative symbol to the parishioners, so much so that it even seems to lend an unusual power to his sermons. The black veil is, indeed, a highly enigmatic symbol, and its meaning seems never to be fully revealed in the story itself. Mr. Richard Harter Fogle is typical when he writes:

> The minister himself believes the veil to be an emblem of the secret sin that poisons the soul of all mankind, but we are not compelled to accept his reading of the matter. We may, if we like, consider it rather a veil upon his understanding, whose gloomy shade conceals from the eyes behind it as much as it discloses.[6]

If we place the story in the perspective that has been described above, its symbolism becomes more intelligible and more effective. The black veil is really a commentary on that area of reality which we have been discussing. Mr. Hooper, the good pastor, dedicates his life to inculcating the most important of all spiritual lessons to his people through this symbol. I shall discuss the nature of this lesson more fully later. But it is at this point that a certain flaw mars the organization of the story. On the symbolic level the veil is presumably teaching certain truths, but on the narrative level of the story it has repercussions in Mr. Hooper's personal life, and Hawthorne has been unable to correlate the two levels completely so that a blurred lack of clarity is the inevitable result. The pastor in his veil should operate wholly as a dramatic symbol, but to a considerable extent he remains a private character in a somewhat ludicrous costume, with a personal life that is far from being perfectly absorbed in his symbolic significance. It is hardly a wonder that many critics have supposed Mr. Hooper himself to have been the prey of some gnawing secret sin when, in fact, he is the perfectly dedicated priest.

The horror of the imprisoned or isolated identity, which is what this story is about, is a recurrent theme in American literature. Perhaps it is because the atmosphere of American democracy paradoxically condemns isolation while it makes, on the social level, anything but isolation undesirable. At any rate, whatever the reason, American writers return to the theme with an insistence that is rare among European writers. For example, Wallace Stevens in his 'Metaphors of a Magnifico' from *Harmonium* writes:

> Twenty men crossing a bridge
> Into a village
> Are twenty men crossing twenty bridges
> Into twenty villages,
> Or one man
> Crossing a single bridge into a village.
>
> This is old song
> That will not declare itself.

It is old song indeed for the American artist. The poem merely means that for man there are two possibilities, either to live in isolation, imprisoned in himself, or to live in community, in some sort of reciprocal sympathy with his fellow-men. If a man lives in isolation, then, even though he is a group of twenty men crossing a bridge into a village, his perception of reality will be unshared, imprisoned in himself; there will be no communication between him and the other men. But if there is a deeply shared sense of emotional and spiritual communion among them, their respective experiences of reality will merge or harmonize. They will be able to communicate what they see and feel and hear, and external reality will not be imprisoned, in the form of sense perceptions, in them. For such men, one bridge and one village will do.

But how does one break through this isolation in oneself? T. S. Eliot, while still an American citizen, expressed it in this way:

> What have we given?
> My friend, blood shaking my heart
> The awful daring of a moment's surrender
> Which an age of prudence can never retract
> By this, and this only, we have existed. . . .

Whatever else these lines may mean, their central meaning is clear: the fullness of life, the release from the prison of one's isolated identity, can only come about through self-surrender, through a refusal to withhold oneself, or any part of one's personality, in a human relationship.

In the last analysis, this was what Hawthorne believed was the essence of human reality. The most compelling truth of all that Mr. Hooper tried to teach by means of his dismal veil is the necessity of self-surrender as a means of entering into the inner sphere of reality. The black veil, of course, does not symbolize self-surrender in any positive sense. Its teaching is negative. It stands as a terrible warning to the parishioners.

It is significant that the two main episodes in this story are concerned with marriage. Hawthorne looked upon marriage as that state in which the magnetic chain of humanity was confirmed, and his positives seem to become more vigorous when he deals with the theme. A true marriage was the supreme example of self-surrender leading on to self-realization. Such a marriage had to be based on perfect mutual trust and love. Concealment was deadly to such a relationship, not because of *what* might be hidden (Hawthorne's talk of 'secret sins' is misleading here), but because the very act of concealing was a denial of all love meant. The symbolism of the veil takes on added density when it becomes the cause of the breach between Mr. Hooper and Elizabeth, the young woman he wishes to marry. The essence of love is self-surrender, but the concealment, of which the veil is a type and symbol, is a denial of love. In refusing to remove the veil for Elizabeth, Mr. Hooper deliberately allows the consequences of the veil to run their tragic course in his own life, and his shattered chance of married happiness confirms, in practical terms, the lesson he wishes to impart to his parishioners.

The other marriage which is treated in the story is equally significant. We recall that in 'The Great Carbuncle' Matthew and Hannah were a type of the perfect wedded couple. The reciprocity between them was complete, and like the new Adam and Eve they possessed the fullness of reality in possessing each other. But the couple whom the minister marries is different. The black veil, like a chemical agent, reveals the hidden stains in their characters which they have mutually concealed— or, if that is too severe an interpretation, it reveals to them the likelihood of such concealment in the future, and hence the terrible threat to their successful relationship. The closing sentences of this episode are particularly important. Having married the couple, Mr. Hooper is about to depart:

> At that instant, catching a glimpse of his figure in the looking-glass, the black veil involved his own spirit in the horror with which it overwhelmed all others. His frame shuddered, his lips grew white, he spilt the untasted wine upon the carpet, and rushed forth into the darkness. For the Earth, too, had on her Black Veil.

Such a passage points not so much towards the moral defection of a given individual as to the whole human condition, and this reading is corroborated by Mr. Hooper's final, dying speech.

Summing up this story, the black veil symbolizes that distrust and suspicion which is the motivation of concealment; it does not symbolize secret sin itself. Concealment, like a black veil, separates men from each other, depriving them of sympathy, love, and understanding. Under such conditions, human reality as Hawthorne thought of it lies like a strip of inaccessible land beyond the reach of their hearts. Mr. Hooper does not directly symbolize the man excluded from human reality because of a defect of heart in the candid way Gervayse Hastings does, but in effect he preaches us a sermon on that condition.

The third relationship, that of the man who for some obscure or apparent reason violates the sanctity of the inner sphere of reality and endeavours to exploit it, has already been discussed in treating 'Ethan Brand'. I have already said that in Hawthorne the artist often appears as the embodiment of this third possible relationship, and in discussing 'Ethan Brand' I tried to show how he himself is intended by Hawthorne to represent the darker side of the artist's role. For Hawthorne, this violation of inner reality represents a complex, often ambiguous, intrusion into the feelings of other people, not from motives of love, but from motives of curiosity, such as characterize the analytic artist; from motives of self-interest, such as we discover in Hollingsworth, the philanthropic reformer in *The Blithedale Romance*, who wishes to utilize the love of others for himself in the interests of his great humanitarian project; or from obscurer motives of jealousy, envy, or vengeance, as with Chillingworth in *The Scarlet Letter*. The theme recurs in American literature outside of Hawthorne. Henry James dealt with it in *The Bostonians*, and the relation of Ahab with his crew is a classic instance. But Hawthorne is unique in seeing the artist as the representative offender. In his hands the theme could be reduced to the Trilby level. The logical story in which to examine the artist as Machiavel is 'The Prophetic Pictures', but apart from the fact that this very poor story gives us the artist as violator or exploiter with peculiar simplicity, it has little intrinsic interest. Moreover, an excellent study has been made of the story by Mary Dichmann (*American Literature*, May, 1951) which leaves little or nothing to be said along these lines. I prefer, instead, to intrude upon the symmetry of my argument at this point by discussing two stories in which Hawthorne endeavours to vindicate the creative vision of the artist, and to show how he also may enter into possession of the inner sphere of reality. It has certainly not been my intention to suggest that Hawthorne's hostility to the role of the artist was a personal feeling cherished for its own sake. His personal life bears sufficient witness to the contrary. But because of the tension between democracy and solitude which I discussed above, he tended to regard the artist with suspicion and as cut off from the most significant reality. But Hawthorne was a great artist and it would be intolerable to suppose that we could not catch sight in his works of a much deeper attitude towards art. When we do so I think it is evident that his views on the subject are unacceptable only when he considers the creative process in its relation to society; rarely, or never, when he considers it in itself. It was his American democratic prejudices which provided the corrupting element.

'The Artist of the Beautiful' is the first of the two stories I wish to consider in this connection. It is the better known of the two, but for reasons I shall point out it is the less successful. It deals with a young man named Owen Warland, who is a watchmaker. He has been unsuccessful in this capacity because he possesses not too little talent, but too much. He is not content with making and repairing watches, but he wants to make objects that will embody his idea of perfect beauty. The symbolism of the story begins to go wrong at an early stage because the intricate mechanisms Owen Warland makes impress the modern reader as rather horrid little things. His final masterpiece, a mechanical butterfly that cannot be distinguished from a living one, has none of the capacity for releasing the imagination that we shall find, somewhat surprisingly, in the ship's figurehead in 'Drowne's Wooden Image'. The mechanical butterfly is too much like an apotheosis of the cuckoo clock. What we are fundamentally irritated by in the story is Hawthorne's assumption that there is such a thing as an abstract, pure beauty, unrelated to life. Paradoxically, although the mechanical butterfly cannot be distinguished from a living one, what it represents is the antithesis of life. Hawthorne is intent on giving us impractical art versus practical reality, the blacksmith Robert Danforth versus Owen Warland. Hawthorne cannot quite make up his mind whether he is in favour of the blacksmith or the artist, but given the respective characters of the two men representing these roles here, the modern reader would hardly hesitate. He would choose Robert Danforth, an intelligent, decent workman, in preference to the insufferable

Owen. 'You are my evil spirit,' cries Owen to a man who has done him some practical favours, 'you and the hard coarse world.' And that is typical.

Unsatisfactory as the development of this story is in some respects, it is one of Hawthorne's most serious attempts to come at the real meaning of the artist's role in life. The concluding sentence of the story is important. The mechanical butterfly has been destroyed without feeling or appreciation by the representatives of the 'hard coarse world', but Owen witnesses its destruction with complacency: 'He had caught a far other butterfly than this. When the artist rose high enough to achieve the beautiful, the symbol by which he made it percep- tible to mortal senses became of little value in his eyes while his spirit possessed itself in enjoyment of the reality.'

Hawthorne is saying here that the creative vision is indeed a means of entrance into the inner sphere of reality, but the pat- tern of the story is seriously impaired by positing a hostility between art and life which amounts to something much more radical than the conflict between what F. R. Leavis has called mass civilization and minority culture. Art is a thing of pure and withdrawn beauty, too fragile to be touched by the world or to have, in its turn, any disciplining effect on life. If the story achieves the fine statement of the concluding sentences quoted above, the movement towards that statement is imperfectly realized in the narrative itself. What 'The Artist of the Beautiful' demonstrates is Hawthorne's inability to reconcile the roles of artist and citizen in the context of American society, or to make a workable creative marriage between solitude and society.

'Drowne's Wooden Image' is a sadly neglected story of Hawthorne's, but it is one of his most appealing. Its attractive- ness centres in the fact that Hawthorne presents the artist in this story in a more amiable and satisfactory light then he does anywhere else. In 'The Artist of the Beautiful' Hawthorne was concerned not only with the value of the creative act to the artist, but with his relation to the community. In treating the latter theme he failed as usual, but so abysmally that he seems to distort his understanding of the significance of artistic creation. Within its limits 'Drowne's Wooden Image' is almost flawless, and the reason is that Hawthorne does not trouble himself about Drowne's relationship with the community. He focuses his attention solely on the meaning and value of the creative process to the artist.

Drowne is a young wood-carver of Boston whose craft is that of making figureheads for vessels. Commissioned by Captain Hunnewell to do a figurehead of a girl for his new ship, Drowne begins a young female figure. Hawthorne's description of this figure is delightfully baroque—a painted image wearing a hat covered with exotic wooden flowers, and carrying a fan. The story is, of course, a variation on the Pygmalion theme, and as usual with Hawthorne there is an ambiguity in the plot. Did the intensity of Drowne's inner vision bring the young woman to life? She was certainly seen walking down the street in her gorgeous hat; or was it, after all, a Portuguese young lady of rank whom Captain Hunnewell was rumoured to have brought across on his ship? But this superficial ambiguity is only a means of leading into a deeper one which embodies Hawthorne's essential meaning. Had Drowne brought the wooden image to life by the intensity of his creative impulse, or had the evolving form in the piece of oak timber awakened Drowne himself into life? Hawthorne's meaning is clear enough. The creative impulse is god-like. The artist in creating finds that his creation in turn creates himself. The question is whether the artist has the inner vision that creates the work, or the discovery of the work gives the artist the vision by which he spiritually lives. When Copley (whose solid historical presence in the story gives ballast to the fantasy) visits Drowne's workshop and notices the figurehead for the first time, he exclaims:

'What is here? Who has done this? . . . Here is the divine, the life-giving touch. What inspired hand is beckoning this wood to arise and live? Whose work is this?'

'No man's work,' replied Drowne. 'The figure lies within that block of oak, and it is my business to find it.' . . .

As Copley departed, happening to glance backward from the threshold, he beheld Drowne bending over the half-created shape, and stretching forth his arms as if he would have embraced and drawn it to his heart; while had such a miracle been possible, his countenance expressed passion enough to communicate warmth and sensibility to the lifeless oak.

Clearly, the vision possessed Drowne, not Drowne the vision, and it is only during the interval that he is under its spell that he is truly alive, that he may be said to possess reality fully. When the image has been completed, 'the light of imagination and sensibility' which had illuminated his face goes out. 'He was again the mechanical carver that he had been known to be all his lifetime.'

As I have said, Hawthorne is not distracted by irrelevant democratic considerations in this story. He confines himself to giving us a splendid statement on the selflessness of the artist and the impersonality of art. To this extent 'Drowne's Wooden Image' conforms to the general argument presented above. Self-surrender in art no less than in human relationships is required if one is to enter into and possess inner reality.

I have tried to uncover the existence of a characteristic motive in the stories I have discussed here. From one point of view they may be called an attempt, unconscious perhaps, to formulate a usable metaphysic in a society whose democratic dogma and practice left little scope for the exceptional individual incapable of being levelled down to the common denominator, or of finding an acceptable corner in the Jacksonian version of reality. In his own way Hawthorne was not less concerned than Cooper had been to close the rift in the American experience. For Hawthorne this rift was characteristically defined in terms of solitude and society, which could be interpreted either on the political or the artistic level. Hawthorne added greatly to his difficulties by attempting to work on both levels at once, with the result that the artist is usually presented as either maladjusted or dangerous. It was only when Hawthorne concentrated on the anguish or the divided individual, as in *The Scarlet Letter* or 'Young Goodman Brown', or when he treated a different set of tensions altogether, as in 'My Kinsman, Major Molineux', that he produced his great masterpieces.

The tension between solitude and society cannot be resolved artistically in the political terms to which Hawthorne so often resorted. That his stories may be said to fail as infrequently as they do is partly owing to his concern with that inner reality which I have tried to analyse here. It is obvious that 'the magnetic chain of humanity', which exists at the level of doctrine in Hawthorne's mind, is a democratic concept as he uses it; but it also transcends those limits and raises Hawthorne to the contemplation of the imprisoned identity, with which our own age is so tragically familiar. The extraordinary thing about those problems which the American experience gave him as subject matter is that questions beginning for him as essentially political enlarged themselves in widening circles until they embraced the most universal aspects of the human heart, and he sometimes returned to those characters whom he seemed to reject under the democratic rubric to reveal in their excluded lives the tragic destiny of the modern world.

But even though a certain set of attitudes and a recurrent subject matter are characteristic of Hawthorne's writing, the means by which he embodied these in his art still remain to be considered. The two most important elements of form in art are surely subject matter or meaning, and the writer's attitude to it. But in addition to these there are the technical means by which the writer makes his communication, the images and terms through which he renders it intelligible and persuasive. My statement here is a little misleading, however, for the artist is no rhetorician obliged to embellish an argument from the outside. He is, rather, a creator whose task is to impose an organic unity on his matter so perfect that the meaning and its expression own one indivisible life.

I have already spoken of certain symbolist elements in Cooper's novels, and with Hawthorne the tradition of American symbolism comes into its own. But before considering how Hawthorne embodies his 'metaphysic' of the inner reality symbolically in his work, I should like to look at a question that was raised by Henry James many years ago. James wrote of Hawthorne that 'the fine thing . . . is that he cared for the deeper psychology, and that, in his way, he tried to become familiar with it'.[7] The statement says so much that, in the end, it really leaves us with very little. Whatever James himself may have meant by it (and the statement is not as clear as it looks), the remark has proved insidiously misleading to some among the later critics who have quoted it with enthusiasm. The phrase itself immediately precipitates the reader of modern fiction into the shadowy subconscious world of the uniquely private, where hidden motives and all the 'secrets' of the inmost self swim fortuitously about. But this is not the world of Hawthorne's interest, and it has nothing to do with the gifts and the realities he bestows on his characters. There is a level at which the psychological becomes an important facet of moral reality— or to put it another way, the psychological is an avenue which, if we pursue it far enough, is bound to issue on a moral field. In reading Hawthorne it is important to remember that if there is a psychological interest, it is a facet, and only a facet, of his moral interest, and that it is this which provides the ultimate reality of his art. The presence of the psychological in Hawthorne's work, as apart from the moral, is deceptive— there is so much less of it than one might suppose.

Hawthorne was interested in the psychology of his characters only in so far as he could use it as a stage on which certain complex moral problems could be dramatically enacted. The final effect of that enactment is that the individual characters themselves dissolve in the transcendent interest of the problem they dramatize. Such a practice of art can have little use for 'the deeper psychology' if this is defined as the field in which personality is individuated, and the ultimate source of private motivation. What Hawthorne leaves us with is not a sense of living characters whom he has endowed with deep psychological complexities, but a set of exploratory symbols which vibrate with a peculiar intensity in a moral ambience that is objectively grounded in Hawthorne's society. Hawthorne's characters have no margin of interest in themselves when they have performed their function in the over-all pattern of the given story. The interest we feel in Hester Prynne is of an essentially different kind from the interest we feel in Isabel Archer. In the last analysis Hawthorne is not interested in Hester's private drama. She exists magnificently in the art as the focus of tangled moral forces, but she is herself as much of a symbol as the Scarlet Letter she wears on her breast. Her role in the novel is to endow that Letter and all it stands for with the life of art, but her own life in our imagination is restricted to those boundaries. James has otherwise focused our interest in Isabel. Both the foolishness and the fineness of her moral nature are uniquely hers. Her ordeal reaches towards the universal, but in the end it remains a very particular and individual modification of it. And one dares say that it is the particularity of it which so compels our interest. It is in this area of the private and the particular, as it impinges on the universal, that we might most reasonably look for satisfactory artistic treatment of 'the deeper psychology'. But it is precisely this area that is missing from Hawthorne's greater characters. This is not a defect, but a condition of the kind of art he was creating, and we shall not get very far towards understanding that art until we either drop James's misleading phrase, or learn to interpret it correctly.

If Hawthorne is not dealing with 'the deeper psychology', just where is his area of operation? I have attempted to answer this question in my examination of Hawthorne's conception of an inner reality, and the various relationships that man may have with it. Here, then, is the level of his interest in man's moral nature, and I should like to demonstrate the way in which he objectifies this interest—or, in other words, projects the inner moral or psychological travail *outward* into a world of external symbols where its significance continues to exist for the imagination apart from the protagonist in whom it had its local origin. The tendency of Hawthorne's art is always outward; it shows a habit of endowing the hidden and the private with a high degree of publicity, and of revealing not the unique differences in men's souls but the hidden samenesses. And as I have pointed out, it undertakes this task with the help of some disturbingly simplifying formulae. I suggest that the artist who is concerned with 'the deeper psychology' would set off in the opposite direction. He would seek out the differences rather than the samenesses, and he would endeavour to focus his discoveries inward rather than outward. Such an artist would not necessarily be a greater artist; perhaps the chances are that he would be smaller. But at any rate he would be a different kind of artist, and he would offer different satisfactions to the reader. He would tell us more about men; possibly less about man. It is man in this second and somewhat portentous sense who is Hawthorne's subject. I have insisted that Hawthorne had a deeply rooted Puritan suspicion of art and the artist all his life, and one may observe, for what it is worth, that this distrust would itself appear to discourage his exploratory excursions into 'the deeper psychology'.

But what is the difference between this sphere of 'inner reality' and 'the deeper psychology'? At first there seems to be a close resemblance between them. Both are concerned with what goes on in the human heart and soul. But 'the deeper psychology', whatever James meant by it, emphasizes for us today the inviduating characteristics of human personality (in its romantic sense) and motivation at their most hidden levels. In its own way the medieval morality play, *Everyman*, is concerned with 'the deeper psychology', and yet no one would think of it under this rubric. It treats the hidden in a public way, and like Hawthorne it is concerned with the profound samenesses rather than with the unique differences between human souls. But my mention of *Everyman* introduces a danger. Hawthorne is not, except at his lower levels, an allegorist, despite the frequency of the attribution. At this point a practical demonstration of what I mean by Hawthorne's symbolism will be of greater value than an abstract discussion. By examining a concrete example, particularly as it appertains to Hawthorne's sphere of inner reality, we shall see how he is able to elevate the problems that confront the deeper consciousness of his characters to an impersonal level where, leaving behind the individuating characteristics of the unique and local, they live with a growing symbolic life in the imagination of his readers. And I think it may be conceded that for its final effect, Hawthorne's interest turns its back on the psychological for the sake of squarely confronting the moral.

The story I wish to consider here by way of illustrating Hawthorne's method is one of his earliest extant stories, 'The Hollow of the Three Hills'. It is one of his shortest; but perhaps it is not as simple as it appears. To make any particular claims for it as a work of art other than to say that for so young a writer it is extremely promising, would be to exaggerate. But when we consider it in the full light of Hawthorne's development, and scrutinize it for hints of Hawthorne's technical methods, the story claims its peculiar interest. His later and better work, although more complex, carries no radical quantity, either of meaning or technique, that is not clearly indicated in this little work, elementary as it is.

There are only two characters in the story, an unhappy young lady and a witch. The young lady is unhappy because she has committed a sin, and, as we know, Hawthorne could sometimes be harder on his sinners than we should feel inclined to be. She has offended against her marriage vow, and burdened with

her sense of guilt she has fled from her past, leaving her parents
to a sorrowful old age, her husband to end in a madhouse, and
her child to die. On a realistic level these are impressive consequences to follow on an act of infidelity; nevertheless, with
the possible exception of the husband, there is no trace of
melodrama here. The reason is that it does not exist as a story
at all, but as a poetically evoked symbol. The lady goes to meet
the witch in a little hollow which is formed by the juncture of
three hills, for she desires to know the fate of her family whom
she has deserted. The witch, just as daylight is beginning to fade,
gives her three magic visions—one of her sorrowing parents,
one of her husband in the madhouse, one of the funeral of her
child.

If we were to respond to this for its 'story' value it would
strike us as intolerable claptrap, but its imagery functions
essentially in the manner of poetry, and we respond to it in that
way. The first paragraph establishes the tone and the mode of
operation at once:

> In those strange old times, when fantastic dreams and mad-
> men's reveries were realized among the actual circumstances of
> life, two persons met together at an appointed hour and place.
> One was a lady, graceful in form and fair of feature, though pale
> and troubled, and smitten with an untimely blight in what should
> have been the fullest bloom of her years; the other was an
> ancient and meanly-dressed woman, of ill-favoured aspect, and so
> withered, shrunken, and decrepit, that even the space since she
> began to decay must have exceeded the ordinary term of human
> existence. In the spot where they encountered, no mortal could
> observe them. Three little hills stood near each other, and down
> in the midst of them sunk a hollow basin, almost mathematically
> circular, two or three hundred feet in breadth, and of such depth
> that a stately cedar might but just be visible above the sides.
> Dwarf pines were numerous upon the hills, and partly fringed the
> outer verge of the intermediate hollow, within which there was
> nothing but the brown grass of October, and here and there a
> tree trunk that had fallen long ago and lay mouldering with no
> green successor from its roots. One of these masses of decaying
> wood, formerly a majestic oak, rested close beside a pool of green
> and sluggish water at the bottom of the basin. Such scenes as this
> (so grey tradition tells) were once the resort of the Power of evil
> and his plighted subjects; and here, at midnight or on the dim

verge of evening, they were said to stand round the mantling pool, disturbing its putrid waters in the performance of an impious baptismal rite. The chill beauty of an autumnal sunset was now gilding the three hill-tops, whence a paler tint stole down their sides into the hollow.

One may have read this story a number of times before one becomes aware that the sense of emotional unity and concentration it imparts to us is related to the symbolic significance of those three hills in the hollow amidst which the action of the story takes place. The hills correspond to the three human ties the lady has violated. They are symbols of her profoundest human relationships; and there is an appropriateness in her symbols, for the relationships in question, that of child to parent, wife to husband, and mother to child, seem as eternal as the hills themselves. The hollow of the three hills, then, becomes a symbol of the lady's heart. It is the point where the three hills, the three most essential relationships possible to mankind, meet. The imagery that Hawthorne uses in describing the hills is significant. It is an imagery of desiccation and death. They are no longer green but clothed with brown October grass, and covered with the decaying trunks of fallen trees. In the final effect, the decaying trunk of the once majestic oak that lies near the centre of the hollow enforces our sense of her husband whom we see in the witch's second vision, the shattered ruin of a man confined in a madhouse. The stagnant pool in the hollow of the hills introduces, in terms of Hawthorne's imagery, a positive suggestion of evil—but it is a suggestion only at this point, for we see it under the melancholy but softening effect of a sunset glow. But it remains in the imagination as a symbol of potential evil, a pool in which, on some future midnight, the Power of Evil may baptize the Lady herself. For the direction of the story is not towards spiritual regeneration.

If the hollow of the three hills is a symbol of the lady's desolated heart, it is also the symbol of that inner sphere which is the locus of Hawthorne's particular reality. Into this hollow comes the visions of the lady's past, images of a reality that once existed for her, but from which she is now forever excluded. This is the tragedy from Hawthorne's point of view: the lady is no longer capable of possessing or communicating with human reality. The hollow of the three hills—that is to say, the lady's heart, her sphere of inner reality—is inhabited only by illusions that have no substance, and she remains tragically alone. The close of the story is significant. By reserving the death of the child to the last, Hawthorne has effectively suggested the death of hope itself, and the cold wind that sweeps down across the hollow of the three hills as the funeral entourage passes through the vision is really the coldness of a hopeless heart.

'The Hollow of the Three Hills' is a story in which we see a human being excluded from participation in reality—the only kind of reality that mattered to Hawthorne—because of an infidelity. In time this theme will grow into *The Scarlet Letter*, but will there take on a magnitude and dimensions that are hardly hinted at here. This story illustrates the way in which the idea of an inner reality dominates Hawthorne's work, and it also demonstrates that his concern is moral rather than psychological, that the focus of his creative method is outward rather than inward. The lady of the story can scarcely be said to be a concretely created character at all in the full fictional sense of the phrase. She exhibits no dimension capable of bearing the burden of a psychological density, and in this she is representative of most of Hawthorne's characters. At most she is a focal point where the force lines that radiate from the symbolic imagery of the story converge. The lady's heart, stricken as it is, is not the subject of Hawthorne's curious psychological probing. He is concerned only with what is widely applicable in her fallen estate, and he is so far from a close or prying scrutiny of private and individual motivation that he discovers nothing that is not readily duplicable in terms of landscape imagery. What the story gives us is a symbolic picture of the curiously moral climate of Hawthorne's New England imagination. The problem that Hawthorne is dealing with is dramatized by universalizing imagery that, in effect, dissolves the lady into nothingness; not once does he approach her with a psychological insight that might particularize or individuate; and one should add that Hawthorne's abstention on this matter is necessary to preserve the pattern of the story's significance. For in the end it is not an account of a private history at all, but a dramatic parable about the inner sphere of reality. And though it is a highly representative story, one looks in vain for anything that might be clearly identified as a felt concern for the claims of 'the deeper psychology'. In the end it is as a delicately poised and finely wrought moralist that we are obliged to evaluate Hawthorne; but it will be prudent to reiterate here that in pressing the claims of the moralist there is no intention of excluding the rights of the psychologist, such as they are in Hawthorne. It remains a matter of priority and emphasis.

But 'The Hollow of the Three Hills' is not only a parable on the inner reality. That subject by its very nature in Hawthorne's mind is intrinsically related, as we have seen, to the American tension between solitude and society. It is this conflict, so remarkably intensified in nineteenth-century America, which is Hawthorne's essential subject, and the lady's crime, like Ethan Brand's, is symbolized by the broken links of her human relationships. In effect, the family whom she has destroyed stands for the great community of men from which she must now forever be excluded in an unreal, solitary world that is the same as Gervayse Hasting's. Cooper endeavoured to heal the rift in the American experience by assuming the role of political and social critic, while Hawthorne approached it always in the role of moralist. It remains for us to see that in the end, their roles had much in common, but the similarity is not on the surface. It is embedded in the very foundations of the American experience and temper, an anguish which only the best of the Americans, aware of the seeds of dissolution in their democratic tradition, could feel. The similarity is so elusive that it sometimes seems to vanish as we look, but it is so real that it binds the great American novelists together in a community and a tradition in terms of which we read their profoundest meaning.

VII

Hawthorne's Novels

I

IN the foregoing chapter I have tried to show the central pattern of Hawthorne's meaning in a representative group of his short stories. In the following discussion of the novels I have no larger intention than to show how they also embody the characteristic tensions and attitudes already discussed. What I have to say will be governed entirely by its relevance to this central pattern. I make this explanatory statement at the beginning because my object in this chapter is necessarily restrictive, and I do not wish to imply that there is not a great deal more to say about the novels than there is appropriate occasion for doing so here.

The Blithedale Romance, published in the summer of 1852, is the third of Hawthorne's major novels, but certain aspects of it present his recurrent subject matter in so forthright a way that it will be convenient to begin our brief survey of the novels with it. It is generally considered his most obscure work. Although something can be said in defence of this obscurity, I think it remains a defect, and is in some measure perhaps attributable to Hawthorne's claim to write romances rather than novels. The absence of a medium of manners in American society in terms of which dramatic action might be sharply delineated made the romance, one is free to surmise, a particularly attractive form to Hawthorne. But how far he was from understanding the real nature of the appeal is evidenced by the 'Preface' to *Blithedale* in which he maintains that it is above all other forms the romance which is difficult to write in the cold, realistic American light. Actually, it is manners by which motive is defined in the novelist's art; manners provide the perspective by which he reveals the significance of human action, and they are a principal means by which that significance is communicated. The romance provided a chiaroscuro which Hawthorne was sometimes tempted to use as a means of concealing the poverty of materials American society provided the novelist to work with. *The Blithedale Romance* is an interesting book, but it is difficult to deny that there are points in it at which Hawthorne uses shadows for refuge rather than for definition. Henry James gave the final word on the romance as a form when he wrote in 'The Art of Fiction' that 'I can think of no obligation to which the "romancer" would not be held equally with the novelist; the standard of execution is equally high for each.' [1]

The principal example to which I would point of an un- justified obscurity in *The Blithedale Romance* is the murky out- line which Hawthorne gives us of Zenobia's relationship to Priscilla. Zenobia certainly seems to be indictable for returning Priscilla, the poor little victim soul, to the power of the sinister mesmerist, Westervelt, and this is a question of absolute im- portance in one's final reading of the novel. Zenobia, even if she falls a little short of Henry James's enthusiasm,[2] is still one of the more attractive characters in Hawthorne's fictions. To all appearances she is a life-symbol in the sterile milieu in which she moves, and the reader who is likely to be rather pleased with her would like to accept her as such; but he is confronted with the intractable fact that her ultimate meaning and value in the novel is grounded in the nature of the Zenobia-Wester- velt-Priscilla triangle, and over this, for reasons of his own, Hawthorne draws a highly charcoal-smudged thumb. The 'romancing' at this point threatens the novelist's integrity. It is quite possible that Hawthorne felt that he had at his disposal an insufficiently dense medium of manners in which to give shape and definition, in a clear light, to the very subtle relation- ships he was treating; but it is also possible that he took refuge in his romantic shadow from the admiration his writing suggests he almost certainly felt for Zenobia. Practically speak- ing, she is a focus of vitality and life in the novel, as Q. D. Leavis has pointed out in her admirable essay, 'Hawthorne as Poet'.[3] But I believe Zenobia is also intended by Hawthorne to bear the brunt of his final displeasure. Her greater fineness, like that of Ethan Brand, is ultimately a thing of death. Haw- thorne's dilemma here reminds one of James's in *The Wings of the Dove*. Kate Croy, who alone gives vitality to that novel, is the character against whom James is sadly committed by the argument of his fiction.

If we eliminate Old Moodie and Westervelt, who are essential figures in the total pattern of meaning but remain in the background, we have three principal characters in the novel: Hollingsworth, the philanthropic reformer; the beautiful and wealthy Zenobia; and Zenobia's half-sister, Priscilla. These two females who, although related by blood, are so different in character and background, are both in love with Hollingsworth; but until quite late in the book at least, Hollingsworth is only in love with his pet project—a new kind of prison to reform criminals. Here, then, is the basis for Hawthorne's favourite theme. As the characters of these protagonists gradually unfold, we see that only Priscilla is capable of disinterested love, of entering into that inner sphere of affection which for Hawthorne provided the only valid human reality. Although Hollingsworth is a man of large nature, he is branded with Hawthorne's special mark of Cain. He is related to all the excluded 'heroes' of Hawthorne's imaginative world, although there are complications in Hollingsworth's case enabling him to give a more strenuous fictional performance than the characters of the short stories were usually asked for. There are also extenuating circumstances that eventually win him a partial pardon (what Hawthorne must have meant for a partial pardon, although it will hardly seem convincing to modern readers) from the fullest penalties of his crime. The most illuminating description of his spiritual state occurs in Chapter VII:

I began to discern that he had come among us actuated by no real sympathy with our feelings and our hopes, but chiefly because we were estranging ourselves from the world, with which his lonely and exclusive object in life had already put him at odds. Hollingsworth must have been originally endowed with a great spirit of benevolence, deep enough and warm enough to be the source of as much disinterested good as Providence often allows a human being the privilege of conferring upon his fellows. This native instinct yet lived within him. I myself had profited by it, in my necessity. It was seen, too, in his treatment of Priscilla. Such casual circumstances as were here involved would quicken his divine power of sympathy, and make him seem, while their influence lasted, the tenderest man and the truest friend on earth. But, by and by, you missed the tenderness of yesterday, and grew drearily conscious that Hollingsworth had a closer friend than ever you could be; and this friend was the cold, spectral monster which he had himself conjured up, and on which he was wasting all the warmth of his heart, and of which, at last,—as these men of a mighty purpose so invariably do,—he had grown to be the bond-slave. It was his philanthropic theory.

This was a result exceedingly sad to contemplate, considering that it had been mainly brought about by the very ardour and exuberance of his philanthropy. Sad, indeed, but by no means unusual: he had taught his benevolence to pour its warm tide exclusively through one channel; so that there was nothing to spare for other great manifestations of love to man, nor scarcely for the nutriment of individual attachments, unless they would minister, in some way, to the terrible egotism which he mistook for an angel of God.

But the obscurities of *The Blithedale Romance* do not spring from a clear-cut case like Hollingsworth's. Rather, they are reserved for the two female characters, and particularly under the aspect of their mutual relationship. In his critical study of Hawthorne, Mr. Hyatt Waggoner is correct when he writes that 'the "mysterious" aspects of Hawthorne's plot are certainly not likely to hold our attention long today'.[4] Nor today only: James was very severe on this part of *The Blithedale Romance* many years ago. I know of no critic who has thought it worth-while to take the 'mystic' and 'hocus-pocus' chapters in which the Veiled Lady dominates, very seriously. Yet it is in these that Hawthorne has lodged the heart of his meaning. I cannot agree with Mr. Waggoner when he goes on to say that 'the veil imagery does not function in terms of an allegorical sort of symbolism'.[5] This is precisely what it does, and the Veiled Lady gives us a commentary on the inner sphere of reality that is no less explicit than the Rev. Mr. Hooper's. It surprises me that a major theme of the book to which so much space is devoted and in which all the characters are involved could be dismissed as easily as it has been; or, if such dismissal is indeed justifiable, how critics could then continue to claim the seri-ously mutilated result as a successful work.

The Veiled Lady, who is giving lyceum performances in Boston under the management (or spell?) of the mesmerist Westervelt (who at one time before the novel opens has been Zenobia's husband or lover), turns out, as the reader tortuously discovers, to be Priscilla's sister. It is in this area that the shadows darken until we never really see anything clearly. On

that blustery winter's night when Hollingsworth turns up at
Blithedale, the experimental Brook Farm to which a group of
intellectualizing reformers, including Zenobia, have retired to
form a progressive community—on that night when he turns up
with the mousy Priscilla, who has been unexpectedly placed in
his care, we have no reason to suppose that Zenobia has ever
seen the girl before, even though Priscilla turns out to be
Zenobia's half-sister in the end. At any rate, Zenobia fails to
recognize her in a way that, on re-reading the text with this
particular question in mind, may strike one as more evasion
than denial. The shadows darken here. If Zenobia does not
know that Priscilla is the Veiled Lady, the legend of 'The
Silvery Veil' which she relates for their entertainment to the
Blithedale illuminati is inexplicable. This occurs in Chapter
XIII. Her legend gives a circumstantial account of the Veiled
Lady, and ends with the direct implication, dramatically
enacted when Zenobia throws a piece of gauze over Priscilla's
head at the climax of the story, that Priscilla is she. This is one
of the points Hawthorne never clears up, and although it is
easy enough to devise an explanation of Zenobia's knowledge,
based on her meeting with Westervelt in the forest, *The Blithedale Romance* is not a detective story. And in any case, such an
explanation would raise more problems than it settled. The
whole thing makes sense only if we accept two propositions that
are not popular with the critics of this novel. Zenobia is not
intended by Hawthorne to be a heroine, but a woman deeply
guilty of violating the sanctity of essential human relationships,
and the novel itself is a straightforward allegory (I shall reserve
the term 'symbolism' for my discussion of *The Scarlet Letter*) on
the inner sphere of reality.

Zenobia's story, 'The Silvery Veil', cannot be dismissed from
the book as a piece of dated and irrelevant decor. It is as
functional in the meaning of the novel as Father Mapple's
sermon in *Moby Dick* or Plotinus Plinlimmon's pamphlet in
Pierre. Zenobia tells of how a fashionable group of young
Bostonian gentlemen fell into a heated discussion of what the
Veiled Lady, under her disguise, looked like. To settle the
dispute one of their number named Theodore agreed to conceal
himself in the Veiled Lady's dressing-room, and, when she
entered after her performance, snatch the veil from her face.

But when, according to plan, Theodore with raised hand stepped from behind the screen where he was hiding, the Veiled Lady created some very Hawthornian difficulties by saying:

'Pause one little instant . . . and learn the conditions of what thou art so bold to undertake! Thou canst go hence, and think of me no more; or, at thy option, thou canst lift this mysterious veil, beneath which I am a sad and lonely prisoner, in a bondage which is worse to me than death. But, before raising it, I entreat thee, in all maiden modesty, to bend forward and impress a kiss where my breath stirs the veil; and my virgin lips shall come forward to meet thy lips; and from that instant, Theodore, thou shalt be mine, and I thine, with never more a veil between us. And all the felicity of earth and of the future world shall be thine and mine together. So much may a maiden say behind the veil. If thou shrinkest from this, there is yet another way.'

'And what is that?' asked Theodore.

'Dost thou hesitate,' said the Veiled Lady, 'to pledge thyself to me, by meeting these lips of mine, while the veil yet hides my face? Has not thy heart recognized me? Dost thou come hither, not in holy faith, nor with a pure and generous purpose, but in scornful scepticism and idle curiosity? Still, thou mayest lift the veil! But, from that instant, Theodore, I am doomed to be thy evil fate; nor wilt thou ever taste another breath of happiness!'

Theodore, with better sense than Hawthorne shows in his control of this plot, refuses the Veiled Lady's first offer, and lifts the veil:

Grasping at the veil, he flung it upward, and caught a glimpse of a pale lovely face beneath; just one momentary glimpse, and then the apparition vanished, and the silvery veil floated slowly down and lay upon the floor. Our legend leaves him there. His retribution was to pine forever and ever for another sight of that dim, mournful face,—which might have been his life-long household fireside joy,—to desire, and waste life in a feverish quest, and never meet it more.

Coming to this from the short stories, we can say that we have heard all this before. Priscilla's veil is not exactly synonymous with Mr. Hooper's veil which was voluntarily assumed as a symbol for the instruction of his parishioners: in her case she has been involuntarily victimized, and she seems to be in the same predicament as the young lady whom Ethan Brand coldly made the subject of a psychological experiment. The villains in this case are, of course, Westervelt and his accessory, Zenobia. Zenobia *is* an accessory, as she first fully reveals by telling this story of 'The Silvery Veil'. The end of the story is particularly significant and it makes direct reference to the chapters immediately preceding in which Zenobia has met Westervelt in the woods around Blithedale. The 'lady' in the following passage is Zenobia who is thus referring to herself in third person:

Just at the moment, so far as can be ascertained, when the Veiled Lady vanished, a maiden, pale and shadowy, rose up amid a knot of visionary people, who were seeking for the better life. She was so gentle and so sad,—a nameless melancholy gave her such hold upon their sympathies,—that they never thought of questioning whence she came. She might have heretofore existed, or her thin substance might have been moulded out of air at the very instant when they first beheld her. It was all one to them; they took her to their hearts. Among them was a lady, to whom, more than to all the rest, this pale, mysterious girl attached herself.

But one morning the lady was wandering in the woods, and there met her a figure in an Oriental robe, with a dark beard, and holding in his hand a silvery veil. He motioned her to stay. Being a woman of some nerve, she did not shriek, nor run away, nor faint, as many ladies would have been apt to do. But stood quietly and bade him speak. The truth was, she had seen his face before, but had never feared it, although she knew him to be a terrible magician.

'Lady,' said he, with a warning gesture, 'you are in peril!'

'Peril!' she exclaimed. 'And of what nature?'

'There is a certain maiden,' replied the magician, 'who has come out of the realm of mystery, and made herself your most intimate companion. Now, the facts have so ordained it, that, whether by her own will or no, this stranger is your deadliest enemy. In love, in worldly fortune, in all your pursuit of happiness, she is doomed to fling a blight over your prospects. There is but one possibility of thwarting her disastrous influence.'

'Then tell me that one method,' said the lady.

'Take this veil,' he answered, holding forth the silvery texture. 'It is a spell; it is a powerful enchantment, which I wrought for her sake, and beneath which she was once my prisoner. Throw it, at unawares, over the head of this secret foe, stamp your foot, and cry, "Arise, Magician! here is the Veiled Lady!' and immediately I will rise up through the earth, and seize her; and from that moment you are safe!'

So the lady took the silvery veil, which was like woven air, or like some substance airier than nothing, and that would float upward and be lost among the clouds, were she once to let it go. Returning homeward, she found the shadowy girl, among the knot of visionary transcendentalists, who were still seeking for the better life. She was joyous now, and had a rose-bloom in her cheeks, and was one of the prettiest creatures, and seemed one of the happiest, that the world could show. But the lady stole noise-lessly behind her and threw the veil over her head. As the slight, ethereal texture sank inevitably down over her figure, the poor girl strove to raise it, and met her dear friend's eyes with one glance of mortal terror, and deep, deep reproach. It could not change her purpose.

'Arise, Magician!' she exclaimed, stamping her foot upon the earth. 'Here is the Veiled Lady!'

At the word, uprose the bearded man in the Oriental robes,— the beautiful, the dark magician, who had bartered away his soul! He threw his arms around the Veiled Lady, and she was his bond-slave for evermore!

This is a long quotation but it contains in microcosm the whole movement of action in *The Blithedale Romance*. The exact nature of Zenobia's relationship with Priscilla, as I have already said, is left deliberately vague in the novel. In Chapter XXV Hawthorne shows us Zenobia, Priscilla, and Hollingsworth in the aftermath of a scene of crisis during which they have threshed things out, and, for a novelist, Hawthorne is spectacu-larly evasive:

And what subject had been discussed here? All, no doubt, that for so many months past had kept my heart and my imagination idly feverish. Zenobia's whole character and history; the true nature of her mysterious relation with Westervelt; her later pur-poses towards Hollingsworth, and, reciprocally, his in reference to her; and, finally, the degree in which Zenobia had been cognizant of the plot against Priscilla, and what, at last, had been the real object of that scheme. On these points, as before, I was left to my own conjectures.

One wonders if, in the whole history of the novel, a serious artist ever found a cheaper way out of the legitimate problems facing him. The total structure of the novel suffers because of this wholesale repudiation of all the questions the reader is entitled to ask. Hawthorne may leave us to our own conjectures, but he does so only within limit. If he is unable to clarify satisfactorily the nature of Zenobia's transgression in terms of the action, he is equally unwilling to leave us in any doubt as to her guilt. She is completely associated with Westervelt's crime in violating the integrity of Priscilla's soul, and her guilt is compounded by virtue not only of her blood relationship with the girl, but because of her rejection of the self-surrendering love Priscilla offers. And, as her 'confession' in 'The Silvery Veil' legend indicates, Zenobia's guilt is wholly conscious and deliberate. In the same chapter from which the last quotation was taken, Miles Coverdale, the narrator, on first encountering Zenobia, Hollingsworth, and Priscilla at the foot of Eliot's pulpit, says:

> But, in truth, as my eyes wandered from one of the group to another, I saw in Hollingsworth all that an artist could desire for the grim portrait of a Puritan magistrate holding inquest of life and death in a case of witchcraft: in Zenobia, the sorceress herself, not aged, wrinkled and decrepit, but fair enough to tempt Satan with a force reciprocal to his own; and, in Priscilla, the pale victim, whose soul and body had been wasted by her spells.

The only significant figure missing from this group is that of Westervelt, who, as Mrs. Leavis has pointed out, is described in imagery that associates him with the Devil. But Zenobia has been able 'to tempt Satan with a force reciprocal to his own'. They have wasted Priscilla's soul, violated her inner sphere of reality, equally between them. Why did Zenobia reject the offer of Priscilla's selfless love? Perhaps for several reasons, but chiefly because she was a rival for Hollingsworth. The veil which Priscilla is condemned to wear during her performances constitutes as much of a prison as Clifford's cell in *The House of the Seven Gables*, and it can only be removed by a love that is self-surrendering. That is the allegorical point of Zenobia's account of Theodore's reluctance to put himself out on a limb by kissing the Veiled Lady, and Zenobia serves unambiguous notice that she also will reject the offer of Priscilla's oppressive devotion—oppressive, that is, to the mind of the contemporary reader. Zenobia (and despite Hawthorne's intention, one admires her for her honest selfishness) will not sacrifice or surrender her identity in any relationship, least of all to a poor creature like Priscilla. The silver veil, which is Priscilla's bondage, is Zenobia's freedom, and Zenobia not only throws the veil over Priscilla's head in the legend she narrates, she does so quite literally in the latter half of the book. Of course Hawthorne makes her pay for it. In the full context of Hawthorne's meaning, Zenobia's crime is infamous. In her rejection of Priscilla's love, she literally aligns herself with the Devil. This is the obvious meaning of *The Blithedale Romance*—so obvious that one hesitates to write it down. Yet I am not aware that it has ever been explicitly stated before. Critics have followed James's cue in taking Zenobia as the heroine, and in doing so they have shown better sense than Hawthorne showed in making her the culprit. I have tried to show elsewhere how James rectified the failures of *The Blithedale Romance* in *The Bostonians*, but even James seems not to have understood what a wicked woman Hawthorne meant Zenobia to be. Having lost Hollingsworth to Priscilla, Zenobia drowns herself, suicide apparently being a natural recourse to those who, like Zenobia and Ethan Brand, break the magnetic chain of humanity. The chapter in which Miles Coverdale, Hollingsworth, and Silas Foster, the old farmer caretaker of Blithedale Farm, drag the river for the body is one of the best pieces of writing in all Hawthorne. We are apt to be so moved by Zenobia's tragedy that we forget Hawthorne wishes to impress on us that Zenobia may well be damned. He is, in fact, quite explicit about it. The description of the river at midnight is superbly and eerily done. Hawthorne's sensibility being what it is, the fact that the search is conducted and the body recovered at midnight is highly significant. The whole thing puts one in mind of the descriptive opening of 'The Hollow of the Three Hills'. The passage (quoted in the last chapter) gives us a sinister pool at the bottom of the little basin formed by the juncture of the three hills: 'Such scenes as they (so grey tradition tells) were once the resort of the Power of Evil and his plighted subjects; and here, at midnight or on the dim verge of evening, they were said to stand round the mantling pool, disturbing its putrid waters in the performance of an

impious baptismal rite.' The suggestion is powerfully present
that Zenobia's death by water may be her final baptism into
evil, and the fact that the contemporary reader may not like
this sort of thing does not change the fact that Hawthorne did.
When the body is recovered rigor mortis has set in, and Miles
Coverdale reads a terrible doubt into the posture of the corpse:

> One hope I had, and that too was mingled half with fear. She
> knelt as if in prayer. With the last, choking consciousness, her soul,
> bubbling out through her lips, it may be, had given itself up to the
> Father, reconciled and penitent. But her arms! They were bent
> before her, as if she struggled against Providence in never-ending
> hostility. Her hands! They were clenched in immitigable defiance.

To return to Hollingsworth with whom I began this consideration of *The Blithedale Romance*, I said that although he was
one of Hawthorne's excluded 'heroes' there were extenuating circumstances in his case that saved him from the fullest
penalty of his crime. These extenuating circumstances centre
in the fact that, at long last, he offers Priscilla the kind of selfless love which alone can remove the veil behind which she is
imprisoned. Chapter XXIII, 'A Village Hall', tells us how
Hollingsworth, attending a performance of the Veiled Lady,
suddenly realizes that she is Priscilla, and saves her from the
power of Westervelt and, presumably, Zenobia:

> 'Come,' said he, waving his hand towards her. 'You are safe!'
> She threw off the veil, and stood before that multitude of
> people pale, tremulous, shrinking, as if only then she had dis-
> covered that a thousand eyes were gazing at her. . . . Within that
> encircling veil, though an evil hand had thrown it over her, there
> was as deep seclusion as if this forsaken girl had, all the while,
> been sitting under the shadow of Eliot's pulpit, in the Blithedale
> woods, at the feet of him who now summoned her to the shelter
> of his arms. And the true heart-throb of a woman's affection was
> too powerful for the jugglery that had hitherto environed her.
> She uttered a shriek, and fled to Hollingsworth, like one escaping
> from her deadliest enemy, and was safe forever.

However contrived this scene may appear to the modern
reader it is the climax of the action. Priscilla, not Zenobia, is
the true heroine of the novel, and it is at this point that she is
finally released from the deadly spiritual peril that has surrounded her, and the values she embodies triumph. We have

been tutored, by the time we reach this scene, to decipher its meaning and read its values, for Zenobia's story of 'The Silvery Veil' has been intended as a direct preparation for Priscilla's victory. The trouble is that Zenobia's story and the later scene in the Village Hall are of a piece, as they were meant to be, and the modern reader is repelled by them. Hawthorne meant to balance this scene with a secondary retributive chapter in which Zenobia should meet her doom, but he destroyed his carefully planned framework by writing something so masterly in his account of Zenobia's death that it completely refocuses, against his intention, the meaning he was trying to convey. James was badly mistaken, but at the same time perfectly right, when he referred to Zenobia's death as the 'dénouement' of the story.[6]

Miles Coverdale, the narrator who observes the action of the entire story, calls for a word of attention here. Henry James, one might have guessed, liked him. He found in the young man a detached observer rather like his own young narrators. But other critics have not been as generous. A recent writer, for example, very ill-naturedly called Miles an ill-natured aesthete. Hawthorne seems to have seen Miles as a kind of symbol of himself, and, in purely autobiographical terms, Miles's arrival at Blithedale on a wintry April day sounds very much like Hawthorne's arrival at Brook Farm. Miles also incorporates Hawthorne's doubts about his own profession. It is true that Miles meddles and snoops to a disconcerting degree. Zenobia takes him to task over and over again throughout the novel for probing into the dark corners of the human heart, and Hawthorne punishes him in the end by condemning him to be forever on the outside of life. This brings me to the real reason for discussing Miles here. The conclusion of *The Blithedale Romance* is rightly held by nearly everybody to be ridiculous. Miles is one of the most charmingly confirmed bachelors in our literature and yet Hawthorne makes him commit the absurdity in the very last line of the novel of stuttering out the grotesque confession:

I—I myself—was in love—with—Priscilla!

It is really too much. But where a gaucherie is as perfect and absolute as this, there must be a reason for it, and this irritating lapse of taste on Miles's part (he is otherwise quite nice) does throw a farther light on the significance Hawthorne attached to Priscilla. As a poet (Miles has published a small volume of poetry, and his character is presented throughout as that of the writer) he comes in for his share of Hawthorne's rebuke to artists in general. He is aloof from men, detachedly observing them in the manner of Holgrave, and indifferent to those life-impulses which move others to action: 'As Hollingsworth once told me, I lack a purpose. How strange! He was ruined, morally, by an over-plus of the same ingredient, the want of which, I occasionally suspect, has rendered my own life all an emptiness.' We know that Hawthorne never lets anyone who has played loose with the magnetic chain of humanity off easily, and so he punishes Miles by equating him with Theodore in Zenobia's story. Of Theodore, who was also afraid to risk self-surrender in a relationship with the Veiled Lady, Zenobia had said: 'His retribution was to pine for ever and ever for another sight of that dim, mournful face,—which might have been his life-long household fireside joy,—to desire, and waste life in a feverish quest, and never meet it more.'

Priscilla occupies a very special place among Hawthorne's heroines. If, on the level of realism, she is merely in our eyes (and Zenobia's) an insignificant, uninteresting girl, Hawthorne meant her, in the role of the Veiled Lady, to be an embodiment of his conception of reality, truth, goodness, imprisoned by the world's artificial system and waiting to be freed by an imaginative, self-surrendering love. As Veiled Lady she is an allegorical figure in relation to whom the other characters define their own respective degrees of reality.

I said earlier *The Blithedale Romance* was an interesting novel, but it is so almost in spite of Hawthorne. We accept it as such only when we interpret in our terms; but they cannot be comprehensive enough to reshape the total framework of Hawthorne's meaning, and we end by admiring the fragment we let pass for the whole. Under such conditions it can be a 'good' novel only in a strictly qualified sense, and I agree with James in finding the value of the book in its occasional touches, which are 'deep and delicate'.[7] James also found a 'certain want of substance and cohesion in the latter portions of *The Blithedale Romance*'. But despite deliberate obscurities, I believe the novel is tightly coherent if we are able to take Priscilla as the reality or life-symbol that Hawthorne asks us to. Frankly, I cannot do so, and this leads me to a conclusion which I think it is time to state openly. Hawthorne was a great artist, and during the past few years he has undergone a critical revival which makes us very much aware of that fact. But there is frequently something defective, or even repellent, in his human sensibility which, although it shows only occasionally, is insistent enough to be extremely disconcerting. I intend no relative evaluation of creative status when I say that of the American novelists treated here, he lacked the intelligence of Cooper, the spirituality of Melville, the spohistication of James, and the final emotional maturity of all three. Q. D. Leavis has written that Hawthorne 'has the indispensable genius for knowing, and communicating, where life flows. . . .' [8] This is certainly true. The existence of Zenobia herself is a vindication of the insight; but the conflict in Hawthorne's character was deep. Hawthorne invests such characters as Zenobia, Hester, and Miriam, with a rich emotional fullness, a deep flow of life. But consider then the hideous fate he deals out to them while apotheosizing the insufferable Priscillas and Hildas to whom he gives his full intellectual approval, and who are, in a degree, portraits of his impossible wife. The rift in the American experience is tragically symbolized here. Hawthorne's three great female characters are essentially European women—two by birth and education, Zenobia by the whole force of her personality. If the fullness of life flows through them, Hawthorne cannot accept it in the end. His intellectualizing, democratic self rebels. Nevertheless, they have provided him with an interval, before their final rejection, long enough for him to prove his genius. Despite the protest of the meaner half of himself, which is never quiet for long, his real interest and affection is centred in them. Like Drowne's wooden image, they awaken the Yankee craftsman into life. But in the end he turns his democratic American back on these evocations of his imagination, and goes back to the company of Matthew and Hannah, back to the Veiled Lady's vapoury version of reality. And even here one suspects that it is the veil more than the lady that Hawthorne prefers—as who, in Priscilla's case, wouldn't?

II

I said earlier that my treatment of the novels would necessarily be restrictive. This is particularly true of such a great
masterpiece as *The Scarlet Letter*. I stated what I believe to be
Hawthorne's limitations before turning to *The Scarlet Letter*
because, finally, all attempts to delimit Hawthorne's achievement in an adverse way must break down before this astonishing performance. I have written elsewhere that *The Scarlet
Letter* is not an allegory on the woman taken in adultery, but a
subtle exploration of moral isolation in America'.[9] I shall con-
fine the present discussion to expanding that remark, and showing how it is Hawthorne's finest analysis of his conception of
reality, and of the ways men possess or are excluded from it.
The schema which I outlined in the chapter on Hawthorne's
short stories is no less valid here than in the work already discussed, but because Hawthorne is creating here at his highest
level, it becomes something of an impertinence, which it was
not before. Nevertheless, it continues to be a useful, if somewhat
blunt, instrument for uncovering those tensions out of which
Hawthorne moulds his art.

We begin with an act that is destructive of that inner sphere
of reality in which the human being finds his fulfilment
through reciprocal sympathy, understanding, and love. The
act, here presented superficially as a sexual transgression, is
conventionally called a 'sin', but as the novel develops the
reader is (or ought to be) left in some perplexity as to the exact
nature of that 'sin' and who the real malefactors are. Even if
the principal 'sinners' prove to be Hester and Dimmesdale,
they are very different kinds of sinners, facing different moral
problems. There is no question of vagueness here, but a
miraculous control that can scarcely be surpassed. Hawthorne
has recreated in his art the complex conditions of life itself; he
has given us, in its shifting uncertainties, the bleak perspective
of doubt in which the heart is compelled to search out its truth.
We are concerned with adultery here only in a transient way.
The act of which Hester and Dimmesdale are guilty partakes of
the 'sins' of Ethan Brand, of the lady in 'The Hollow of the
Three Hills', of Goodman Brown; and, again, it is the sin
exemplified by Mr. Hooper's black veil. It is all of these and, of

F

course, none of them, for it has the unique, induplicable life that belongs to all great, fully realized art. It escapes easy definition, but we can begin by saying that its essence lies in the centrifugal nature of its effect. We have this revealing passage at the close of Chapter XXII in which the effect of the scarlet letter, which symbolizes Hester's 'sin' in all its complexity, is described:

> There were many people present, from the country round about, who had often heard of the scarlet letter, and to whom it had been made terrific by a hundred false or exaggerated rumours, but who had never beheld it with their own bodily eyes. These, after exhausting other modes of amusement, now thronged about Hester Prynne with rude and boorish intrusiveness. Unscrupulous as it was, however, it could not bring them nearer than a circuit of several yards. At that distance they accordingly stood, fixed there by the centrifugal force of the repugnance which the mystic symbol inspired.

The act of which Hester and Dimmesdale are guilty is not only destructive, as we shall see, of interior fulfilment in private human relations, it is also destructive of social relationships in the largest sense of the word. But it is worth noting that, even in the passage just quoted, Hawthorne maintains our sense of ambivalence very subtly. If the scarlet letter creates a sphere of emptiness in the midst of which Hester stands, it has by this time become a 'mystic symbol' in relation to which the sin of society defines itself. If, in the beginning, the scarlet letter symbolized an act by which Hester violated her relationship with her husband and society, the focus has now shifted and it is seen as a symbol of exclusion from reality of those whose intrusive curiosity violates the magnetic chain of humanity. The scarlet letter represents here a magic ring that can only be penetrated by selfless love, and at this point it suggests the later symbol of Priscilla's veil, but done with immeasurably greater subtlety.

I do not wish, however, to exchange one simplification for another. Hawthorne does not end by pointing an accusatory finger at the intolerance of Puritan society while exonerating Hester and Dimmesdale. While condemning its intolerance, Hawthorne shows that it is also part of a larger human world against which the two protagonists have transgressed. The symbol lives in its various meaning at one and the same time. If Hawthorne gives us a society in which children play at whipping Quakers in the street, to leave it at this would be to elicit our sympathy and forgiveness for Hester and Dimmesdale far too easily. It would be to invite a disastrously facile moral judgement along 'liberal' lines, and to reduce the living complexity of art to the comparative vulgarity of a pat resolution. And so, while showing us the eccentric and fanatical side of the Puritan community, Hawthorne also gives it to us as a substantial microcosm of the great world. This sense of the microcosm is partly kept in the reader's mind by images suggesting the relationship between England and America. We are shown men whose dress and manners, and the order of whose minds, introduce echoes of another society beyond the seas.

I shall point to only one instance in which Hawthorne impressively creates, not merely a picture of a small puritan coterie, but a microcosm capable of enlarging, and affording a major perspective to the human tragedy we witness. It comes near the end of the book, and is only the last of a succession of such passages. It is the final crisis and death of Dimmesdale on Election Day. This crisis is enacted against a solidly realized background of civil and military order, and at this crucial moment of the novel the background has the effect of powerfully personifying that society from which Hester's and Dimmesdale's sin has alienated them. It clearly represents much more than was suggested by the rude inquisitiveness of the boors who gathered around Hester in the market-place. Without the resonance provided by this richly communicated sense of a more-than-Puritan society which we are given in such passages, the whole tragedy would lose stature. The fact that the tragedy itself occurs on Election day has more than one importance. It focuses the whole action at one of civic society's most public and ceremonial moments. The dramatic effect of this device is, of course, overwhelming, but Hawthorne has a deeper reason: it symbolizes the fact that as Dimmesdale's sin has consisted essentially in concealment, its expiation must be public. But the intolerant, Quaker-whipping society about which Hawthorne can be so eloquent would not be the proper audience for Dimmesdale's final expiation. At bottom, his sin has not been against society in such a limited or distorted sense as this, and so Hawthorne metamorphosizes the little Puritan village into what seems substantially an image of the outside world. The passage is given in Chapter XXII, which describes the Election Day procession to the meeting-house:

This body of soldiery—which still sustains a corporate existence, and marches down from past ages with an ancient and honourable fame—was composed of no mercenary materials. Its ranks were filled with gentlemen, who felt the stirrings of martial impulse, and sought to establish a kind of College of Arms, where as in an association of Knights Templars, they might learn the science, and, so far as peaceful exercise would teach them, the practices of war. The high estimation then placed upon the military character might be seen in the lofty port of each individual member of the company. Some of them, indeed, by their services in the Low Countries and on other fields of warfare, had fairly won their title to assume the name and pomp of soldiership. The entire array, moreover, clad in burnished steel, and with plumage nodding over their bright morions, had a brilliancy of effect which no modern display can aspire to equal.

And yet the men of civil eminence, who came immediately behind the military escort, were better worth a thoughtful observer's eye. Even in outward demeanour, they showed a stamp of majesty that made the warrior's haughty stride look vulgar, if not absurd. It was an age when what we call talent had far less consideration than now, but the massive materials which produce stability and dignity of character a great deal more. The people possessed, by hereditary right, the quality of reverence; which, in their descendants, if it survive at all, exists in smaller proportion, and with a vastly diminished force, in the selection and estimate of public men. The change may be for good or evil, and is partly, perhaps, for both. In that old day, the English settler on these rude shores, having left king, nobles, and all degrees of awful rank behind, while still the faculty and necessity for reverence were strong in him, bestowed it on the white hair and venerable brow of age; on long-tried integrity; on solid wisdom and sad coloured experience; on endowments of that grave and weighty order which gives the idea of permanence, and comes under the general definition of respectability. These primitive statesmen, therefore,—Bradstreet, Endicott, Dudley, Bellingham, and their compeers,—who were elevated to power by the early choice of the people, seem to have been not often brilliant, but distinguished by a ponderous sobriety, rather than activity of intellect. They had fortitude and self-reliance, and, in time of difficulty or peril, stood up for the welfare of the state like a line of cliffs against a tempestuous tide. The traits of character here indicated were well represented in the square cast of countenance and large physical development of the new colonial magistrates. So far as a demeanour of natural authority was concerned, the mother country need not have been ashamed to see these foremost men of an actual democracy adopted into the House of Peers, or made the Privy Council of the sovereign.

It is to a society which Hawthorne is careful to elevate above the claustrophobic limitations of New England Puritanism that Dimmesdales makes his public confession. This confession at the close of *The Scarlet Letter* when Dimmesdale stands on the scaffold in front of the assembled crowd balances that other great chapter in which he stands on the same scaffold at midnight and proclaims his guilt to the darkened houses of the village. The two scenes taken together provide a highly successful dramatization of Dimmesdale's almost intolerable urgency to rid himself of the sense of concealment—concealment of the kind that Hawthorne had already analysed in 'The Minister's Black Veil'.

The sin, then, of Hester and Dimmesdale is what Hawthorne refers to, at least once, as a centrifugal sin, separating the guilty ones from society, but this separation occurs in different ways for each of them. In Dimmesdale's case, the nature of the sin, and its progress in him, is relatively easy to understand. At one point in the novel Hawthorne writes that *originally* the sin was one of passion, not of principle. The crime might have been easily thrown off by another nature, but, says Hawthorne: 'Crime is for the iron-nerved, who have their choice either to endure it, or, if it press too hard, to exert their fierce and savage strength for a good purpose, and fling it off at once! This feeble and most sensitive of spirits could do neither, yet continually did one thing or another, which intertwined, in the same inextricable knot, the agony of heaven-defying guilt and vain repentance.'

The poisonous nature of Dimmesdale's guilt springs, not from the act of adultery itself, but from the fact that he is unable to reveal it, and this inability Hawthorne presents as something bordering on a constitutional incapacity, but hardly the less culpable for that. As I said, Dimmesdale's midnight appearance

on the scaffold dramatizes his desire, but inability, to communicate his secret sin. And Hawthorne has other passages
where the problem is stated very explicitly, as in Dimmesdale's
repudiation of his own life of penance in an exchange with
Hester in Chapter XVII:

> 'There is no substance in it! It is cold and dead, and can do
> nothing for me! Of penance, I have had enough! Of penitence,
> there has been none! Else, I should long ago have thrown off
> these garments of mock holiness, and have shown myself to man-
> kind as they will see me at the judgement-seat. Happy are you,
> Hester, that wear the scarlet letter openly upon your bosom!
> Mine burns in secret! Thou little knowest what a relief it is, after
> the torment of a seven years' cheat, to look into an eye that
> recognizes me for what I am! Had I one friend—or were it my
> worst enemy!—to whom, when sickened with the praises of all
> other men, I could daily betake myself, and be known as the
> vilest of all sinners, methinks my soul might keep itself alive
> thereby. Even thus much of truth would save me! But, now, it is
> all falsehood!—all emptiness!—all death!'

Here again is the world of Gervayse Hastings—the moral
desert in which no reality exists behind the appearances of
things, and in which apparent movement is only a sign of death.
Dimmesdale's constitutional incapacity to throw off concealment as a means of once again entering into a living relationship with society relates to the short, unimportant story,
'Wakefield', in which a man walks from his home one day and,
for no assignable reason, goes into hiding for twenty years while
his wife believes him dead. Such a story seems to indicate that
Hawthorne believed in the possibility of some perverse sickness
of the will closely related to that native defect of the heart
already discussed, for which the individual was not wholly to
blame, but for which he had to bear the fullest responsibility.
In the passage quoted, the original sexual transgression is
almost lost sight of, while the actual guilt springs from the
festering concealment that poisons the whole context of human
relationships in which Dimmesdale must find the real meaning
of his life. Paradoxically, the relation with Hester from which
the tragic sequence of events began, now promises, or seems to,
a possibility of spiritual renewal. But I shall speak of this later.
    The nature of Hester's sin is different from Dimmesdale's,

and it is more difficult to analyse. It differs, first of all, in not being a secret sin. As far as the adultery itself goes, it is probable that Hawthorne would have considered the public penance imposed on Hester in the opening pages of the novel a sufficient retribution. The tragedy of her life was, not that she had sexually transgressed, but that a penalty was imposed which induced alienation in her, and in the imposition of such a penalty society itself is deeply guilty. There are points at which the guilt of society almost seems to absorb the personal guilt of Hester. But such a resolution would be highly uncharacteristic of Hawthorne, and in the end we find the problem complicated by certain factors in Hester's own mind and character which suggest that inherent moral flaws have found nutriment in the social penalty under which she has had to suffer. Thus, the symbol of the scarlet letter stands for a pervasive guilt in which all have their respective shares. There is a passage from Chapter XIII which, despite its length, it is imperative to quote here, for it gives us very clearly the two points I have made above— that the social penalty inflicted upon Hester, because it struck at the very roots of her human nature, was itself sinful; but that, among its consequences, was the development of a speculative turn of mind which Hawthorne, to a degree not often recognized today, found sinful, and imputable to Hester alone.

The effect of the symbol,—or, rather, the position in respect to society that was indicated by it—on the mind of Hester Prynne herself, was powerful and peculiar. All the light and graceful foliage of her character had been withered up by this red-hot brand, and had long ago fallen away, leaving a bare and harsh outline, which might have been repulsive, had she possessed friends or companions to be repelled by it. Even the attractiveness of her person had undergone a similar change. It might be partly owing to the studied austerity of her dress, and partly to the lack of demonstration in her manners. It was a sad transformation, too, that her rich and luxuriant hair had either been cut off, or was so completely hidden by a cap, that not a shining lock of it ever once gushed into the sunshine. It was due in part to all these causes, but still more to something else, that there seemed to be no longer anything in Hester's face for Love to dwell upon; nothing in Hester's form, though majestic and statue-like, that Passion would ever dream of clasping in its embrace; nothing in Hester's bosom, to make it ever again, the pillow of Affection.

Some attribute had departed from her, the permanence of which had been essential to keep her a woman . . . She who has once been a woman, and ceased to be so, might at any moment become a woman again if there were only the magic touch to effect the transfiguration. We shall see whether Hester Prynne were ever afterwards to be touched, and so transfigured.

Much of the marble coldness of Hester's impression was to be attributed to the circumstance, that her life had turned, in a great measure, from passion and feeling, to thought. Standing alone in the world,—alone, as to any dependence on society, and with little Pearl to be guided and protected,—alone, and hopeless of retrieving her position, even had she not scorned to consider it desirable,—she cast away the fragments of a broken chain. The world's law was no law for her mind. It was an age in which the human intellect, newly emancipated, had taken a more active and wider range than for many centuries before. . . . Hester Prynne imbibed this spirit. She assumed a freedom of speculation, then common enough on the other side of the Atlantic, but which our forefathers, had they known it, would have held to be a deadlier crime than that stigmatized by the scarlet letter. In her lonesome cottage, by the sea-shore, thoughts visited her, such as dared to enter no other dwelling in New England; shadowy guests, they would have been as perilous as demons to their entertainer, could they have been seen so much as knocking at her door.

In the first paragraph, Hawthorne points to the guilt of society in depriving Hester of her essential womanhood; but in the second paragraph she complements society's guilt with her own. Speculative freedom of mind, although presumably at a more vulgar level, also characterized Zenobia in *The Blithedale Romance*: 'She made no scruple of oversetting all human institutions, and scattering them as with a breeze from her fan. A female reformer, in her attacks upon society, has an instinctive sense of where the life lies, and is inclined to aim directly at that spot.' This speculative freedom, as we have seen, characterized various types of the artist in Hawthorne's short stories. We get a significant clue to what this freedom of mind signified for Hawthorne at the beginning of Chapter XVIII:

Her intellect and heart had their home, as it were, in desert places, where she roamed as freely as the wild Indian in his woods. For years past she had looked from this estranged point of view at human institutions, and whatever priests or legislators had established; criticizing all with hardly more reverence than the Indian would feel for the clerical band, the judicial robe, the pillory, the gallows, the fireside, or the church. The tendency of her fate and fortunes had been to set her free. The scarlet letter was her passport into regions where other women dared not tread. Shame, Despair, Solitude! These had been her teachers,—stern and wild ones,—and they had made her strong, but taught her much amiss.

The modern reader may be inclined to discount Hawthorne's criticism of Hester's speculative freedom as ironic, but Hawthorne means what he says. Her 'latitude of speculation' is as disastrous in its effects on her personality as Ethan Brand's 'star-lit eminence' of mind was on his, and the imagery Hawthorne uses in describing the two cases is strikingly similar. Of Hester, Hawthorne, says: 'Standing in the world alone . . . she cast away the fragments of a broken chain.' This is, of course, that same magnetic chain that figures so largely in the short story. If society has a hand in the breaking of that chain for Hester, Hawthorne is careful to show that Hester is ultimately guilty in her own right:

> A woman never overcomes these problems by any exercise of thought. They are not to be solved or only in one way. If her heart chance to come uppermost, they vanish. Thus Hester Prynne, whose heart had lost its regular and healthy throb, wandered without a clew in the dark labyrinth of mind. . . .

If Dimmesdale's sin moves us towards the worlds of Mr. Hooper and Gervayse Hastings, a passage like the above unmistakably relates to the Unpardonable Sin of Ethan Brand:

> Then ensued that vast intellectual development, which, in its progress, disturbed the counterpoise between his mind and heart. . . . But where was the heart? That, indeed, had withered,—had contracted,—had hardened,—had perished! It had ceased to partake of the universal throb. He had lost his hold of the magnetic chain of humanity.

Hester's exclusion from the inner sphere of reality is complete:

> In all her intercourse with society, however, there was nothing that made her feel as if she belonged to it. Every word, every gesture, and even the silence of those with whom she came in contact, implied, and often expressed, that she was banished, and as

much alone as if she inhabited another sphere, or communicated with the common nature by other organs and senses than the rest of human kind. She stood apart from moral interests, yet close beside them, like a ghost that revisits the familiar fireside, and can no longer make itself seen or felt; no more smile with the household joy, nor mourn with the kindred sorrow; or, should it succeed in manifesting its forbidden sympathy, awakening only terror and horrible repugnance. These emotions, in fact, and its bitterest scorn besides, seemed to be the sole portion that she retained in the universal heart.

There are certain qualities in this passage that remind one of the lady's predicament in 'The Hollow of the Three Hills'. Because of an infidelity to her husband, that lady is also forever excluded from moral interests, and the relationship between her and her family is a communion of ghosts. Hawthorne's death-imagery is applied, in Hester's case, with a good deal of insistence: 'Her face, so long familiar to the townspeople, showed the marble quietude which they were accustomed to behold there. It was like a mask; or rather, like the frozen calmness of a dead woman's features; owing this dreary resemblance to the fact that Hester was actually dead, in respect to any claim of sympathy, and had departed out of the world, in which she still seemed to mingle.'

The essence of Dimmesdale's sin is concealment; Hester's is more complicated, but it is essentially a withdrawal from society on her part; for if Hester is banished, Hawthorne insists that she similarly banishes mankind from her own heart. The result is a living death. But in Chapters XVII and XVIII a rather extraordinary and un-Hawthornian thing happens. Meeting in the forest after their seven years of penitential misery, Hester persuades Dimmesdale to flee back to Europe with her: in other words, to re-establish their illicit union as a permanent thing. As a symbol of her decision, she tears the scarlet letter from her breast and throws it away:

There played around her mouth, and beamed out of her eyes, a radiant and tender smile, that seemed gushing from the very heart of womanhood. A crimson flush was glowing on her cheek, that had been long so pale. Her sex, her youth, and the whole richness of her beauty, came back from what men call the irrevocable past, and clustered themselves, with her maiden hope, and a happiness before unknown, within the magic circle of this hour. And, as if the gloom of the earth and sky had been but the effluence of these two mortal hearts, it vanished with their sorrow. All at once, as with a sudden smile of heaven, forth burst the sunshine, pouring a very flood into the obscure forest, gladdening each green leaf, transmuting the yellow fallen ones to gold, and gleaming adown the grey trunks of the solemn trees. The objects that had made a shadow hitherto, embodied the brightness now. The course of the little brook might be traced by its merry gleam afar into the wood's heart of mystery, which had become a mystery of joy.

Such was the sympathy of Nature—that wild, heathen Nature of the forest, never subjugated by human law, nor illumined by higher truth—with the bliss of these two spirits! Love, whether newly born, or aroused from a death-like slumber, must always create a sunshine, filling the heart so full of radiance, that it over-flows upon the outward world. Had the forest still kept its gloom, it would have been bright in Hester's eyes, and bright in Arthur Dimmesdale's!

Perhaps it would be too much to maintain that the husband of Sophia Peabody was arguing a case for adultery here, and he tries to cover any tracks he may have made in that direction by a discreet reference to 'higher truth'. But the passage clearly establishes that it is *not* adultery as such that constitutes the crime of *The Scarlet Letter*. The possible renewal of the adulterous union is seen here as a resurrection into life, and as a means of once again possessing, or entering into, the inner sphere of reality.

Hawthorne was always ruthless in the way he punished those characters who broke the magnetic chain of humanity. This seems, quite literally, to have been the Unpardonable Sin as far as he was concerned. Ethan Brand and Zenobia commit suicide, Gervayse Hastings dies in despair, Goodman Brown's poisoned faith in men haunts him to the grave. One would not expect Hawthorne to let Hester off easily, then, if the essence of her sin was indeed that she had broken the magnetic chain. It is part of Hawthorne's artistic triumph in this novel, as contrasted with some of the others, that he is able to suggest (or make the reader believe that he does) the possibility of a final redemption for Hester. But the closing lines, which describe her grave, are far from the light-filled forest scene in the above quotation.

Hawthorne in the end emphatically rejects the possibility of escape which seemed to be offered there, and even in death Hester does not free herself from the awful symbol which shows more gloomily on her tombstone than it ever had on her breast. In the shadow of such a final paragraph all talk of redemption seems a little superfluous.

In view of the inexorable fate that overtakes the men and women who err in Hawthorne's stories and novels, his inability completely to forgive them, or to mark a termination to their punishment—in view of these things, it is tempting to say that Hawthorne's conception of human nature continued to be corrupted by Calvinism, even though, intellectually, it was unacceptable to him. The native defect of heart, or the inherited malaise of the will, which are so recurrent throughout Hawthorne and which I have remarked on many times in these pages, comes at last to impress one as some taint of the soul with which man is born, and for which, though hardly responsible, he must be endlessly punished. There are perhaps other possible explanations. I shall discuss a political one in the following chapter in attempting to understand the motives of disillusionment and despair in Melville's later novels. But I should merely like to say here that Hawthorne and Melville resemble each other more than one might expect, and the resemblance is closer in the darker aspects of their minds than anywhere else. There is a passage in Chapter LXI of *White Jacket* in which Melville gives us a symbol that might be used equally for both his and Hawthorne's visions of the universe. I think, in its way, it suggests useful reflections on the effective but depressing closing pages of *The Scarlet Letter*, which really tell us so much less than they seem to. The passage describes a plaster cast in the cabin of Dr. Cuticle, the Surgeon of the Fleet:

> Like most old physicians and surgeons who have seen much service, and have been promoted to high professional places for their scientific attainments, this Cuticle was an enthusiast in his calling. . . . In particular, the department of morbid anatomy was his peculiar love; and in his state-room below he had a most unsightly collection of Parisian casts, in plaster and wax, representing all imaginable malformations of the human members, both organic and induced by disease. Chief among these was a cast, often to be met with in the Anatomical Museums of Europe,

and no doubt an unexaggerated copy of a genuine original; it was the head of an elderly woman, with an aspect singularly gentle and meek, but at the same time wonderfully expressive of a gnawing sorrow, never to be relieved. You would almost have thought it the face of some abbess, for some unspeakable crime voluntarily sequestered from human society, and leading a life of agonized penitence without hope, so marvellously sad and tearfully pitiable was this head. But when you first beheld it, no such emotions ever crossed your mind. All your eyes and all your horrified soul were fast fascinated and frozen by the sight of a hideous, crumpled horn, like that of a ram, downward growing out from the forehead, and partly shadowing the face; but as you gazed, the freezing fascination of its horribleness gradually waned, and then your whole heart burst with sorrow, as you contemplated those aged features, ashy pale and wan. The horn seemed the mark of a curse for some mysterious sin, conceived and committed before the spirit had entered the flesh. Yet that sin seemed something imposed, and not voluntarily sought; some sin growing out of the heartless necessities of the predestination of things; some sin under which the sinner sank in sinless woe.

The most 'hopeful' part of *The Scarlet Letter* centres in Hester's little daughter, Pearl, and her role should be borne in mind as a necessary qualification of the pessimism I have emphasized in the conclusion. Pearl represents the wild, heathen nature of Hester's and Dimmesdale's love, which is symbolized by her intimate communion with the wild creatures of the forest. And simultaneously the little girl's hostility to society symbolizes the unconventional nature of their union—for Hawthorne explicitly presents Pearl as a symbol of their love in its full play of complex contradictions. The emotional transformation of little Pearl as she kneels by her dying father on the scaffold may be read to symbolize a kind of spiritual resurrection for both her parents:

> Pearl kissed his lips. A spell was broken. The great scene of grief in which the wild infant bore a part, had developed all her sympathies; and as her tears fell upon her father's cheek, they were the pledge that she would grow up amid human joy and sorrow, nor forever do battle with the world, but be a woman in it. Towards her mother, too, Pearl's errand as a messenger of anguish was all fulfilled.

But all we can really be sure of is that the scattered parts of the magnetic chain are to be brought together once again in Pearl's life. For Hester and Dimmesdale the dark ambiguity remains, and almost the last words of Dimmesdale are, 'I fear! I fear!'

The Scarlet Letter has essentially the same meaning as nearly everything Hawthorne wrote—the same meaning, that is, if we resort to analytic paraphrase, for in *The Scarlet Letter* that recurrent meaning is incarnated in a symbolism that represents the highest triumph of his art. Hawthorne's inner sphere of reality is really little more than the quiet and pure communion of a human mind and heart with others in love and charity. Using the symbol of a magnetic chain of humanity which, in some ways, corresponds to the Christian idea of a mystical union among the faithful—using this symbol of spiritual fellowship, Hawthorne is always concerned to show the multiple and subtle ways in which the chain can be broken, and the effects this violation has on the human spirit. It is rather as if a Christian novelist were to set out to write a body of fictions dealing with the effects on the human heart of a fall from grace, of the subtle and hidden effects of sin on the soul. But with Hawthorne, the whole drama of which he writes, and which he analyses, is not conceived primarily in terms of sin, at least in the theological sense. His concern with the sanctity and purity of human relationships is ultimately as secular in nature as Henry James's. His interest is focused on an analysis of the barriers which arise between human spirits in a conventional society when its code has been transgressed, and of the subtle poisons that are generated because of those barriers. *The Scarlet Letter* is a study of isolation on the spatial plane. From Hester's and Dimmesdale's original transgression we see widening circles of isolation radiating outwards until Hester is left stranded in the midst of a terrible solitude which, to Hawthorne's thinking, is the negation of reality. Hester is simply cut off from life. And yet, in the subtly woven novel, her guilt is shown to be balanced by that of the surrounding social medium, the intolerant element. The conflict between Hester and the community is the most poised statement Hawthorne ever made of the tension between solitude and society, and at no point does he simplify by allowing the guilt of the one to cancel out the guilt of the other.

III

If *The Scarlet Letter* is a study of the breaking of the magnetic chain of humanity on a spatial plane, *The House of the Seven Gables* may be described as a variation on the theme from a temporal point of view. It is a study of guilt transmitted through time, from generation to generation, rather than of guilt seen in a widening circle which gradually encompasses surrounding society. The focus is less psychological than historical, and the political note is more dominant than in *The Scarlet Letter*. The original transgression from which the whole action of the story begins is not, as with Hester and Dimmesdale, a private moral action, but a public one—an action involving laws of inheritance and the transference of property from one generation to the next. We encounter here another of those basic tensions in American life of which I spoke earlier—the tension between past and present. In *The American Renaissance*, F. O. Matthiessen writes: 'A peculiar kind of social understanding made Hawthorne hold to both the contradicting terms of this paradox of being at once a democrat and a conservative.' [10] Matthiessen is not very enlightening on the nature of this 'social understanding', but it would seem to go back to that fundamental ambivalence in American experience which created the apparent contradiction between Cooper's European political novels and the Littlepage trilogy. I think we might simply define this ambivalence as the recognition on the part of the best Americans that either the excessive democracy or the excessive conservatism of the extremists on either side of the equation was impracticable. In *The House of the Seven Gables* Hawthorne carries on the same kind of debate between the respective claims, on one hand, of the past, inherited wealth, and aristocratic status; on the other, of the present, and of democratic equality, both financial and social. But the debate does not come off successfully. The resolution is as slippery for Hawthorne as for Cooper. This conflict can be illustrated by juxtaposing two quotations from *The House of the Seven Gables*. The first is from Chapter XII:

'Shall we never, never get rid of this past?' cried he [Holgrave], keeping up the earnest tone of his preceding conversation. 'It lies upon the Present like a giant's dead body! In fact, the case is just as if a young giant were compelled to waste all his strength in carrying about the corpse of the old giant, his grandfather, who died a long while ago, and only needs to be decently buried. Just think a moment, and it will startle you to see what slaves we are to bygone times,—to Death, if we give the matter the right word!'

'But I do not see it,' observed Phoebe.

'For example, then,' continued Holgrave: 'a dead man if he happen to have made a will, disposes of wealth no longer his own; or, if he die intestate, it is distributed in accordance with the notions of men much longer dead than he. A dead man sits on all our judgement seats; and living judges do but search out and repeat his decisions. We read in dead men's books! We laugh at dead men's jokes, and cry at dead men's pathos! We are sick of dead men's diseases, physical and moral, and die of the same remedies with which dead doctors killed their patients! We worship the living Deity according to dead men's forms and creeds. Whatever we seek to do, of our own free motion, a dead man's icy hand obstructs us! Turn our eyes to what point we may, a dead man's white immitigable face encounters them, and freezes our very heart! And we must be dead ourselves before we can begin to have our proper influence on our own world, which will then be no longer our world, but the world of another generation, with which we shall have no shadow of a right to interfere. I ought to have said, too, that we live in dead men's houses; as, for instance, in this of the Seven Gables!'

'And why not,' said Phoebe, 'so long as we can be comfortable in them?'

'But we shall live to see the day, I trust,' went on the artist, 'when no man shall build his house for posterity. Why should he? . . . If each generation were allowed and expected to build its own houses, that single change, comparatively unimportant in itself, would imply almost every reform which society is now suffering for. I doubt whether even our public edifices—our capitols, state-houses, courthouses, city-hall, and churches— ought to be built of such permanent materials as stone or brick. It were better that they should crumble to ruin once in twenty years, or thereabouts, as a hint to the people to examine into and reform the institutions which they symbolize.'

Basically, this is the purest and extremest Jeffersonianism. Jefferson's philosophy of constitutions was based on the principle that the earth belongs to the living. Each generation was, or should be, independent of those who had lived and legislated before it, and consequently every constitution required revision every nineteen years. Albert Jay Nock points out in his *Jefferson* that for Jefferson the length of a generation was counted as a majority of men 'born on the same day, reaching maturity at twenty-one years of age, dying on the same day, thirty-four years later',[11] hardly a very logical point of view. The laws and constitutions made by one generation could be preserved in existence only by the will of the majority of men of that generation which devised them. If they were 'enforced longer it is an act of force and not of right':

> . . . no society can make a perfect constitution, or even a perpetual law. The earth belongs always to the living generation. They may manage it then, and what proceeds from it, as they please during their usufruct. They are masters of their own persons, and consequently may govern them as they please. But persons and property make the sum of the objects of government. The constitution and the laws of their predecessors, extinguished them, in their natural course, with those whose will gave them being. This could preserve that being till it ceased to be itself, and no longer. . . .[12]

We may assume that the words Hawthorne puts into Holgrave's mouth are to be taken with some seriousness, for the same sentiments can be duplicated easily in *The English Notebooks*. The sudden transition which occurs in Holgrave's character in the final chapter is, then, not only disconcerting—it fails to the point of appearing grotesque:

> Very soon after their change of fortune, Clifford, Hepzibah, and little Phoebe, with the approval of the artist, concluded to remove from the dismal old House of Seven Gables, and take up their abode for the present, at the elegant country seat of the late Judge Pyncheon. . . .
> 'The country house is certainly a very fine one, so far as the plan goes,' observed Holgrave, as the party were discussing their future arrangements. 'But I wonder that the late Judge—being so opulent, and with a reasonable prospect of transmitting his wealth to descendants of his own—should not have felt the propriety of embodying so excellent a piece of domestic architecture in stone, rather than wood. Then, every generation of the family might have altered the interior, to suit its own taste, and convenience; while the exterior through the lapse of years, might have been adding venerableness to its original beauty, and thus

giving that impression of permanence which I consider essential to the happiness of any one moment.'

'Why,' cried Phoebe, gazing into the artist's face with infinite amazement, 'how wonderfully your ideas are changed! A house of stone, indeed! It is but two or three weeks ago that you seemed to wish people to live in something as fragile and temporary as a bird's nest!'

'Ah, Phoebe, I told you how it would be!' said the artist, with a half-melancholy laugh. 'You find me a conservative already! Little did I think ever to become one.'

The juxtaposition of these two passages illustrates the tension in Hawthorne, but at its dullest level. The quotations confront each other with the nerveless, lumpish opposition of two lifelessly held ideas that can generate no creative activity between them. Matthiessen's kindly attempt at justification, which I have cited above, is as good as any that can be made about the ending, but it remains unconvincing. When he was dealing with ideas, Hawthorne was inferior. His mind lacked the intellectual rigour, consistency, and logical courage of Cooper's. If he was greater as an artist, as a dealer in ideas he was a conventional bore, and in these passages the fatigue that would later overwhelm him is anticipated. The form of the whole novel seems to split up at the end on Holgrave's schizophrenia. The conflict in attitudes is nowhere absorbed into a more comprehensive viewpoint. At best, it is a matter of petty weighing, measuring and counting to see which has the larger balance on the credit side.

In a novel like *The Spoils of Poynton*, Henry James was able to build up an attitude around the same theme, but with a subtle complexity we do not find in *The House of the Seven Gables*. Mrs. Gereth's house, with its wonderful antiques, becomes a symbol of what can happen when the values of the past—represented by her purchased treasures—are substituted for human values. And yet so delicate is James's touch that the whole thing is capable of being stated from several conflicting points of view, in contrast to which Holgrave's sudden reversal is heavy and embarrassing. It is not that, carefully analysed, James's attitudes would have been greatly different. But he retained a wonderful control of tone that was to disappear from Hawthorne's novels after *The Scarlet Letter*. For example, we can see this tone operating at an elementary but marvellously effective level in Arthur Townsend's speech in *Washington Square* in which he speaks of the virtues of the perennial New York habit of tearing down the city every few years for the sake of putting up something equally unsure of itself:

'At the end of three or four years we'll move. That's the way to live in New York—to move every three or four years. Then you always get the last thing. It's because the city's growing so quick —you've got to keep up with it. It's going straight up town— that's where New York's going. If I wasn't afraid Marian would be lonely, I'd go up there—right up to the top—and wait for it. But Marian says she wants some neighbours—she doesn't want to be a pioneer. She says that if she's got to be the first settler she had better go out to Minnesota. I guess we'll move up little by little; when we get tired of one street we'll go higher. So you see we'll always have a new house; it's a great advantage to have a new house; you get all the latest improvements. They invent everything all over again about every five years, and it's a great thing to keep up with the new things. I always try to keep up with the new things of every kind. Don't you think that's a good motto for a young couple—to keep 'going higher'? That's the name of that piece of poetry—what do they call it?—*Excelsior!*'

The playful Jamesian irony that permeates Arthur Townsend's speech is itself a delightful commentary on this exhibition of the tension between past and present in the American mind. And one may well pause to consider if Arthur Townsend, for all his rather attractive giddiness, was any more of a featherbrain than the solemn young Holgrave whom Hawthorne takes so seriously. My point simply is that the tension we have been considering here can be resolved in art only in terms of finely controlled tone. It is not amenable to the sort of intellectual solemnity into which Hawthorne falls so disastrously.

But if *The House of the Seven Gables* at one level treats of the American tension between past and present, it also makes another statement on Hawthorne's old theme of human isolation, of the individual cut off from society and reality. This aspect of the story is centred in Clifford, and the parts of the story in which he appears are the most significant. The House of the Seven Gables is a richly evocative symbol. While Hawthorne's control is not as sure as in *The Scarlet Letter*, the decayed

old house carries with it almost as many meanings as Hester's
ambiguous A. It symbolizes all those human motives—greed,
selfishness, pride—that explains Clifford's unjust imprisonment
thirty years before the novel opens, and at the same time it
renders visible his isolation from human society, his exclusion
from the inner sphere of reality. Out of prison after thirty years
of unjust confinement, Clifford at Seven Gables continues to be
imprisoned in himself, shut off from the world as much as he
had been before. When the reader encounters Clifford for the
first time in Chapter VII, Hawthorne describes him in terms
that bring Gervayse Hasting's inner emptiness to mind:

> The guest seated himself in the place assigned him, and looked
> strangely around. He was evidently trying to grapple with the
> present scene, and bring it home to his mind with a more satis-
> factory distinctness. He desired to be certain, at least, that he was
> here, in the low-studded, cross-beamed, oaken-panelled parlour,
> and not in some other spot, which had stereotyped itself into his
> senses. But the effort was too great to be sustained with more than
> a fragmentary success. Continually, as we may express it, he faded
> away out of his place; or, in other words, his mind and conscious-
> ness took their departure, leaving his wasted, grey, and melan-
> choly figure—a substantial emptiness, a material ghost—to
> occupy his seat at table. Again, after a blank moment, there
> would be a flickering taper-gleam in his eyeballs. It betokened
> that his spiritual part had returned, and was doing its best to
> kindle the heart's household fire, and light up intellectual lamps in
> the dark and ruinous mansion, where it was doomed to be a
> forlorn inhabitant.

There is one important difference between Clifford and all
the other characters in Hawthorne's work who are excluded
from the inner sphere of reality. Clifford is the only one who is
perfectly innocent, and entirely the victim. He has not, like
Hester, co-operated with the guilt of society by developing a
bold speculativeness of mind. Possibly he resembles Owen
Warland in 'The Artist of the Beautiful' more than anyone else:
'the hard coarse world' has proved too much for him. There is
an episode at the close of Chapter XI which tells us something
of the meaning Hawthorne meant to embody in him. He shows
us the aged Clifford blowing soap bubbles into the street from
the window in Seven Gables: 'Little impalpable worlds were

those soap-bubbles, with the big world depicted, in hues bright as imagination, on the nothing of their surface.'

Hawthorne more than most artists husbanded his technical resources, and this passage reminds one of the similar symbolism employed in 'Endicott and the Red Cross' and *The Scarlet Letter* in passages in which the surrounding features of the Puritan world are reflected in the armour of Endicott and Governor Bellingham respectively. In those passages, as Mr. Yvor Winters has pointed out,[13] we have the disparate and scattered elements of Puritan society reduced to a symbolic microcosm in the rounded, burnished steel of the breastplate and helmet—images providing us a commentary on the hard martial quality, and intolerant spirituality of Puritanism. But here the world of Clifford's vision is reflected, not in martial steel, but on the surface of bubbles. Clifford is a type of the artist for Hawthorne, and the one 'creative' character in his work to whom he shows any generosity. But Clifford provides an even sadder commentary on Hawthorne's conception of the artist than the others. Those soap bubbles are significant, and one's spontaneous embarrassment is wholly justified. They come out of the same part of Hawthorne's mind in which Owen Warland's ghastly little mechanical butterfly flutters limply about. Art is not for 'the hard coarse world', but, presumably, for the illustrated souvenir gift books.

But the passage is not intended to be at Clifford's expense. Perhaps it exemplifies Hawthorne's meaning as much as anything in the novel. Unlike houses of stone and timber, or landed estates, or gold, soap bubbles are too perishable to be inherited or willed to posterity, and yet (Hawthorne thinks) their momentary beauty embodies a life that is denied to more durable things. But once in touch with more durable things, they break and vanish, just as Clifford's own life had broken on the crude and harsh unscrupulousness of Judge Pyncheon.

The sign of Clifford's saving grace is that he endeavours to break down the barriers that keep him isolated from men. He does not welcome his solitude as Wakefield seemed to do, nor accept his exclusion from inner reality with Gervase Hasting's sense of inevitability. There are two occasions in the novel in which he makes a great effort to break out from his solitude and become a living part of the democratic community. Sitting at an upstairs window, he observes a tawdry political procession going down the street with banners and a band and he is irresistibly impelled to join it:

> He shuddered; he grew pale; he threw an appealing look at Hepzibah and Phoebe, who were with him at the window. They comprehended nothing of his emotions, and supposed him merely disturbed by the unaccustomed tumult. At last, with tremulous limb, he started up, set his foot on the window-sill, and in an instant more would have been in the unguarded balcony. As it was, the whole procession might have seen him, a wild, haggard, figure, his grey locks floating in the wind that waved their banners; a lonely being, estranged from his race, but now feeling himself man again, by virtue of the irrepressible instinct that possessed him. Had Clifford attained the balcony, he would probably have leaped into the street; but whether impelled by the species of terror that sometimes urges its victim over the very precipice which he shrinks from, or by a natural magnetism, tending towards the centre of humanity, it were not easy to decide. Both impulses might have wrought on him at once.
> 'Clifford, Clifford! are you crazy?' cried his sister.
> 'I hardly know, Hepzibah,' said Clifford, drawing a long breath. 'Fear nothing,—it is over now,—but had I taken that plunge, and survived it, methinks it would have made me another man!'

One is reminded here (at least as far as meaning goes; there is no artistic equality between them) of how Robin in Hawthorne's most masterly story, 'My Kinsman, Major Molineux', by momentarily participating in the terrible merriment of the torch-light procession which is persecuting his noble old kinsman, proves his worthiness to become a part of the new American humanity which, it must be added, looks even less attractive than Clifford's political procession. Hawthorne frequently suggests that some violent act of the will, possibly involving a high degree of sacrifice, is sometimes necessary either to sustain the magnetic chain of humanity in unbroken integrity, or make it whole again. And Clifford shows himself ready for such a sacrifice: 'Had I taken that plunge and survived it, methinks it would have made me another man!'

The second occasion on which Clifford endeavours to establish communication with society is in the chapter called 'The Flight of the Two Owls', in which he and Hepzibah flee through a storm to the railway station, and take their aimless excursion on the train. The chapter is beautifully done, and as it closes with Hepzibah and Clifford standing in the cold rain on the deserted platform, Hawthorne's artistry reaches a higher point, perhaps, than elsewhere in the book. He has managed in his description here to externalize very skilfully the hopelessness and emptiness that have followed this aged couple in their flight to the world, and in the course of the chapter he has managed to present visible everyday reality in such a way that it seems more of a dream than the visions that haunt Clifford in the shadowy corners of Seven Gables itself.

I have already commented on the happy story-book ending of *The House of the Seven Gables*. It has been praised recently for its positive affirmation of life-values which, supposedly, stand out in dominant contrast to the elements of the past represented by the old house itself.[13] The dialectic is certainly there: tradition and the past disputing with the American future. But the most casual reader can hardly escape recognizing that the successful portions of the novel are those in which Hawthorne, forgetting his democratic American axe, describes the shadows of the ancient house, and not the plumbing improvements of the suburban villa into which everybody moves at last.

IV

The last of Hawthorne's four major novels, *The Marble Faun*, is the least inviting of them, and I do not propose to consider it at much length here. My account of the inner sphere of reality in Hawthorne has become repetitious, and the briefest treatment must serve to indicate that *The Marble Faun* is no exception to Hawthorne's central theme. Despite the obtrusive clutter of the fringes and tassels of romance which make this such an irritating book, the theme of the effects of sin and isolation on the human heart are held under firm control. The accents are a little changed, however. The emphasis is on sin, here treated for the first time from what seems a Christian point of view, and the theme of isolation is a little scanted. But it runs true to form in passages like the following, where Miriam meets the young American copyist Hilda (disgusting girl) for the first time after Donatello and she have murdered the mysterious model (Westervelt done over Roman style) at the Tarpeian Rock. Hilda has accidentally witnessed the murder, and now, pure, virtuous American that she is, she'll have nothing to do with her old European friend, Miriam:

> Hilda was standing in the middle of the room. When her friend made a step or two from the door, she put forth her hands with an involuntary repellent gesture, so expressive, that Miriam at once felt a great chasm opening itself between them two. They might gaze at one another from the opposite side, but without the possibility of ever meeting more; or, at least, since the chasm could never be bridged over, they must tread the whole round of Eternity to meet on the other side. There was even a terror in the thought of their meeting again. It was as if Hilda or Miriam were dead, and could no longer hold intercourse without violating a spiritual law.

The effects of sin run their course in Miriam and Donatello, the modern faun, but there is a somewhat different attitude present than Hawthorne had shown before. The novel revolves around the concept of the Fortunate Fall with a good deal of tediousness. Hilda, the angelic, outraged young American Puritan will, of course, have no such nonsense discussed in her presence, but Hawthorne, despite his sympathy for this most repulsive of all his characters, insists that there has been spiritual growth in Donatello just because of his sin. More than half a dozen passages might be cited, but one from Chapter XXXI will do. The self-righteous American sculptor, Kenyon, whom Hawthorne uses as a mouthpiece of goodness and truth, is speaking:

> 'A wonderful process is going on in Donatello's mind. . . . The germs of faculties that have hitherto slept are fast springing into activity. The world of thought is disclosing itself to his inward sight. He startles me, at times, with his perception of deep truths; and, quite as often, it must be owned, he compels me to smile by the intermixture of his former simplicity with a new intelligence. Out of his bitter agony, a soul and intellect, I could almost say, have been inspired into him.'

Hawthorne's generosity is not large enough to prevent him from suggesting in the last chapter that Donatello nevertheless spends the remainder of his life in the dungeons of a prison, but his emphatic and repeated assertions that Donatello has matured both intellectually and spiritually are more outspoken than his darker suggestions concerning Hester. But then no one would accuse Donatello of the bold speculativeness of mind that Hawthorne distrusted so much in Hester and Ethan Brand. But there is no need to dwell on this novel, which is a complicated five-finger exercise on themes that had been better treated before. What Hawthorne brings to his treatment that is new (with the exception of a guidebook knowledge of Rome) is hardly original enough, or deftly enough used, to sustain much interest or invite protracted analysis.

The work of Hawthorne forms a curiously tight little unity. All artists return to familiar themes and images, but there are few whose creative impulse is as confined in such small quarters as Hawthorne's. His meaning is perfectly expressed in *The Scarlet Letter* and five or six short stories which are masterpieces of a high order, but if these had been lost the remainder of his performance would be uninspiring enough. Both Melville and Henry James are deeply in Hawthorne's debt, however, and this alone would be enough to argue a very large stature in the man. That two writers so dissimilar should have learned so much in the practice of their respective art from a man so different from either is important in any assessment of Hawthorne, for the Hawthorne of Melville is not the Hawthorne of James. He is undoubtedly large enough to incorporate, at least partially, both images of himself; and yet, as Hawthorne's art is nearer to James's than to Melville's, it is reasonable to assume that James was more nearly correct in his version of the earlier writer. I have discussed the influence of Hawthorne on James's fictions in detail in the opening chapters of *The Complex Fate*, and I shall only say here that they apply themselves to the same problems and they have the same moral concerns; and that the same pervasive doubt that runs through Hawthorne has its counterpart in James. It is worthwhile observing, in view of the argument of Chapter V, that they draw nearest to each other, not in their dedication to the possibilities of symbolism, but in their approach to, and treatment, of a characteristic subject matter. Basically, this subject matter is the same that Cooper was concerned with, although it is seen from different points of view, and treated towards different ends. Within the context of their

American experience it is a weighing of two ways of life, the American and European; it is a protracted debate between the merits of democracy and aristocracy, between the past, present, and future; and finally (and this is especially true of Cooper and James) it is an uneasiness, carrying with it its own creative problems and motives, over the sources of wealth in American society. This essential subject matter is not treated as programmatically by Hawthorne and James as Cooper treated it. It is, nevertheless, at the very heart of their work, and in all three cases there is a drive to explore American experience and to justify the ways of the Americans. In the two foregoing chapters, I have discussed Hawthorne's work principally from the viewpoint of the recurrent tension between solitude and society —a tension that reflects many of the others. However, I have explicitly treated the conflict between past and present, Europe and America, as it provides motives for his art, in the relevant chapters of *The Complex Fate*, and there seems little point in repeating myself here. But in concluding I should like to say that this difference exists between Cooper and the two later writers: that whereas Cooper was primarily interested in the tensions themselves, for their own sakes, and as they affected America, Hawthorne and James were interested in them as they affected the moral action and outlook of men, not primarily as citizens, but as private human beings. The difference between these two approaches is not absolute; there is a great overlapping in the interests of all three as they converge on these dominant points; nor do I wish to suggest that Hawthorne and James are identical in their approaches. Hawthorne's approach, as I tried to make clear in discussing 'The Hollow of the Three Hills', is impersonal and moralistic with a minimum of interest in the psychology of the individual.

VIII
Melville

I

DEMOCRACY is based on a belief in the perfectibility of man. At heart democracy is always optimistic. But the very idea of perfectibility, of progression in specific directions which are indicated by the requirements of man's social nature and the political goals he sets for himself, introduces the idea of an ordered universe. Perfectibility and progress are intelligible concepts only in relation to certain objective norms and goals which, at least for practical purposes, are taken as absolutes. Behind the belief in social and political improvement, in perfectibility, there lies, at any rate by implication, a working idea of good and evil. The historical democrat is traditionally reluctant to face the issue when couched in theological terms, and perhaps this reluctance shows his wisdom, for a God who works through democratic machinery afflicts his followers with many cruel paradoxes. This was one of the discoveries it was the lot of the Adams family to make. Brooks Adams in his remarkable introduction to his brother's volume, *The Degradation of the Democratic Dogma*, describes the anguish of his grandfather, John Quincy Adams, when he was forced to recognize, through the events of history, the double-dealing character of a God conceived in democratic terms:

> Mr. Adams as a scientific man was a precursor of the later Darwinians who have preached the doctrine of human perfectibility, a doctrine in which the modern world has believed and still professes to believe. Granting that there is a benign and omnipotent Creator of the world, who watches over the fate of men, Adams' sincere conviction was that such a being thinks according to certain fixed laws; that these laws may be discovered by human intelligence and when discovered may be adapted to human uses. And if so discovered, adapted, and practised they must lead man certainly to an approach to perfection, and more especially to the elimination of war and slavery. The theory was pleasing, and since the time of Mr. Adams it has been generally accepted as the foundation of American education and the corner

187

stone of democracy. But mark how far it led Mr. Adams astray in 1828, and how at last it broke his heart. Eli Whitney's cotton gin was certainly one of the most famous and successful of the applications of science to a supremely bountiful gift of God, in making American cotton serviceable and cheap to the whole human race. But it propagated slavery, it turned the fair state of Virginia into an enormous slave-breeding farm, whence forty-thousand blacks were annually exported to the South, and thus inexorably induced the Civil War; so with the public lands which Mr. Adams would willingly have given his life to save for his contemporaries and their posterity. Railroads and canals raised the price of these lands by making them accessible. And this is what Mr. Adams saw in the House of Representatives in 1838, and this is his comment on the humanizing effect of applied science. It was the triumph of Benton and Jackson, of the very essence of evil, over him. 'The thirst of a tiger for blood is the fittest emblem of the rapacity with which the members of all new states fly at the public lands. The constituents upon whom they depend are all settlers, or tame and careless spectators of the pillage. They are themselves enormous speculators and land-jobbers. It were a vain attempt to resist them here.' This was written on June 12, 1838, and thus had the bargain of Benton with the planters been consummated by means of applied science. Such bargains were to have been anticipated and would have been taken as a matter of course by an ordinary political huckster, but Mr. Adams, though after his defeat in 1828 he did practically, as he states here give up the contest, because he had ceased to believe that God supported him, never could nor ever did reconcile himself to the destiny which this betrayal by God entailed on the world.[1]

Although the terms in which the problem is presented here are so different, a moment's reflection will persuade one that the kind of theological doubt engendered in John Quincy Adams by his contemplation of the democratic process is similar to the doubts that were to torment Melville. At bottom, it is an inability to keep the terms of good and evil distinct from each other; and it comes about because the democrat in the beginning making a close identification between God and democratic society, later carries this spurious identification over to the defects and failures of democracy. When the human perfectibility that God seemed to promise when he crowned the great American experiment with brotherhood from sea to shining sea conspicuously fails to develop, the disillusioned democrat proceeds from his earlier faith—which itself had been tainted with materialism—either to cynicism or hatred, and God is cast in the role of the great betrayer. That this was not quite the fate of John Quincy Adams was merely a matter of his great personal integrity; but the general proposition helps to explain why Americans have often found it easy to reject the idea of Original Sin one day, and to express the utmost hatred of creation the next. Democracy tends to make it a case of all or nothing.

Democracy, as I said, demands an ordered universe in which good and evil are distinguishable; but at the same time it makes it extremely difficult to tell them apart. Cooper, Hawthorne, and James avoided this dilemma by approaching it on a pragmatic level. It may be recalled that in discussing Leatherstocking's symbolic significance I remarked that 'the ability to distinguish good from evil is the ultimate note of Natty Bumpo's character' and that Cooper refers to this faculty as 'the choicest —perhaps the rarest—gift of nature'. Cooper himself was an Anglican, and particularly during the latter part of his life he was interested in theological problems. *The Sea Lions* (1849), for example, in addition to being an adventure story laid among the Antarctic wastes, is also a tract on Trinitarianism. Cooper's temperament naturally graviated towards a hieractic theology corresponding to his sense of status and class. Although Natty is no churchman, the security of his moral distinctions, as well as a hagiographic quality with which Cooper has invested him, point to a distinctly theological bent in his creator's character— and one that has nothing to do with New England Calvinism. But with Cooper, theology seems to have social or class roots. He reserves his intensities most often for such questions as whether or not the Littlepage family pew in the parish church is to be permitted to retain its distinguishing canopy, symbol of aristocratic status. It is with a good deal of reluctance that Cooper allows it to be removed. Cooper, in short, is concerned with religion in almost the same way that he is concerned with the American political and social tensions.

It is obvious that these tensions on the political, economic, and social levels have made it easier for Cooper to deal with the problem of good and evil in his fiction. By equating good with that side of the conflict on other levels that he favours, and evil with the opposite side, Cooper really cancelled the metaphysical aspects of the problem. The metaphysical ordering of the universe proceeds directly from his ordering on the lower levels rather than vice versa. And in different ways this is also true of Hawthorne and James. For Hawthorne, evil springs from an incorrect relation with the 'inner sphere' of reality, both in oneself and in others. But the integrity of one's relation to this area of reality is guaranteed only by maintaining the most delicate adjustments with society, which are themselves dependent on the way one resolves the political and social tensions of American experience. The metaphysical ordering of James's universe is more difficult to analyse, but it appears to have been fundamentally pragmatic. One constructed a universe of good or evil from the truth or falseness of one's perceptions and relationships, and that moral universe was finally validated or rejected by the *process* of events.[2] It is easy to see how, in all three cases, the problems naturally raised by the rift in American experience would ultimately issue in certain moral positions that implied a metaphysic, and a certain predictable grouping of good and evil. It we except Calvinism which, as an active theology, had already given way before the growing popularity of Transcendentalism at the time Hawthorne began to write, America inherited no great theological system with which to order experience. To some extent, the structural tensions we have considered here were a substitute. They raised certain recurrent and fundamental questions, and the questions themselves moulded the answers. We should not be surprised, then, to find certain basic elements in common among Cooper, Hawthorne, and James, when they come to treat such a problem as that of good and evil, since they frequently arrive at their conclusions by way of certain common questions. Making allowances always for the Christian orthodoxy in Cooper which his Anglicanism dictated, we find that all three are primarily interested in good and evil as it affects men living in society and as it enriches or degrades their relations with other human beings. The problem of eternal sanctions never really bothers any of them very much. But Melville's concern was metaphysically more pure.

Apart from his actual works we do not know very much about the state of Melville's mind, and in attributing to him a profound disillusionment with American democracy I am look-ing ahead to that appalling picture of the American mind and heart he has given us in *The Confidence Man*. It is in this book that his despair, though so much more ferocious and intense than John Quincy Adams's, takes on certain characteristics of the elder man's disillusionment. Melville was not a political writer in the sense that Cooper was, but the profound disillusionment that fills his later books strikes one as being, partly at least, political in character. The rift in American experience, which Cooper, Hawthorne, and James dealt with pragmatically, was approached more directly by Melville, who, undercutting these proximate tensions, struck at the metaphysical heart of the dilemma. Yet, paradoxically, what finally confronted him was not a polarity between good and evil, corresponding to the polarity of the others' tensions, but a tragic confusion in which good and evil were indistinguishable. As for the elder Adams, so for Melville—the very texture of the American universe revealed the way it had been betrayed by God. Democracy existed only in ruthless competition, and God, who alone might have redeemed it, was unequal to the task: that, if anything, seems to be the meaning of the final chapter of *The Confidence Man*.

But before that stage had been reached, Melville made a tremendous effort, in *Moby Dick*, to introduce order into his moral universe, and to establish a polarity between good and evil without which he could not give form either to his experi-ence or to his art. In terms of this one book he succeeded magnificently; but in *Pierre* and *The Confidence Man* the distinc-tion he had made in his great masterpiece could not be sustained, and a pursuit of the knowledge of good and evil was replaced by a suffocating sense of the ambiguity which he formally and cynically seemed to formulate and preach as the ultimate knowable moral truth. In other words, moral action (which is to say, *human* action) became an impossibility. With no metaphysical poles of good and evil, and no dialectical pattern on the pragmatic levels of life to guide them, Melville's heroes became incapable of development or progression. They became the passive victims of their situation in life, trapped in the endless unfolding of moral ambiguities whose total signifi-cance was to drain all possible meaning from life. Reality which is conceived as endlessly ambiguous, never coming to rest in any certainty, is the negation of form. Because it is everything, it can be determined as nothing specifically. Such a reality cannot be interpreted as an action in that sense in which we predicated it of Cooper. It is, at most, a commotion that must sooner or later collapse into stasis through sheer exhaustion. I shall speak of this phase of Melville, later, but first I wish to discuss *Moby Dick* from that point of view I have already suggested—as his single but heroic attempt to distinguish good from evil: his single attempt, that is, if we disregard *Billy Budd*, which seems to me, at best, a very partial recovery after the collapse following *Moby Dick*, and a rather uninteresting recovery at that.

II

The magnitude and complexity of *Moby Dick* is discouraging. There is so much to say that if one were to say all, even of the little oneself has to say, emphasis would be lost and accent blurred. Read, one after the other, what any three or four critics say of *Moby Dick*: take, for example, Richard Chase, Newton Arvin, William Sedgwick, Lewis Mumford, and Lawrance Thompson—the result is painfully indigestible, both in the mind and in the emotional response one brings to Melville, which is not to say anything to the discredit of these critics. Where the possibilities of exegesis are so vast, the result must inevitably be a loss of salience. I begin in this fashion, not only by way of apology for resorting to an exegetical approach myself, but in particular to mark out the limits of my interest in the following discussion, which will be concerned *only* with Melville's attempt to distinguish between good and evil, and to establish that polarity in a universe in which it seemed to him in radical danger of dissolving.

In a recent book on Melville, *Melville's Quarrel with God*, Mr. Lawrance Thompson has undertaken to cast Melville in the role of God-hater. His position will provide a convenient foil for presenting its opposite. In *Moby Dick* Melville is not attacking God; he is attempting to rescue the idea of the good, to push back from his darkening consciousness that instinctive reaction of the disillusioned American: hatred of creation itself. A large part of Mr. Thompson's argument is based on Melville's intense dislike of the Dutch Reformed Church in which he grew up, and a good many of the insults against Christianity that Mr. Thompson uncovers are delivered at the level of the Calvinism preached by that bleak institution. The trouble with using Melville's attitude to that form of Calvinism as a touchstone by which to gauge his attitude to religion generally is simply that one is compelled to simplify disastrously.

Early in his discussion of *Moby Dick* Mr. Thompson takes up the question of Ahab's name, which derives from the wicked King of Israel in the First Book of Kings. This is a crucial problem in any interpretation of *Moby Dick*, for it helps us guard against that romantic exaltation of Ahab which has resulted in missing Melville's point. A just appreciation of Melville's reasons for choosing this name, among all others, for his monomaniac captain, will reveal a great deal about his creative intentions. Mr. Thompson, in conformity with his general argument, sees in Melville's choice an instance of his habit of beguiling Christian readers:

> But there is one other correlation, far more interesting, between these two Ahabs. Each of them is seduced to his death by a prophet, and Captain Ahab's misleading prophet is Fedallah. . . . Consider, however, the hint in First Kings as to how it happened that King Ahab was similarly victimized: 'I saw the Lord sitting on his throne, and all the host of heaven standing by him, on his right hand and the left. And the Lord said, Who shall persuade Ahab, that he may go up and fall at Ramoth-gilead? . . . And there came forth a spirit, and stood before the Lord, and said, I will persuade him. And the Lord said unto him, Wherewith? And he said, I will go forth, and I will be a lying spirit in the mouth of all his prophets. And the Lord said, Thou shalt persuade him, and prevail also: go forth and do so.'
>
> For Melville's anti-Christian purposes, that passage lends itself nicely to a correlated series of insinuations that God is a malicious double-crosser, a deceiver, who is not above employing a 'lying spirit' . . . to lead a man to his death. . . .' [3]

Mr. Thompson's reading of the twenty-second chapter of First Kings is so unusual that one's best alternative, in commenting on it, is to digress for several paragraphs in the role of

G

Biblical commentator. The meaning of *Moby Dick* is, I think, in deep accord with a somewhat less 'sinister' reading of the scriptural chapter.

It may be recalled that as the chapter opens, King Jehosophat has arrived from Judah on a social visit to King Ahab of Israel. During an early conversation, Ahab raises the question of Ramoth-gilead, formerly a tributary city of his in the north, but for some time since, by the power of possession, in the hands of the King of Syria. Ahab wants it back, and persuades Jehosophat to assist him in a military expedition. Being more devout than Ahab, Jehosophat insists that the prophets be officially consulted to insure that Jehovah's blessing rest on the undertaking. So at Jehosophat's insistence, Ahab summoned four hundred prophets—that is to say, four hundred of the clergy of the Established Church—to appear and prophesy before them in a public place. Two thrones were erected, and at the appointed time the two Kings in full royal regalia took their places. The four hundred prophets, passing before them, prophesied great success for their arms. One of them went so far as to wear iron horns to suggest the way in which Ahab would crush his enemies. It is perfectly clear from the chapter as a whole that they were not unaware of the private expediency of their tack. In fact, ever since their day the clergies of most countries have not found it difficult to prophesy glory for the arms of their temporal sovereigns. But apparently Jehosophat was not deceived, for turning to King Ahab, he asked: 'Is there not here a prophet of the Lord besides, that we might enquire of him?' Why, yes: Ahab admitted that there was, but he never had anything agreeable to say. But Jehosophat would not be put off, and so Ahab had to send a messenger to summon the prophet Micaiah. But it is clear that he instructed his messenger to have a private talk with Micaiah, for coming before him the messenger said: 'Behold now, the words of the prophets declare good unto the King with one mouth; let thy word, I pray thee, be like the word of one of them, and speak that which is good.' It was, as who should say, an order; and as an obedient subject of his temporal ruler, Micaiah obeyed. But Ahab understood well enough the way in which he had sealed the lips of his prophet. It is intriguing to speculate what compulsive drive led him to blurt out at the crucial moment, just when Micaiah had prophesied good as the King had commanded him to do through the messenger: 'How many times shall I adjure thee that thou tell me nothing but that which is true in the name of the Lord?' Nothing could be clearer than that this is an implicit confession that he hadn't believed the lying four hundred prophets in the first place, being so aware of the way he had projected his royal will into their servility. Being thus adjured to speak, not in the name of his King but of his God, Micaiah prophesied the defeat of Ahab's army, and his death. Ahab's response to this, apart from putting Micaiah into prison, was to turn to Jehosophat and enquire: Didn't I tell you he would only speak evil about me? It is the perfect picture of a man who will not admit a truth that he knows to be true. It is, then, at this point, before being led away to gaol for having prophesied truly, that Micaiah turns to Ahab and speaks that passage about the 'lying spirit' and the four hundred prophets leading Ahab to destruction—the passage that leads Mr. Thompson to speak of God as a malicious double-crosser, at least for the purposes of his critical argument. It is a little difficult to see how Mr. Thompson's reading can be accepted as plausible at any level of interpretation. Mr. Thompson has radically criticized the immaturity of meaning with which Melville invested Captain Ahab. Actually, Melville was as aware of the moral limitations of Ahab as Mr. Thompson, and a proof of it is that he chose the name Ahab for very different reasons than those Mr. Thompson attributes to him.

What, in fact, did Melville see in the Biblical King? So far from being a victim, King Ahab is one of the most petulant self-asserters among Israel's rulers. His God-defiance never really got above the level of a foot-stamping 'I won't!' Ahab didn't have a great will, but he had a leech-like will. Once he had fastened it to a purpose it was a little difficult to disengage it. With a blue-print of his own destruction in his hand he deliberately followed it to the last line and letter. He is one of the most remarkable delineations of a perverse will in sacred or profane literature, and what we see is not a Titan but a weakling. Melville's Ahab is certainly not a weakling in the usual sense—but then the King was never more typical than when he insisted on going to war with the knowledge that he would be killed, and much of his army also. This, I think, was what influenced Melville in First Kings, chapter twenty-two. The flaw in the King and the Captain is identical.

But Melville might, conceivably, have found other congenial elements in the Biblical passage. The persons in the chapter are operating under two distinct ideas of God. There is the true God of Micaiah, and the false God of the prophets—yet he is ostensibly the same. Actually, the verses which Mr. Thompson quotes with such dark designs, so far from representing God as a malicious double-crosser and deceiver, are a divine satire on the time-serving prophets, and if one wishes to believe that Melville connected them in his imagination with the clergy of the Dutch Reformed Church (though Mr. Thompson doesn't make this point) I see no objection to doing so. It at any rate suggests what ample scope Melville might have found in First Kings for ecclesiastical satire and censure without the necessity of shaking his fist in God's face, or proclaiming that the universe was essentially evil.

Another scriptural correspondence, also made in the interests of a God-hating Melville, seems equally unfortunate—at least in the way Mr. Thompson interprets it, for the correspondence itself is undeniable. Melville, according to this argument, hated God because God is the creator of evil as well as good, and Mr. Thompson argues that the White Whale is essentially a symbol of evil to Melville, though not an abstract, but a very specific, theological kind of evil that corrupts the universe. One of the great chapters of *Moby Dick* is the one in which Starbuck's whaling boat harpoons an old bull whale, crippled and en-feebled by age. The chapter is moving because of the power-fully evoked pity—a pity that exists at a much higher level of the imagination than one of R.S.P.C.A. decency. The scriptural correspondence of which I spoke a moment ago is the one which Mr. Thompson draws between the imagery of this chapter, describing the sufferings of the harpooned old whale, and the forty-first chapter of Job, in which Jehovah describes the im-pregnable attributes of Leviathan, thereby, as it were, taunting the afflicted man. According to Mr. Thompson, Melville's chapter is built up of concealed sarcasms at God's expense—a case of taunting the Taunter, dismembering the Dismemberer. The correspondence is there, but this reading of it promotes a sad falling off in Melville. Prefiguring the sufferings of Christ, the Psalmist cried: 'They have pierced my hands and feet, they have numbered all my bones.' This seems a better commentary on those chapters in *Moby Dick* in which we are presented with lengthy commentaries on the dismembering of the whales than the charge that Melville is insulting God thereby. Read from this point of view, we have in the image of the suffering Leviathan not only an image of the suffering God, but simultaneously the agonized whale, as a magnificent image of created nature, reveals the awful wrack in that creation which men themselves cause.

If the image of Leviathan can, at one level, be interpreted as the image of the suffering God, we would expect to find in the record of his afflictions some allusions to Christ. And I think we do. I would cite as a single instance at this point the passage which Mr. Thompson quotes as an example of Melville's concealed jibing against God—a passage which describes a harpooned whale attached by lines to three whaling-boats from the Pequod:

> Seems it credible that by three such thin threads the great Leviathan was suspended like the big weight to an eight day clock. Suspended? and to what? To three bits of board. Is this the creature of whom it was once so triumphantly said—'Canst thou fill his skin with barbed irons? or his head with fish-spears? The sword of him that layeth at him cannot hold, the spear, the dart, nor the habergeon: he esteemeth iron as straw; the arrow cannot make him flee; darts are counted as stubble; he laugheth at the shaking of a spear!' This the creature? this he? Oh! that unfulfilments should follow the prophets. For with the strength of a thousand thighs in his tail, Leviathan had run his head under the mountains of the sea, to hide him from the Pequod's fish-spears.

As one returns to this chapter with the whole of *Moby Dick* in mind, I think it not unreasonable to see something reminiscent of the three arms of the cross from which Christ hung in those three bits of wood from which Leviathan is suspended. 'Oh! that unfulfilments should follow the prophets!' It seems probable to me that this is a rhetorical exclamation calling attention to the fact that the old prophecies have indeed been fulfilled. The tormented Leviathan, running his head under the mountains of the sea, recalls Psalm 69, which is commonly accepted as prefiguring the sufferings of Christ and the malice of his persecutors:

> Save me, O God; for the waters are come in unto my soul.
>
> I sink in deep mire, where there is no standing: I am come into deep waters, where the floods overflow me.
>
> I am weary of my crying: my throat is dried: mine eyes fail while I wait for my God. . . .
>
> Deliver me out of the mire, and let me not sink: let me be delivered from them that hate me and out of the deep waters.
>
> Let not the waterflood overflow me, neither let the deep swallow me up, and let not the pit shut her mouth upon me.

The connection is at least not as tenuous as some Mr. Thompson proposes. And one might, to sustain the spirit of the counter-argument, surmise that since Christ was pierced by a spear, and since the Fish was an early symbol of Christ, it is possible that Melville's reference to the Pequod's fish-spears is, most deeply, at the expense of Ahab and his crew rather than at the expense of God. I am trying here to point to the function that this idea of the suffering Leviathan performs in the novel. It is a symbol in which Melville was not only able to express his growing horror of evil in the universe, but his positive affirmation of an indestructible good. It is a deeply tragic symbol redeemed by a yet profounder religious intuition.

D. H. Lawrence in an early essay on Melville said that probably Melville himself did not know what the White Whale meant.[4] But Lawrence did not mean that the White Whale was a vague symbol that could mean everything or nothing. He only meant that what it actively realized in itself—realized with the complexity and mystery of a living thing—was incapable of being neatly itemized or systematized. The White Whale is Melville's profoundest intuition into the nature of creation, and it is an intuition in which God and nature are simultaneously present and commenting on each other.

The evil of the world filled Melville with horror, and there is little doubt that because of that horror a Manichean element colours his sensibility. Many critics before Mr. Thompson have seen in the White Whale a symbol of God, and some of them have viewed that God as predominantly an evil one. And yet it seems to me that Melville makes some clear distinctions which, if not necessarily pointing towards a rigorously orthodox

Christian God, exonerate the White Whale from that burden
of malignancy that Ahab's own perverse will has projected into
his image. I would point particularly to Chapter LIX entitled
'Squid'. It is one of the most imaginatively terrifying chapters
in the novel, and also one of the most beautifully written. On
a beautiful blue morning 'when the slippered waves whispered
together as they softly ran on'—just such a morning as would
banish any thought of evil from the mind—the crew of the
Pequod is given a vision of pure evil, and at first they mistake it
for the White Whale. From his lookout post on the mainmast,
Daggoo, the harpooner, sights a huge rolling mass of white in
the sea ahead, and cries out to those below, 'The White Whale,
the White Whale!'

Instantly four boats and their crews are lowered in pursuit,
but as they approach the floating mass it is not Moby Dick they
see:

> Soon it went down, and while, with oars suspended, we were
> waiting its reappearance, lo! in the same spot where it sank, once
> more it slowly rose. Almost forgetting for the moment all thoughts
> of Moby Dick, we now gazed at the most wondrous phenomenon
> which the secret seas have hitherto revealed to mankind. A vast
> pulpy mass, furlongs in length and breadth, of a glancing cream
> colour, lay floating on the water, innumerable long arms radiating
> from its centre, and curling and twisting like a nest of anacondas,
> as if blindly to catch at any hapless object within reach. No per-
> ceptible face or front did it have; no conceivable token of either
> sensation or instinct; but undulated there on the billows, an
> unearthly, formless, chance-like apparition of life.

In Zoroastrianism, with which Melville, to some extent at
least, was familiar, the world is divided between a good and an
evil principle, and they are twin brothers. In the end the good
will triumph, but their conflict is for the length of time. The
giant Squid was surely meant by Melville for his symbol of
evil. It is, as one would expect, evil in a Manichean rather than
in a Christian sense, but the Squid's horrid anaconda arms
invoke the Christian serpent; and they also give an added
meaning to a later reference to Captain Ahab as an anaconda
of an old man—for he also has blindly caught at the hapless
members of his crew, and carried them down to destruction.
But what is most significant is the resemblance of this symbol of

evil, when viewed at a little distance, to the White Whale. They are, as one might say, twin brothers. They resemble each other most in their whiteness and their facelessness, and both of these attributes signify the inscrutability of the divided yet impenetrable universe in which it is so difficult to distinguish good from evil. And as between the twin brothers of Zoroastrianism, so between the White Whale and the White Squid there is eternal enmity:

> . . . the spermaceti whale obtains his food in unknown zones below the surface; and only by inference is it that anyone can tell of what, precisely, that food consists. At times, when closely pursued, he will disgorge what are supposed to be the detached arms of the squid; some of them thus exhibited exceeding twenty and thirty feet in length. They fancy that the monster to which these arms belonged ordinarily clings by them to the bed of the ocean; and that the sperm whale, unlike other species, is supplied with teeth in order to attack it.

One of the most striking threads of imagery in *Moby Dick* is the 'feeding' imagery. What is fed upon becomes assimilated into the body of the feeder, and this idea sounds throughout *Moby Dick* as a deep and ominous note of resonance. In an oddly subterranean way it keeps the perception bubbling that, through all this mutual devouring, good and evil become inextricably confused with each other, assimilated into each other's being until it is impossible to distinguish between them. In its vulture or sharkish aspect, which reflects Melville's shocked recoil from the world he saw, it comes to a head in the devastating chapter called 'Shark Massacre', in which the sharks

> . . . viciously snapped, not only at each other's disbowelments, but like flexible bows, bent around and bit their own, till those entrails seemed swallowed over and over again by the same mouth, to be oppositely voided by the gaping wound.

It is almost like *Maldoror*; but Melville, in the great orgy of cannibalism and inter-feeding that goes on throughout the novel, is searching for some sacramental essence of good that persists through all devourings.

Significant from this point of view is the opening sentence of

Chapter LXV where the second mate, Stubb, has had the cook
prepare a whale steak for him:

> That mortal man should feed upon the creature that feeds his
> lamp, and, like Stubb, eat him by his own light, as you may say;
> this seems so outlandish a thing that one must needs go a little
> into the history and philosophy of it.

If the White Whale is a symbol of God, Melville's recurrent
references to the light that is derived from his broken body are
certainly important, and the metaphysical image of Stubb eat-
ing the whale by its own light is a sarcasm, not at God's
expense, but at the expense of a hypocritical and savage world
that, like the false four hundred prophets of King Ahab, uses
the light of God for its own profit while lacerating the body of
truth. The meaning of this image is enriched in what follows,
for as Stubb eats the whale steak in his cabin, a ravenous shoal
of sharks devour the body of the murdered whale that is tied
to the side of the Pequod. When Stubb forces the old negro
cook to preach a sermon to the sharks to quiet them down,
before he goes onto the deck Stubb says to him: ' "Here, take
this lantern," snatching one from the sideboard: "now, then,
go and preach to them." ' So the old cook preaches over the
ship's side to the sharks by the light of the whale they are
devouring. No doubt it is an indictment of the perversions of
Christianity in the world. But it is Christianity *in the world*; and
it is the light of God, one might say by way of gloss, that
reveals the horrors.

So far I may have seemed inconclusive in assuming, in
opposition to Mr. Thompson's position, that the image of
Leviathan is the symbol of a *good* God, although I have already
given a number of reasons for taking such an attitude. The
greatest chapter in *Moby Dick* is Chapter LXXXVII, 'The
Grand Armada'. It is even more important than the chapter on
the White Squid for determining what Leviathan meant for
Melville. As the voyage of the Pequod approaches its end, the
ship sails through the straits of Sunda into the China seas, and
it is confronted there by an immense aggregation of sperm
whales, by what seemed thousands and thousands of them. The
look-out first becomes aware of them as a great semi-circle of
spouting jets, 'a continuous chain . . . up-playing and sparkling

in the noon-day air', and embracing one half of the level horizon. The Pequod sets off in pursuit, and the crew soon realizes that the crescent has come full circle, and that they are entirely surrounded by a vast circle of spouting jets—by what, as the chapter progresses, one feels might be called a heavenly host of whales. Three boats are lowered. The one in which Ishmael has his place fastens its harpoon in a whale which, plunging forward, heads into the heart of the great herd, drawing the boat behind it. There is something mystically portentous in the entry of Ishmael's whaling boat into the quiet centre of the circling whales:

> . . . at last the jerking harpoon drew out, and the towing whale sideways vanished; then, with the tapering force of his parting momentum, we glided between two whales into the innermost heart of the shoal, as if from some mountain torrent we had slid into a serene valley lake. Here the storms in the roaring glens between the outermost whales, were heard but not felt. In this central expanse the sea presented a smooth satin-like surface. . . . Yes, we were now in that enchanted calm which they say lurks in the heart of every commotion. And still in the outer distance we beheld the tumults of the outer concentric circles, and saw successive pods of whales, eight or ten in each, swiftly going round and round, like multiplied spans of horses in a ring; and so closely shoulder to shoulder that a Titanic circus rider might easily have over-arched the middle ones, and so have gone round on their backs. . . .
>
> Now, inconclusive of the occasional wide intervals between the revolving outer circles, and inconclusive of the spaces between the various pods in any one of those circles, the entire area at this juncture, embraced by the wide multitude, must have contained at least two or three square miles. At any rate . . . spoutings might be discovered from our low boat that seemed playing up almost from the rim of the horizon.

It seems obvious to me that the source (though probably the unconscious source) of this vision of circling whales is Canto XXVIII of the *Paradiso*. We know that Melville's mind was filled with *The Divine Comedy* when he began writing *Pierre* almost immediately after finishing *Moby Dick*, and at least from 1848, when Melville bought a copy of Cary's Dante, allusions are frequent.[5] The passage in question from *Moby Dick* seems to me to be indubitably such an allusion. In Canto XXVIII, it

will be recalled, Dante, turning from Beatrice, beholds a point
of intensest light around which spin the nine concentric circles
of the angelic intelligences—great wheels of fire which, as they
revolve, shoot forth sparkles. Visually, the circles of whales
present a startingly similar image to the imagination as their
water-spouts catch the light of the sun in great concentric rings
that are enclosed by the horizon only. The visual similarity is
enhanced by the water imagery in which Dante describes the
revolving angelic orders. Thus, he compares them to the
luminous ring of vapour that sometimes surrounds the moon;
and, again, he compares the reach of the circles with the rain-
bow's arc.

Beatrice, explaining to Dante the centre of intense light about
which the concentric circles eternally revolve, says: 'From that
point doth hang heaven and all nature.' Now the question is,
what did the Pequod's whaling boat, when it broke through
the living circles into the enchanted calm, find there? It is here
that Melville's writing achieved a beauty that he never surpassed, or equalled:

But far beneath this wondrous world upon the surface, another
and still stranger world met our eyes as we gazed over the side.
For, suspended in those watery vaults, floated the forms of the
nursing mothers of the whales, and those that by their enormous
girth seemed shortly to become mothers. The lake, as I have
hinted, was to a considerable depth exceedingly transparent; and
as human infants while suckling will calmly and fixedly gaze
away from the breast, as if leading two different lives at the time;
and while yet drawing mortal nourishment, be still spiritually
feeding on some unearthly reminiscence;—even so did the young
of these whales seem looking up towards us, as if we were but a bit
of Gulf-weed in their new-born sight. Floating on their sides, the
mothers also seemed quietly eyeing us. One of these little infants
that from certain queer tokens seemed hardly a day old, might
have measured some fourteen feet in length and some six feet in
girth. He was a little frisky; though as yet his body seemed scarce
yet recovered from that irksome position it had so lately occupied
in the maternal reticule; where, tail to head, and all ready for the
final spring, the unborn whale lies bent like a Tartar's bow. The
delicate side-fins, and the palms of his flukes still freshly retained
the plaited crumpled appearance of a baby's ears newly arrived
from foreign parts.

What we have here is a vision of the world in its primal innocence, an image of the life principle presented in an intuition so profound that it seems a part of God's being. The whale mother and her beautiful infant, still attached by the umbilical cord, is an image as tender and reverent, essentially as religious, as a Della Robbia Madonna and Child. The sheer loveliness of that 'enchanted calm' into which the whaling boat intrudes is such that, leaning over its side and looking down into the transparent depths wherein is reflected one of the most astonishing images of the purity and mystery of life ever conceived by an artist—the sheer loveliness of it is such that we almost say with Beatrice: From this point hangs heaven and all nature.

Leviathan is not the tyrant, and Melville would leave us in no doubt. Into this paradisal context Melville, with the effect of almost unbearable shock, unexpectedly reintroduces his savage 'feeding' imagery. Describing the breasts of the nursing whales he says: 'When by chance these precious parts in a nursing whale are cut by the hunter's lance, the mother's pouring milk and blood rivallingly discolour the sea for rods. The milk is very sweet and rich; it has been tasted by man; it might do well with strawberries.' It is not only that the twin images of the milk and blood, churned together in the sea, open into terrible perspectives for the imagination that dwells on them—there is also a kind of horrible-sweet facetiousness in the tone, and suddenly one realizes why the mediaeval mysteries presented Herod as a comic figure. Melville is here operating at that depth and height of the imagination.

In what I have just said of the influence of Dante I have had no intention of suggesting that Melville is trying to use Leviathan as a kind of symbol for the Beatific Vision—but the emotional impact of Dante's Canto on Melville clearly seems to be an important element in the wonderful achievement represented by 'The Grand Armada'. And the significance of this for determining what Leviathan meant for Melville when he wrote *Moby Dick* can hardly, I think, be exaggerated. The image of God that Leviathan symbolizes is an image, certainly not beyond, but *outside* a *specific* theology. It represents a religious intuition of life itself in some of its most basic and positive affirmations. At the same time, it is essentially a tragic intuition, and

Leviathan is a suffering God. If the image is not Christian, it is
filled with Christian overtones, and they lend Leviathan a
large part of his evocativeness. It is hardly too much to say
that if we have seen Leviathan dismembered and his bones
numbered by his enemies, we see him rise again after three
days in Moby Dick's final victory over the Pequod at the end
of the third day's chase.

Captain Ahab is the focus of attention in the novel, and as
the symbolic embodiment of the representative nineteenth-
century American the fate that overtakes him is an indication
of Melville's own reaction to the American world of his day.
There is no need here to argue this representative quality in
Ahab. Nearly all critics are agreed on it.[6] But perhaps it is
worthwhile remarking that in nothing is Ahab more representative (I use 'representative', of course, in this context not to
indicate the average but the paradigmatic) than in the transition he illustrates between the American democratic acceptance
of creation, and hatred of that creation. Ahab is sometimes
mistakenly identified with Melville's viewpoint in the novel,
and, indeed, to some extent he represents a part of Melville's
mind; and a much larger part if we consider the Melville of a
year or so later. But it is Ishmael with whom we must identify
Melville's viewpoint in the end; and this identification is
essential if we are to discover a positive and coherent form in
Moby Dick.

Leviathan, I have argued, represents the *good* in Melville's
universe, but through Ahab's and Ishmael's eyes we are given
two different visions of him. Thus, the ambiguity that, in *Pierre*,
will be rooted in the nature of reality itself, is, in *Moby Dick*,
restricted to the point of view. But beyond that point of view
we sense a universe of objective values in which moral action
and direction are still possibilities, though difficult to achieve.
That Ishmael *does* achieve them constitutes the formal justification of the novel. Ishmael's solitary survival at the end of the
novel is, in a sense, the validation of his vision; and it represents
Melville's momentary triumph in having introduced an element
of moral order into his universe, in having re-established, in the
face of his growing doubts, the polarity of good and evil. I wish
to consider here, as briefly as I may, the meaning of Ishmael's
point of view, as opposed to Ahab's which usually gets most of

the attention. For it is through Ishmael that Melville makes his positive affirmation.

The experiences in which Ishmael participates on the Pequod are, in a sense, his. They constitute a kind of passion play for him from which he is almost literally resurrected in the Epilogue into new life.[7] The opening paragraph indicates the problem that faces Ishmael, and to which the action of the novel brings a cosmic solution:

> Whenever I find myself growing grim about the mouth; whenever it is a damp drizzly November in my soul; whenever I find myself involuntarily pausing before coffin warehouses, and bringing up the rear of every funeral I meet; and especially whenever my hypos get such an upper hand of me, that it requires a strong moral principle to prevent me from deliberately stepping into the street, and methodically knocking people's hats off—then, I account it high time to get to sea as soon as I can.

Though so casually expressed, Ishmael's malaise as described here represents the essence of that despair, though then greatly exaggerated, which overtook Melville in *Pierre* and *The Confidence Man*. But in *Moby Dick* there will be, as the opening paragraph indicates, no submission to it, but a vigorous resistance. The sea is the source of life in the world, and it is to the sea that Ishmael returns whenever he feels symptoms of this depression. Ishmael, then, hardly less than Ahab may be said to do, sets out on the voyage on a quest, but it is a different quest from Ahab's. It is a quest for spiritual health, a desire to enter into a new and deeper harmony with creation. Ishmael accepts the mystery of creation—particularly as embodied in Leviathan—which Ahab does not. Ishmael's attitude towards Moby Dick is one of respectful reverence and wonder, and although from time to time during the course of the Pequod's voyage Ishmael comes under the influence of Ahab's intellectual domination, such occasions are momentary.

From the very beginning, Moby Dick is not a symbol of evil to Ishmael, but a magnificent symbol of creation itself. Creation is not a pasteboard mask for Ishmael, to be broken through in some excess of spiritual pride, as it was for Ahab, whose attempt to penetrate visible creation, not through love but hatred, could only end in a material vision. The measure of Ishmael's contrast in this respect is given in the following passage. Ishmael is paying a visit to the whaling chapel in New Bedford:

'Methinks that in looking at things spiritual, we are too much like oysters observing the sun through water, and thinking that thick water the thinnest air. In fact, take my body who will, take it, I say, it is not me. And therefore three cheers for Nantucket; and come a stove boat and stove my body when they will, for stave my soul Jove himself cannot.'

We are sometimes inclined to lose sight of the elementary fact that the whole complex movement of *Moby Dick* originates in Ahab's inability to resign himself, after Ishmael's fashion as indicated here, to the loss of a leg. Ahab is guilty of that most democratic of sins—of denying hierarchy between the body and soul, eternal and temporal values. He can proceed from a severed limb to a condemned and guilty universe with the greatest of ease. We are back at John Quincy Adams once again, who discovered in Eli Whitney's cotton gin God's great betrayal of the world. Essentially, democracy is the denial of degree, and, by implication, of limit also. But the very principle of form is boundary and limitation. Thus, the democratic aspiration that would deny the hieratic element in creation ends in a monstrous negation. It is the very essence of form-lessness.

The degrees of knowledge are the most important of all for they most directly reflect the degrees of order and value in the spiritual world. It is an important element in Ahab's comprehensive significance that, in Chapter CXVIII, 'The Quadrant', he symbolically destroys the instrument of knowledge by which he should determine his location—his place in creation, as it were:

Then gazing at his quadrant, and handling, one after the other, its numerous cabalistical contrivances, he pondered again, and muttered: 'Foolish toy! babies' plaything of haughty Admirals, and Commodores, and Captains; the world brags of thee, of thy cunning and might; but what after all canst thou do, but tell the poor, pitiful point, where thou thyself happenst to be on this wide planet, and the hand that holds thee: no! not a jot more!'

The manner in which the official hierarchy of the navy is merged here with the ordered knowledge for which the quadrant stands, is worth noting. The importance of this chapter is generally recognized; but there is still reason to insist that it is not science as such that Ahab is rejecting here. Rather, it is the idea of degree. It is precisely Ahab's *place* in the universe which he does not wish, indeed refuses, to know. And it is only his *place* that the quadrant can tell, his place with reference to the sun. Thus, the paradox of the democratic dogma that refuses to recognize anything above it exists in its being forced back on the degrees below: 'Curse thee, thou quadrant!... no longer will I guide my earthly way by thee; the level ship's compass, and the level dead-recokoning, by log and by line; *these* shall conduct me, and show me my place on the sea.' Once the ordered framework that controlled and directed the political vision of John Adams, Cooper, and even of Jefferson, is rejected, we are confronted by a breed of nineteenth-century Titans whose offspring is ultimately degraded to the 'common man' of the twentieth century.

Ahab's attitude is the antithesis of life because it represents a rejection of creation. The analysis of this attitude forms the main substance of the novel, but its great formal achievement exists in the beautiful way that Melville placed the action in an evaluative perspective so that its final effect is one of positive affirmation. He achieved this in two ways. First, he built up the symbol of Leviathan, layer on layer, so that it became one of the most magnificent images in the language of the positive aspects of creation. Leviathan, especially in his greatest role of the White Whale, is the affirmation of all that Ahab denies. The impact of this recognition on the imagination is the greater because, if Melville leads one towards it irresistibly, we yet make the discovery in the midst of all the gargantuan suffering of the whaling ground. We learn the triumph of life that the White Whale represents only because we come to it through such seas of death. This is the most deeply Christian note that Melville ever strikes.

Secondly, Melville achieved the evaluative perspective for the action of *Moby Dick* through his use of Ishmael, and particularly by means of his 'resurrection' in the Epilogue. Ishmael, as I said, enrolls in the crew because he himself wishes to recover spiritual health. The long voyage that is finally brought to its disastrous termination in the China Seas, to repeat an earlier remark, is a kind of long drawn out passion play for Ishmael, ending in his symbolical 'resurrection', from which he returns to life, as we may surmise, cured of that spiritual malady from which we see him suffering in the first chapter of the book.

The relevant portions of the novel which deal with this symbolic resurrection are Chapter CX, and the Epilogue. It will be recalled that Ishmael's cannibal friend Queequeg is for a time so grievously afflicted with fever during the course of the voyage that his life is despaired of. As he seems to be dying, the ship's carpenter is asked to construct a coffin for him. But after the coffin is built, Queequeg recovers. The coffin itself has been strongly constructed, and Queequeg decides to use it for a sea chest, in his leisure moments covering the lid of it with a fancy design:

> With a wild whimsiness, he now used his coffin for a sea-chest; and emptying into it his canvas bag of clothes, set them in order there. Many spare hours he spent, in carving the lid with all manner of grotesque figures and drawings; and it seemed that hereby he was striving, in his rude way, to copy parts of the twisted tattooing on his body. And this tattooing had been a work of a departed prophet and seer of his island, who, by those hieroglyphic marks, had written out on his body a complete theory of the heavens and the earth, and a mystical treatise on the art of attaining truth; so that Queequeg in his own proper person was a riddle to unfold; a wondrous work in one volume; but whose mysteries not even himself could read, though his own live heart beat against them; and these mysteries were therefore destined in the end to moulder away with the living parchment whereon they were inscribed, and so be unsolved to the last.

Somewhat later in the novel it is discovered that the life-buoys on the Pequod, which are sealed casks, have been warped by the sun so as to be useless. It occurs to Queequeg that his coffin might, if the lid were sealed on, substitute admirably for the ruined buoys, and so the coffin takes its place on the ship as a life-preserver. No more is heard of it until the Epilogue. After the Pequod has been rammed by Moby Dick and has disappeared under the sea, Ishmael is saved by its means, and in such a manner as to make it almost appear, when he is picked up by the Rachel, as if he had been resurrected from his own coffin. And the coffin itself is a very special one. It belonged to

his friend Queequeg, one of the noblest savages in literature—
a primitive prince whose whole way of life is based, not on
enmity to nature, as with Ahab, but on harmony with nature.
And we know from Queequeg's whole life, as Melville gives it
to us, that he represents a kind of instinctive charity and adjustment to the world that is the antithesis of Ahab's madness. To
recapture the full flavour of Queequeg's moral implications,
we have to go back to Chapter X:

> As I sat there in that lonely room; the fire burning low, in that
> mild stage when, after its first intensity has warmed the air, it
> then only glows to be looked at; the evening shades and phantoms
> gathering round the casements, and peering in upon us silent,
> solitary twain; the storm booming without in solemn swells; I
> began to be sensible of strange feelings. I felt a melting in me. No
> more my splintered heart and maddened hand were turned
> against the wolfish world. This soothing savage had redeemed it.
> There he sat, his very indifference speaking a nature in which
> there lurked no civilized hypocrisies, and bland deceits. Wild he
> was; a very sight of sights to see; yet I began to feel myself mys-
> teriously drawn towards him.

What have we noticed particularly about Ishmael's survival
is that it happens, in fact, virtually through Queequeg's agency.
By virtue of the carving on the lid which duplicates the tattoo-
ing on Queequeg's body, the coffin stands in proxy for the
savage himself. And we should remember what the design
represented: '. . . a complete theory of the heavens and the
earth, and a mystical treatise on the art of attaining truth.'
Although not obtrusive, this symbolism is nevertheless straightforward and clear. Ahab himself represents hatred of creation
—an extremity of madness, symptoms of which Ishmael had
begun to show when he took to the sea for a cure. He is saved,
or cured, by an acceptance of nature, of the earth and the
heavens. This is what the hieroglyphics on Queequeg's coffin
lid symbolize, and Ishmael's physical survival by its means
stands also for his spiritual recovery.

Moby Dick is, then, Melville's great attempt to create order
in a universe in which a break-down of the polarity between
good and evil is threatened. This threat comes from Ahab,
whose hatred of creation is the symptom, or perhaps the
consequence, of that democratic disillusionment with the

universe I have spoken of—that resentment of the spirit's betrayal of matter, and of God's betrayal of the world. In so far as Melville's own thought is to be equated with any particular person's, it is with Ishmael's. Ishmael represents Melville's resistance against the temptation to follow Ahab which was so powerful for him; he represents Melville's hold on the world of reality and of nature. But as Melville plunged almost immediately into the writing of *Pierre* when he had finished *Moby Dick*, the sanity and grace that had shaped the earlier of the two books was to vanish for good.

III

I have discussed *Moby Dick* at some length because it represents a high point of form in the American novel. The structural tensions that Cooper, Hawthorne, and James employed were elevated here to a metaphysical level, and the struggle between good and evil not only became the form of the action, but the very terms themselves were newly carved out of the ambiguous element of the American experience by the creative fiat of the artist. But they were still grounded in an objective moral framework as it has been traditionally understood in the western world. Alexander Cowie perhaps phrased it as well as any when he wrote: 'Melville was a sceptic but not by any means an atheist. Like many who question orthodoxy, he did so in order to prepare a place in which to build a faith for himself. Ironically, he was castigated for blasphemy when he was in search for spiritual security.'[8] But he proved incapable of sustaining the elaborately achieved form of *Moby Dick* in his later work. Mr. Henry A. Murray in his 'Introduction' to *Pierre* suggests persuasive reasons for this:

> Wearied and exasperated by the relentless underlying conflict and confounded by the constant inversions of value from positive to negative and negative to positive, the man may finally arrive at a state of virtual paralysis with no capacity for decision, one effect of which is the constant apprehension that everything is almost equally meaningless and worthless—'all objects are seen in a dubious, uncertain, and refracting light . . . the most immemorially admitted maxims of men begin to slide and fluctuate, and finally become wholly inverted.' By pursuing the trial of

thought so far, an explorer 'entirely loses the directing compass of his mind; for arrived at the Pole, to whose barrenness only it points, there, the needle indifferently respects all points of the compass alike.' This state of feeling accounts for most of the remaining ambiguities, as well as for the pervasive moral of the book, which is that there is *no* moral; it is impossible for a man to reconcile this world with his own soul, and impossible to make a clean decision for one or for the other; there is evil in the good and good in the evil, gloom in the light and light in the gloom; a step beyond this bitter knowledge carries one to the indifferent thought that good and evil are but 'shadows cast from nothing', the mind of man. 'It is all a dream—we dream that we dreamed that we dream.' [9]

I only wish to glance at *Pierre* and *The Confidence Man* here sufficiently to indicate the relaxation of form, the general impression of motionlessness, that occurred after *Moby Dick*. I am not speaking of conventional, externally imposed form here. From this point of view *Pierre* is more conventional than anything Melville had written so far. Referring to *Pierre*, Arvin writes:

> Nor was he more fortunate in the form he was attempting than in his manner. He had evolved a great and highly idiosyncratic form in *Moby Dick*—as, in *Redburn* and *White-Jacket* he had moved toward it—and now, as if he were not a master but a disciple and a tyro, he put aside all that he had learned in doing this, denied himself all his most personal resources, and undertook to express himself in a hybrid form that had come to him, quite mistakenly, from a hodge-podge of models.[10]

To revert to a definition of form I used in Chapter IV, form is an action, and action is 'the intensified motion of life in which the moral and spiritual faculties of men are no less engaged than their physical selves'. The passage from Mr. Murray quoted above ends with a sentence from *Pierre*, and to understand what was happening in Melville, we can do nothing better than quote the context from which that sentence is taken. It occurs at the close of Book XIX:

> 'Thou, Pierre, speakest of Virtue and Vice; life-secluded Isabel knows neither the one nor the other, but by hearsay. What are they in their real selves, Pierre? Tell me first what is Virtue:— begin!'

'If on that point the gods are dumb, shall a pigmy speak? Ask the air!'

'Then Virtue is nothing.'

'Not that!'

'Then Vice?'

'Look: a nothing is the substance, it casts one shadow one way, and another the other way; and these two shadows cast from one nothing; these, seems to me, are Virtue and Vice.'

'Then why torment thyself so, dearest Pierre?'

'It is the law.'

'What?'

'That a nothing should torment a nothing; for I am a nothing. It is all a dream—we dream that we dreamed we dream.'

It is clear that all Melville had achieved in *Moby Dick* is lost here. The polarity he had been at such pains to establish in his masterpiece—a polarity within the field of which moral action could occur without the danger of stasis setting in—gives way before a poisoned ambiguity that undermines the very foundation of reality itself. Pierre is engulfed by a nihilism which, as it proves the destructive element for him, is also the negation of form in the novel in so far as form is defined as the intensified motion of life:

The old mummy lies buried in cloth on cloth; it takes time to unwrap this Egyptian king. Yet now, forsooth, because Pierre began to see through the first superficiality of the world, he fondly weens he has come to the unlayered substance. But, far as any geologist has yet gone down into the world, it is found to consist of nothing but surface stratified on surface. To its axis, the world being nothing but superinduced superficies. By vast pains we mine into the pyramid; by horrible gropings we come to the central room; with joy we espy the sarcophagus; but we lift the lid—and no body is there!—appallingly vacant as vast is the soul of man!

In such a passage we see the terrifying degree to which reality is drained from appearances. There has always been a tendency for the American to separate appearance and reality. I have discussed this tendency at some length, as it occurs in the works of Henry James, in *The Complex Fate*. But James employed this ambiguity as a positive principle of form, whereas in *Pierre* it is a principle of dissolution. It carries all before it, and the result is catastrophic. The role of the mind in moulding the appearances of reality was fully exhibited in *Moby Dick* through the conflicting visions of Ahab and Ishmael; but Melville masterfully suggested there the objective existence of a reality beyond appearances. If Ishmael's vision corresponds to reality more nearly than Ahab's, it is a *correspondence*, and not a creation. Leviathan is, in the last word, the validation of Ishmael's vision of creation; that is to say, the whale is not, as Mr. Feidelson might argue, a symbol of a symbol—a complex image that reverberates with ultimate hollowness. It represents reality itself, suggestively constructed on the material plane through the long sequence of cetological chapters and issuing at last, for the imagination, as a principle of metaphysical order in the universe. But in *Pierre*, the mind does not correspond to, it *creates*, its reality, and we are left with almost no sense of an extramental world of things to corroborate the images formed in the mind. Mr. Feidelson's appreciation of the symbolic process, as described in his *Symbolism and American Literature*, can work admirably with second-rate examples of art, and it is only fair to add here that his analysis of *Pierre* (pp. 186–207) is brilliant. He shows, for example, how even the most physical facts and relationships of Pierre's life are, for him at least, not grounded in any objective reality, that he is incapable of distinguishing between the external and the internal, and that for him 'the fiction is the thought and the fact' (p. 192). The dream-like movement that this induces, and the insufficiently grounded relations between the characters, defeat the physical action of *Pierre* almost as surely as the moral action is defeated by the pervading ambiguity that cancels all positive directions and motives. Viewed detachedly, this state of moral nihilism could become a successful subject for art. In his great short story, 'Bartleby the Scrivener', Melville raised a somewhat similar condition of existence to a level of superb achievement. But, however much Bartleby may represent certain aspects of Melville's own plight and personality,[11] he yet avoided the kind of identification with Bartleby that he succumbed to in *Pierre*. In the story, we have a sense of an objective world with which Bartleby stands in tragic relation; but in *Pierre* the world itself is the tragic emanation of Melville's mind as it comes to a paralysingly personal focus in Pierre's consciousness. All that is significant in reality is a mood, a cast of mind:

> Say what some poets will, Nature is not so much her own ever-sweet interpreter, as the mere supplier of that cunning alphabet, whereby selecting and combining as he pleases, each man reads his own peculiar lesson according to his own peculiar mind and mood.

As we know, Melville had never been much concerned at any level with that practical dialectic out of which Cooper, Hawthorne, and James evolved the form of their fiction; which is to reaffirm once more that he had little interest in European as opposed to American experience, or in the interplay between them. What we are left with, in the absence of this dialectic, after the struggle with good and evil has subsided, is the terrible emptiness and solitude of the American sensibility, forced back upon itself in utter isolation, with no theology or faith, no sense of intimacy with the European past and present to impart significance to its own dissenting forms, and with a growing distrust of its own democratic credo. As Melville's work grows increasingly sombre, one is reminded of a passage from Santayana's *Reason in Common Sense*:

> An earnestness which is out of proportion to any knowledge or love of real things, which is therefore dark and inward, and thinks itself deeper than the earth's foundations—such an earnestness, until culture turns it into intelligent interests, will naturally breed a new mythology. It will try to place some world of Afrites and shadowy giants behind the constellations, which it finds too distinct or constant to be its companions or supporters; and it will assign itself vague or infinite tasks, for which it is doubtless better equipped than for those the earth now sets before it. . . . All will be a tossing servitude and illiberal mist, where the parts will have no final values and the whole no pertinent direction.[12]

The intellectual seriousness of the several novelists we have been concerned with in the main body of this book is a different thing from the disproportionate earnestness of which Santayana is speaking. The dialectical questions raised by the rift in American experience turned their creative drive towards intelligent interests that shaped the form of the novels they wrote. With them, we remain in a lightened air that is free of obscurantist ambiguities. Boundary or limit is essential to intelligibility and form. This is the lesson that the Old World had to teach the New above all others; and it was through their sense of the European experience that Cooper, Hawthorne, and James avoided that provincial formlessness that overtook Melville after *Moby Dick*. In *Pierre* Melville wrote:

> Deep, Deep, and still deep and deeper must we go, if we would find out the heart of a man; descending into which is as descending a spiral stair in a shaft, without any end, and where the endlessness is only concealed by the spiralness of the stair and the blackness of the shaft.

It is usual to speak of this as illustrating Melville's interest in the unconscious. Perhaps it does; but the image itself suggests even more powerfully Melville's retreat from the real world. The task that he proposes here with so much earnestness is both vague and infinite in Santayana's sense, and pursued to the end which the image itself proposes—or, to be more accurate, pursued through its endlessness and indetermination—would terminate in a negation of consciousness itself, an attempt to stretch a measurable meaning to infinity, and to escape the limits of the rational and the real. But one can escape from them only into nothingness.

That other profoundly American writer, Mark Twain, wrote the logical conclusion to the process of Melville's thought as it was developing through *Pierre*, at the very end of *The Mysterious Stranger*:

> 'You perceive, *now*, that these things are all impossible except in a dream. You perceive that they are pure and puerile insanities, the silly creations of an imagination that is not conscious of its freaks—in a word, that they are a dream, and you the maker of it. The dream-marks are all present; you should have recognized them earlier.
>
> 'It is true, that which I have revealed to you; there is no God, no universe, no human race, no earthly life, no heaven, no hell. It is all a dream—a grotesque and foolish dream. Nothing exists but you. And you are but a *thought*—a vagrant thought, a useless thought, a homeless thought, wandering forlorn among the empty eternities!'
>
> He vanished, and left me appalled; for I knew, and realized, that all he had said was true.

There are no doubt very good reasons why a disproportionate earnestness that is in excess of a love of real things should be more than a mere possibility in America. The democratic philosophy places an intolerable burden on the world of real things: it is doubtless only in America that cotton gins could have symbolized God's great betrayal. And the earnestness is deepened in America because, feeling alien to the intellectual, spiritual, and cultural answers of the Old World, the American is much impressed by the magnitude of his task, and inclined to be unaware that others have preceded him more brilliantly. But this proposes questions that are beyond the scope of the present argument.

I only wish to indicate that as Melville lost touch with that polarity he had created in *Moby Dick* the possibility of a moral action began to recede from him, and as a consequence, an element of formlessness entered his novels. If there is motion at all, it is circular and descending, and as the terminus of departure is a world of shifting and ambiguous forms about which there is little certainty for Pierre, so the terminus of arrival is lost sight of 'among the empty eternities'.

In its own way *The Confidence Man* continues the same process of negation that we have glanced at in *Pierre*, but focused so emphatically against an American democratic background that it reveals for us, as nothing had before, how profoundly American were the roots of Melville's despair. Mr. Richard Chase has argued that *The Confidence Man* is Melville's attack on the progressive-liberalism of his day.[13] Mr. Chase's argument is persuasive, and from one point of view it is undoubtedly correct. But the novel itself leaves one with a sense of darker dimension that Mr. Chase allows. It is less a criticism than a denial of life, and Melville succeeds, with a skill he had never exhibited in *Pierre*, in lifting the lid of the sarcophagus that rests in the central room—to reveal that no body is there. The one certain fact about the confidence man is that he does not exist. He is appearance drained of all reality. Lift any one of the masks that pass in succession before one: one encounters only vacancy. He is the great and ultimate joke of the April Fool's Day voyage of the Fidèle. The endless and repetitious conversations between the confidence man and his fellow travellers on the Fidèle represent the exact opposite of that structural dialectic

we have examined earlier. The confidence man is the antithe-
tical shadow of the Americans with whom he argues: 'nothing
is the substance, it casts one shadow one way, and another
another way'. The book as a whole is a practical commentary
on Melville's exploration of the American heart, 'descending
into which is as descending a spiral stair in a shaft, without any
end, and where the endlessness is only concealed by the spiral-
ness of the stair and the blackness of the shaft'. As such a descent,
in Melville's view, has no end, the final sentence of the book,
which has puzzled so many critics, was inevitable: 'Something
further may follow of this Masquerade.'

Such a process is obviously related to disillusionment with
the democratic experience, but it is also the expression of a
deeper metaphysical malaise. In this connection the following
passage from Allen Tate is illuminating. It occurs in the first of
the chapters on Poe in *The Forlorn Demon*:

> [Poe] is progressively mastered by one great idea, deeper than
> any level of conscious belief and developing to the end of his life
> at an ever increasing rate, until at last he is engulfed by it. It is
> his own descent into the maelstrom.
>
> He arrives at it, or reaches the bottom of it, in *Eureka*, which
> he wrote in 1848, the year before his death. I shall not go so far
> as to connect, symbolically or prophetically, his death and the
> vision of the pit at the end of *Eureka*. We may only observe that
> the complete vision, of which the early works represent an
> approximation, immediately precedes his death. The proposition
> of which *Eureka* is to provide the 'proof' he states at the beginning:
>
> > In the original unity of the first thing lies the secondary
> > cause of all things, with the germ of their inevitable annihilation.

This 'nothingness' is a dialectical conversion, not of one symbol
into its opposite by analogy, as we see it in Dante, or even in
Donne, but of an abstraction into its antithesis. Thesis: the omniscient intellect of man (Poe as man) achieves a more than angelic
knowledge in comprehending the structure and purpose of the
created universe. Antithesis: the final purpose of the created
universe is the extinction in its own unity of the omniscient intellect of man. There is no Hegelian synthesis. After the original act
of divine creation, God withdraws into his deistic aloofness,
leaving the separate and local acts of creation to man. This is the
sphere of secondary creations which man as angelic delegate of

God is empowered to perform. Thus, says Poe at the end of *Eureka*, not only is every man his own God, every man *is* God: every man the non-spatial centre into which the universe, by a reverse motion of the atoms, will contract, as into its annihilation. God destroys himself in the eventual recovery of this unity. Unity equals zero. If Poe must at last 'yield himself unto death utterly', there is a lurid sublimity in the spectacle of his taking God along with him into a grave which is not smaller than the universe.[14]

This is also the trend of Melville's thought after *Moby Dick*. Ahab was, indeed, the man who tried to equal God, but as I have said above, Melville did not ultimately assent to Ahab's role. But Pierre's world, as we have seen, is literally a secondary act of his own creation—an emanation of his own symbol-making mind, grounded in ultimate nothingness. Mr. Tate's last sentence recalls very vividly the last scene of Melville's book in which the confidence man leads away into the darkness the old man who is his last victim, and who, Mr. Chase says, is both Uncle Sam and 'the Old God and Father of all the planets sitting at his death-white table at the centre of the universe'. The endless descent of the spiral stair ends in the dissolution of everything no less than the universe of Poe that Mr. Tate has described.

I quoted Sir Herbert Read: 'We are concerned' not so much with ' "the life of form" . . . but rather the form of life'. Despite its repetitious monotony, which was inevitable when we consider the endless circling theme of *The Confidence Man*, the novel is executed with a good deal of incisive energy, and in its peculiar way it is tightly and effectively organized. And its meaning is realized in its form. But it is the form of death, and not the form of life.

IX

Henry James and 'Life'

THE art of Henry James illustrates so richly the tensions which make up the characteristic subject matter of the American novelist that there is some difficulty in treating him within reasonable compass. But where his work supports my argument most conspicuously, in presenting a sustained debate between America and Europe, it is also obvious enough at this date in the history of Jamesian criticism to make extended analysis and comment a superfluous duty. Some years ago, F. R. Leavis in an article in *Scrutiny*[1] which has not been reprinted wrote an account of *The Europeans* that ought to be a classic of its kind. He demonstrates the way in which James dramatically and symbolically embodies the American and European values, holding them in poised suspension in an international dialectic that never vulgarly collapses into mere national commitment. This dialectic is both the form and the subject matter of James's novels and stories, and for anyone undertaking James for the first time there is possibly no better point to start from than *The Europeans*, and no criticism better to begin with than Dr. Leavis's essay. The discrimination of international values in James is, in fact, a search for a reality precipitated by the inadequacy of the home product when unqualified by the alleviations of Europe.

The international novel has a long but tentative history in America.* When it finally reaches its climax in James, what we have is not merely a spectacle of divergent national manners and attitudes played off against each other in carefully selected areas, but a serious attempt to resolve these conflicts, to escape from the restrictive categories of the provincial, local, and native, into a more spacious, humane, and comprehensive reality. This is a passage outward and upward for the European hardly less than for the American component. It is not an accident that the great wave of James's popularity has coincided with the Second World War and the beginning of the United Nations. The suggestion is not as simple-minded as it

* See Appendix C.

may sound, for the desire for international understanding, deeply intensified in those years, created an ideal climate in which to read James's subtle explorations of international social relations. What had once seemed frivolous to many now seemed fraught with significance. To say this is not to credit James's art with a merely adventitious importance or appeal, but to recognize his international theme for the deeply serious thing it is.

James searches throughout his fictions for a reality that is poised in suspension among the multiple possibilities that Europe and America offer him, but which is really the property of neither. It is a reality to which he attaches as much importance as Hawthorne does to his 'inner sphere', but it is more elusive than that. James begins with two distinct advantages over Hawthorne. The double edge of the international theme gives him an instrument that can probe more deeply than anything at Hawthorne's disposal; and James's reverence for the role of the artist in society gives him a security in his art that Hawthorne never had. For Hawthorne, the New England conscience in its decline was a divisive element that tended to separate the moral from its human context. It provided no medium in which the complex aspects of the problem could coalesce into a symbolic unity. In 'Henry James' Portrait of the Artist' [2] Matthiessen writes that James, in his stories of writers and artists, dealt with 'problems which [he] knew from the inside and whose urgency was ever with him, problems of the writer and his audience, of the lack of intelligent appreciation and of the demands of his craft. They also dramatize the issue which is still our issue, the relation of the artist to society.' Hawthorne approached these problems, but he did so with moral preoccupations that were essentially alien to the nature of the problems themselves. These issues raised by the artist in society carry their own moral problems, but they cannot be solved by truckling to the remnants of a dead Calvinism, or the exigencies that American democratic flank-rubbing would foist on them.

In Henry James, this conflict between the artist and social morality, which proved a stumbling block to Hawthorne, is dramatized in 'The Author of Beltraffio'. Mark Ambient, the writer who represents the aesthetic movement in England in the 'eighties, is describing the differences in temperament and outlook between himself and his morally conventional wife:

> 'The difference between us is simply the opposition between two distinct ways of looking at the world, which have never succeeded in getting together, or making any kind of common ménage, since the beginning of time. They have borne all sorts of names, and my wife would tell you it's the difference between Christian and Pagan. I may be a pagan, but I don't like the name; it sounds sectarian.'

And later James describes the character of the wife herself in these terms:

> Certainly, at first, she looked like a woman with as few passions as possible; but if she had a passion at all, it would be that of Philistinism. She might have been—for there are guardian spirits, I suppose, of all great principles—the angel of propriety.

James modelled Mark Ambient on John Addington Symonds, and his remarks in *The Notebooks* show that he was dramatizing impersonally the same conflict in which Hawthorne was too personally involved to be sure of himself:

> March 26, 1884. Edmund Gosse mentioned to me the other day, a fact which struck me as a possible *donnee*. He was speaking of J. A. S., the writer (from whom, in Paris, the other day I got a letter), of his extreme and somewhat hysterical aestheticism, etc.: the sad conditions of his life, exiled to Davos by the state of his lungs, the illness of his daughter, etc. Then he said that, to crown his happiness, poor S.'s wife was in no sort of sympathy with what he wrote; disapproving of its tone, thinking his books immoral, pagan, hyper-aesthetic, etc. 'I have never read any of John's works. I think them most *undesirable*.' It seemed to me *qu'il y avait un drame—un drame intime*; the opposition between the narrow, cold, Calvinistic wife, a rigid moralist; and the husband, impregnated—even to morbidness—with the spirit of Italy, the love of beauty, of art, the aesthetic view of life, and aggravated, made extravagant and perverse, by the sense of his wife's disapproval. *Le drame pourrait s'engager—si drame il y a*—over the education of their child—the way he is to be brought up and to be taught to look at life; the husband drawing him one way and the wife another. The father wishes to make him an artist—the mother wishes to draw him into the church, to dedicate him to morality and religion, in order to expiate, as it were, the coun-

tenance that the family have given to godless ideas in the literary career of the father, who, however, is perfectly decent in life.[3]

Dolcino, Mark Ambient's son in the story, is the victim who is wasted and destroyed by this conflict between his parents. His danger is more real than Esther's or little Joe Bartram's in 'Ethan Brand'. It is clearly the wife's conventional code which proves the destructive one, and not Ambient's aesthetic approach to life. Both attitudes, however, are vulnerable in the pattern of the story, the aesthetic attitude finding its adequate 'placing' in the figure of Ambient's absurd sister who 'made up very well as a Rossetti'. This balanced pattern has nothing of that irresolution that characterizes Hawthorne's fear of the artist as a danger to society and the individual. As for the danger to the artist in withdrawing from the intimacy of personal relationships, James's story, 'The Lesson of the Master', is perhaps his finest commentary on that. Ultimately for the artist security lies, in James's world, where Hawthorne would sense danger—or so Henry St. George and Paul Overt would seem to teach us: in sophisticated detachment from the world and from personal relationships capable of imposing obligations on the artist strong enough to encourage him to betray his own genius as Henry St. George betrayed his. Hawthorne's sense of his 'stern and black-browed' Puritan ancestors was too strong to permit him ever, on such a subject as art, to rise to the magnificence of Dencombe's dying speech in 'The Middle Years':

> 'We work in the dark—we do what we can—we give what we have. Our doubt is our passion and our passion is our task. The rest is the madness of art.'

I said a page or two ago that James's international theme provided him with a double-edged instrument which could cut out a more subtle version of reality than Hawthorne ever achieved with his inner sphere. Both artists were deeply aware of the tension between appearance and reality which frequently reached the snapping point in their respective works. What I shall say here on this subject should be implemented by my fuller discussion of this tension in *The Complex Fate*, but at the moment I am only concerned with showing how James used the international theme to probe under the appearances of life towards a moral reality that remained essentially uncommitted to any national pattern or allegiance. James was a confessed pragmatist to whom moral values were acceptable only when they had proved and validated themselves in terms of human experience. Life proved itself in the living. But as social conventions and attitudes are frequently dissociated in the actual world from the sources of life and refreshment, the social surfaces of James's fictions are often screens behind which we have to look to discover the values he believed in and the judgements he was making. They are often different from what they appear to be at first. This is not a contrivance in James: in some ways it is the level at which his art approaches life most closely. I shall consider only one example here, and content myself with pointing to the relevant pages in *The Complex Fate* for corroboration.

'Madame de Mauves' is a story of less than a hundred pages which James wrote in 1873, and it is a first-rate piece of work. *The American*, which it slightly resembles in some ways, was not written for several more years, and it is not nearly as good. 'Madame de Mauves' may be taken as a paradigm of Henry James's technique and intentions in dealing with the international theme, and I present it here as a beautifully representative story. Its representativeness is of a highly significant kind, and it illustrates the way in which the international theme could become not only the subject but the form of James's fiction at one and the same time.

The story tells of how Euphemia Cleve, a rich young American girl at a French convent school, is introduced to the older brother of one of her classmates, Richard de Mauves, a French aristocrat of highly questionable morals, and is enticed into a marriage that will salvage the wavering financial fortunes of the old family. The story opens some few years after this marriage has taken place when Bernard Longmore, a young American visiting Europe, chances to meet Madame de Mauves through a mutual friend. She is beautiful, and obviously unhappy, and Bernard falls more or less in love. At least he pities her and wishes to cheer her. Her husband, M. de Mauves, is currently involved in an affair, and finding the American stiffness of his wife in such matters an inconvenience. To justify his own conduct, and in the interests of easier

practical management, he tries to arrange for a love affair
between Bernard and his wife: he has his mistress, she should
have her lover. Being only a French nobleman, he innocently
fails to realize that passion in Americans is always controlled
by conscience. Towards promoting this affair, M. de Mauves
enlists the services of his redoubtable sister, Madame Clairin,
who is a splendid comic creation of the morally sinister sort
that James could do so well. In an interview with the reluctant
Longmore—an interview which has the redeeming grace of
being exquisitely funny—Madame Clairin lays all the shocking
cards on the table while Bernard grows hot under the collar:

> 'My brother, in a single word, is in love with another woman.
> I don't judge him; I don't judge my sister-in-law. I would have
> kept my husband's affection, or I would frankly have done with-
> out it, before this. But my sister is an odd compound; I don't
> profess to understand her. Therefore it is, in a measure, that I
> appeal to you, her fellow-countryman. Of course you'll be sur-
> prised at my way of looking at the matter, and I admit it's a way
> in use only among people whose family traditions compel them
> to take a superior view of things.' Madame Clairin paused, and
> Longmore wondered where her family traditions were going to
> lead her.

They lead her far enough to make a clear-cut distinction
between the American and European codes in the hands of
their more extreme proponents. Madame Clairin's speech is a
splendid achievement of monumental vulgarity. She is the
Countess Gemini without the finer touches and the saving
graces, but still superb in her soiled assurance. Her brassy
cynicism is, in the end, not really distinguishable from a wilting
sentimentality: 'The De Mauves are real Frenchmen, and their
wives—I may say it—have been worthy of them. . . . They were
femmes d'esprit. When they had a headache, they put on a
little rouge and came to supper as usual; and when they had a
heartache, they put a little rouge on their hearts.'

As opposed to critical opinion a generation ago, Jamesian
critics today concede that James favours his Americans, and
surely, one thinks, Madame Clairin and her dissolute brother,
who doesn't even have the grace of being amusing, will prove
easy moral foils to the two noble Americans, and that *seems* to be
the way James plays it. Madame de Mauves and Bernard have

H

all the unbending puritan righteousness of Hilda and Kenyon in *The Marble Faun*. Even their speech accents are similar. At one of their meetings Madame de Mauves says to Bernard:

> 'I believe, Mr. Longmore, . . . that I have nothing on earth but a conscience,—it is a good time to tell you so,—nothing but a dogged, clinging, inexpugnable conscience. Does that prove me indeed to be of your faith and race, and have you one for which you can say as much? I don't say it in vanity, for I believe that if my conscience will prevent me from doing anything very base, it will effectually prevent me from doing anything very fine.'
>
> 'I am delighted to hear it,' cried Longmore. 'We are made for each other. 'It's very certain I too shall never do anything fine. And yet I have fancied that in my case this inexpugnable organ you so eloquently describe might be blinded and gagged awhile, in a fine cause, if not turned out of doors. In yours,' he went on with the same appealing irony, 'is it absolutely invincible?'
>
> But her fancy made no concession to his sarcasm. 'Don't laugh at your conscience,' she answered gravely: 'that's the only blasphemy I know.'

They are made for each other, but made for each other at a distance. Bernard returns to America, and Madame de Mauves remains with her husband where her indignant morality scores the final triumph. Her husband, we hear indirectly on the last page, puts a bullet through his head when his wife (whom he has now perversely learned to love) refuses to forgive him his infidelities: 'She was stone, she was ice, she was outraged virtue.'

A certain ambiguity has been remarked in this story by critics before, but it has usually been attributed to changing fashions in heroines and emotions which, quite apart from James's intentions, have swung our sympathies away from the virtuous Americans to take a more indulgent view of the French characters. Actually, this ambiguity seems to me to be central to the formal structure of the story, and to rest at the very heart of James's moral meaning as we see it developing throughout his work.

I disapprove of diagramming structures in novels: it is the activity of the literary machine shop. But there is a symmetry so perfect in 'Madame de Mauves', and so significantly embodying the interaction of the American and European traditions, that it can do no harm for once to map out in one's mind the main lines of development in the action. This action may be thought of as represented by two parallel lines, horizontally placed. The top line, down which Madame de Mauves and Bernard Longmore move, is the line of the American conscience, signifying sacrifice and renunciation. The bottom line represents the primrose path of M. de Mauves and Madame Clairin. It is the French way, and signifies acceptance of the senses, and, in a very qualified way, life. James's task is to achieve some kind of communication between the two lines, to discover a field in which the mutual hostility of the two ways can be artistically resolved, for the marriage of Madame de Mauves and her husband represents only an arbitrary yoking together of what is essentially irreconcilable. There is a prefatory communication between the two lines at the very beginning of the story in the comprehensive consciousness of the French grandmother, who understands the implications of both traditions, and foresees disaster if they are joined, but who nevertheless encourages the marriage between Euphemia and her grandson in the interests of the family fortune. But this is only a prelude to the two attempts in the narrative, one attempt being made from either side in the direction of the other, to bring the two traditions together in some kind of harmony.

These two attempts occur in the major scenes of the novel before the climax on the terrace, when Madame de Mauves sends Bernard back to America in the name of conscience. The first scene is that one which I have already described in which Madame Clairin does her best to arrange a love affair between Bernard Longmore and her sister-in-law for the convenience of her brother. This scene constitutes a strenuous effort on the part of the French line to communicate with the American line, the nature of which it fails abysmally to understand. The result is that they remain as parallel as ever, and Bernard flees into the countryside in a state of moral shock.

The second scene which balances this one follows immediately afterwards, and represents the contrasting attempt of the American to move in the direction of the French level. I said a moment ago that after his interview with Madame Clairin the two lines remained as parallel as ever, but this is not quite true. The interview was clearly a necessary introduction to Bernard's interlude at the French inn, from which he returns with a less rigid conception of correct behaviour. This scene gives us what I take to be James's essential values in this story, and in much of his later work as well, and it is finely done. James's description of landscape (and this is unusual with him) enforces the moral meaning he wishes to communicate. After leaving Madame Clairin, Bernard has wandered for a couple of hours in the forest, and at last he emerges into a rural countryside that is strange to him:

> The fields and trees were of a cool metallic green; the grass looked as if it might stain your trousers, and the foliage your hands. The clear light had a sort of mild greyness; the sunbeams were of silver rather than gold. A great red-roofed, high-stacked farm-house, with whitewashed walls and a straggling yard, surveyed the high road, on one side, from behind a transparent curtain of poplars. A narrow stream, half choked with emerald rushes and edged with grey aspens, occupied the opposite quarter. The meadows rolled and sloped away gently to the low horizon, which was barely concealed by the continuous line of clipped and marshalled trees. The prospect was not rich, but it had a frank homeliness which touched the young man's fancy. It was full of light atmosphere and diffused sunshine, and if it was prosaic, it was soothing.
>
> . . . In twenty minutes he came to a village which straggled away to the right, among orchards and *potagers*. On the left, at a stone's throw from the road, stood a little pink-faced inn, which reminded him that he had not breakfasted. . . . In the inn he found a brick-tiled parlour and a hostess in sabots and a white cap, whom, over the omelette she speedily served him,—borrowing license from the bottle of sound red wine which accompanied it, —he assured that she was a true artist. To reward his compliment, she invited him to smoke his cigar in her little garden behind the house.

While lounging on 'a bench against the pink wall, in the sun, which was not too hot', he begins to ask himself certain questions which will be asked repeatedly by James's characters through the full course of his career:

> To renounce—to renounce again—to renounce forever—was this all that youth and longing and resolve were meant for? Was experience to be muffled and mutilated, like an indecent picture?

Was a man to sit and deliberately condemn his future to be the black memory of a regret, rather than the long reverberation of a joy? Sacrifice? The word was a trap for minds muddled with fear, an ignoble refuge of weakness.

If we are to realize, finally, the importance James attached to these questions he gives Bernard, it will be well to turn to Book Fifth, Part II, of *The Ambassadors*, and read again that famous speech of Strether's in Gloriani's garden in which he tells little Bilham to live: 'Live all you can; it's a mistake not to. It doesn't so much matter what you do in particular, so long as you have your life. If you haven't had that, what *have* you had?' The question of what James means by 'life' is as radical for him as the question of the 'inner sphere' is for Hawthorne. It is the one great overwhelming problem that most of his characters have to face sooner or later, in one way or another, just as Hawthorne's characters are all brought up against that 'inner reality' which was 'life' for the earlier novelist.

As Bernard sits in the garden of the French inn, the answers to the questions he has been asking himself seem to be given to him by the appearance of a young French couple, an artist and his mistress, who are living there. The young man has gone ahead with his artist's equipment down to the meadow stream to paint, and presently the girl, Claudine, comes from the inn to join him:

. . . she came out of the house with her hat and parasol, prepared to follow her companion. She had on a pink muslin dress and a little white hat, and she was as pretty as a Frenchwoman needs to be to be pleasing. She had a clear brown skin and a bright dark eye, and a step which seemed to keep time to some slow music, heard only by herself. Her hands were encumbered with various articles which she seemed to intend to carry with her. In one arm she held her parasol and a large roll of needlework, and in the other a shawl and a heavy white umbrella, such as painters use for sketching.

This young couple embodies the positive values James wishes to give us. They are a part of the fresh summer afternoon, the sunshine and the greenery. They are young, happy, spontaneous, and although Bernard later learns from the land-lady that they are not married, they are certainly innocent with the kind of innocence that matters. They represent a positive health that glows radiantly when put beside the aristocratic Frenchwoman, Madame Clairin, or equally when put beside Madame de Mauves. It is not possible to reproduce their effect in the story by quotation, but they are as near as James ever came to giving us the kind of young people that one meets everywhere in D. H. Lawrence. They are the best commentary in James's fictions on what Strether meant by his rather tired recommendation of 'life'. James has carefully built up an atmosphere of cheerful domesticity in the kitchen and garden of the inn, and he has given us a sense of sun- and air-filled countryside as the background which enforces the values he wishes the young couple to suggest. I do not mean that James absolutely commits himself to them as the ideal embodiment of what he believes in. They are, after all, only figures that we glimpse at a strategic moment for a paragraph or two. But their happy, exuberant existence is a reproach to the moral characters of the American woman and her French sister-in-law: as much to the festering righteousness of the American as to the more amiable corruption of Madame Clairin. And they are a reproach despite the somewhat tentative character of their union:

> Longmore was puzzled for a moment. Then, 'You mean she's not his wife?' he asked.
> She shrugged her shoulders. 'What shall I tell you? They are not *des hommes serieux*, those gentlemen! They don't engage themselves for an eternity. It's none of my business, and I've no wish to speak ill of madame. She's a very nice little woman, and she loves her *jeune homme* to distraction.'

If, and when, they cease to love each other, one can be sure that Claudine will not put a little rouge on her heart as she dresses for dinner before going downstairs to fulfil the conventional social duties for a husband whom she hates; and on the other hand she will not hover over him like a female Chillingworth to exact the terrible moral vengeance that Madame de Mauves claims in the end. This young couple are free of the moral limitations of *both* the American and European traditions as they are embodied in the two principal female characters in this story. They may not be quite as respectable as Hawthorne's Matthew and Hannah, but it is clear that James's sense of 'life' is related to Hawthorne's 'inner reality' even though an obvious improvement on it. Claudine's and her artist's sphere of reality is somewhere between the two diagrammatic lines I posited in the beginning, for they both accept the senses and live (so the image James gives us suggests) with an emotional integrity and vitality which acts effectively as a conscience, even if it is not quite up to New England standards.

Bernard is to some degree susceptible to the lesson Claudine and her lover have given him, and he returns to Madame de Mauves in a softened mood. She senses the change, and in twilight on the terrace she plays her 'renunciation' scene for all it is worth. When one compares the histrionics of her speech to Longmore, filled with its little vanities and self-regarding rhetoric, in which she forewarns him to make her no profession of affection—when one compares this with the simple naturalness of the young lovers at the inn, one must admit that James clinches his point. Here is Madame de Mauves to Longmore:

'When I said just now that I had a very high opinion of you, I meant it very seriously. It was not a vain compliment. I believe there is no appeal one may make to your generosity which can remain long unanswered. If this were to happen,—if I were to find you selfish where I thought you generous, narrow where I thought you large,'—and she spoke slowly, with her voice lingering with emphasis on each of these words,—'vulgar where I thought you rare,—I should suffer keenly. I should say to myself in the dull days of my future, "There was one man who might have done so and so; and he, too, failed." But this shall not be. You have made too good an impression on me not to make the very best. If you wish to please me forever, there's a way.'

I have quoted this speech here, unnecessarily from some points of view, because it shows what rare but unobtrusive control the early James had over the language of his characters. The whole moral pose rings false in the over-niceness of Madame de Mauves's phrasings. This was not James's way of writing at any time, and all one has to do is compare almost any of Madame de Mauves's speeches with any of Madame Clairin's to see how sure James was of himself. The 'way' that Madame de Mauves refers to in the last line is naturally that Bernard should return to America and see her no more. Back in America, Bernard settles down to a life which, as the years go by, one feels will come to resemble Miles Coverdale's at the close of

The Blithedale Romance, and which looks forward to Marcher's empty career in 'The Beast in the Jungle'.

This is a splendid story. It is representatively Jamesian in the best sense of the word, but one wishes that he had returned to the type offered in the young couple at the inn a little more often, and developed them a little further. What the story indicates clearly enough is that James's concern with the international theme is a concern with life—although being an American one feels that reality would be the more appropriate word. They more or less mean the same thing, but the American writer usually prefers, or did in the past, the more abstract, non-sensuous term. Hawthorne would have been a little embarrassed to be told that his 'inner sphere of reality' was really a comment on life after all. James deserves a great deal of credit for having brought the term 'life' as explicitly and as largely into his working intentions as he did, and if his attempts to define what he meant by it sometimes seem a little dry, he leaves us in no doubt in the end. 'Madame de Mauves' is one of his most direct answers.

Hawthorne had his conception of the magnetic chain of humanity. When that was broken, men ceased to live significantly. James's international theme as he uses it is, after all, merely the magnetic chain of humanity envisaged on a trans-Atlantic scale. And just as Hawthorne's characters were always breaking the chain, accidentally or by deliberate intention, so James's characters have abundant troubles of their own.

In 'Madame de Mauves' we saw that 'life' meant for James pretty much what it has meant for all great artists from Shakespeare to Lawrence, but every artist has to reach towards life in his art in those images and Symbols which his sensibility and his time allow him, whether they are images of inner spheres, dark gods, positive visions of Byzantium or negative ones of the Unreal City. For James, the image of life was Europe, but it was a far more complicated image than the simple statement suggests. It was not simply the great good place to which Americans went; it was, more than anything else, a test of integrity, the field of honour on which the young man proved his worth. It was the Green Chapel towards which the young knight worked his way through the winter waste land and through many dangers to bring back the spring to his own heart. Few, if any, reached it; most fell by the way, and James's fictions celebrate the failures more than those who succeeded. Poor Bernard Longmore was among the first who fell.

If Europe exists in James's imagination as a condition of the personal fulfilment which is life, it is a condition only, not life itself, and Europe is a treacherous guide. The narrator in James's early story, 'Four Meetings', says to the pathetic little teacher who longs to go to Europe, Caroline Spencer:

> 'You've the great American disease, and you've got it "bad"—the appetite, morbid and monstrous, for colour and form, for the picturesque and romantic at any price. I don't know whether we come into the world with it—with the germs implanted and antecedent to experience; rather perhaps we catch it early, almost before developed consciousness—we *feel*, as we look about, that we're going (to save our souls, or at least our senses) to be thrown back on it hard. We're like travellers in the desert—deprived of water and subject to the terrible mirage, the torment of illusion, of the thirst-fever. They hear the plash of fountains, they see green gardens and orchards that are hundreds of miles away. So we with *our* thirst—except that with us its *more* wonderful: we have before us the beautiful old things we've never seen at all, and when we do at last see them—if we're lucky!—we simply recognize them. What experience does is merely to confirm and consecrate our confident dream.'

Europe considered merely as the 'picturesque and romantic' is not reality but an illusion of reality; it is not life but a mirage of life. It can assist the inhibited American to break through the provincial and Puritan barriers which have excluded him from his own inner sphere of reality, it can open up to him the life of the senses and the world of imagination and colour, but much more frequently James's Americans do not know how to use the gifts and clues that Europe gives them towards that inner life which *no* tradition can give, but which each man must discover and cultivate in himself. James's novels and stories compose a full and tragic record of the many different ways in which his American pilgrims fail to reach the Celestial City. The young New England artist, Roderick Hudson, comes early in the tragic roster.

For Caroline Spencer, Europe was mainly the possibility of

romantic ruins and picturesque views. Because her essential conception of life was as two dimensional as a picture postcard's, there is little point in considering her 'case' here. But the handsome, appealing young Roderick was looking for life in a very different sense, and *Roderick Hudson* is one of James's most interesting early explorations of the theme. The thirst of the nineteenth-century American for life is admirably symbolized in the opening pages of the novel by Roderick's statuette, which Rowland Mallett admires so much:

> The statuette, in bronze, something more than two feet high, represented a naked youth drinking from a gourd. The attitude was perfectly simple. The lad was squarely planted on his feet, with his legs a little apart; his back was slightly hollowed, his head thrown back; his hands were raised to support the rustic cup. There was a loosened fillet of wild flowers about his head, and his eyes, under their dropped lids, looked straight into the cup. On the base was scratched the Greek word Δίψα, Thirst. The figure might have been some beautiful youth of ancient fable —Hylas or Narcissus, Paris or Endymion. Its beauty was the beauty of natural movement; nothing had been sought to be represented but the perfection of an attitude.

One can't help wondering if, down the years, this gourd doesn't a little relate, in the subconscious depths of James's imagination, to the golden bowl. But here, of course, the thing to recognize—as Rowland Mallett immediately does—is what an un-New England type this naked youth, in his beauty of natural movement, is. What he symbolizes relates to the values represented by the young couple in the French inn garden. The danger that often confronts James's characters is that, having been deprived for so long, they really can't be trusted with the cup when it finally comes into their hands. There is an exchange between Rowland and Roderick in Chapter II that is a warning for the wary reader, of danger ahead:

> 'Tell me this,' said Rowland. 'Did you mean anything very particular by your young Water-drinker? Does he represent an idea? Is he a pointed symbol?'
> Hudson raised his eyebrows and gently stroked his hair. 'Why, he's youth, you know; he's innocence, he's health, he's strength, he's curiosity. Yes, he's a lot of grand things.'
> 'And is the cup also a symbol?'

'The cup is knowledge, pleasure, experience. Anything of that kind.'

'Then he's drinking very deep,' said Rowland.

Hudson gave an approving nod. 'Well, poor wretch, you wouldn't have him die of thirst, would you?'

It is typical of Rowland Mallett that he would reach the conclusion all by himself that it was water in that gourd. At any rate, Roderick carries a thirst to Europe that can easily match his bronze boy's, and he is not prepared to satisfy it with water. Roderick represents the American who takes to Europe too readily, who loves it perhaps too much, and whose facility of assimilation is unleavened by judgement and experience. After a short interval Roderick feels that he has come to know and understand Europe, but James's point is that he hasn't. America has not provided him with the experience necessary for assimilating the experience of Europe on a level of emotional maturity. His death is, in fact, symbolic. He falls from the 'heights'—heights which, with his talents, he has been able to scale easily enough, but upon which he cannot maintain a secure footing. Roderick is as unable as Longmore in 'Madame de Mauves' to bring the two traditions significantly together. He behaves in a manner exactly opposite to Longmore's: he rejects the American or the New England tradition in favour of the European, but he is unable to become a part of that tradition simply because he, too, has the 'appetite, morbid and monstrous, for colour and form, for the picturesque and romantic at any price'. Desiring to drink deeply of life, he mistakes, in his innocence, the mirage of colour and plashing fountains for the reality itself.

James's queerest treatment of the American's thirst for 'life' which overreaches itself is his rather macabre little story, published in 1899, 'Europe'. In this story James imagines the cup to have been inordinately withheld, far beyond even Strether's long term of deprivation, with results that are grotesque, and perhaps a little monstrous. The story tells of three Boston spinsters, Rebecca, Maria, and Jane, the daughters of an ancient woman, Mrs. Rimmle, whose life span has been prodigious and whose future duration is unpredictable. The daughters long for Europe—long with the passionate intensity of the specially deprived—but they delay their journey until the

death of their mother will leave them free. James's story is not
explicit about the ages of these women, but we learn from an
entry in *The Notebooks*⁴ that the mother is approaching her
century, and that at least one of the daughters is seventy. The
selfish, ancient mother has detained them at home each time
they prepared for Europe by announcing her imminent death,
and keeping to her bed until the plans were abandoned and
the trip postponed. Miss Jane alone breaks free of this deadlock,
and accompanies an elderly, respectable couple, the Hathaways, on their trip to Europe. Poor Miss Jane's thirst for 'life'
seems greater than Roderick's in proportion as she is decades
and decades older—he, twenty-four or five; she, more or less
seventy. The subject, by its very nature, carries overtones of
the morally sinister and these are notes which James knows
how to strike with rare skill. In Florence, Miss Jane simply
refuses to return to America with the now shocked and dumb-
founded Hathaways. The narrator of the story is given the facts
in an exchange with his informant, who is an old acquaintance
of the Rimmles:

'Then she simply refused——'
'To budge from Florence? Simply. She had it out there with
the poor Hathaways, who felt responsible for her safety, pledged
to restore her to her mother's, to her sister's hands, and showed
herself in a light, they mention under their breath, that made their
dear old hair stand on end. Do you know what, when they first
got back, they said of her—at least it was *his* phrase, to two or
three people.'
I thought a moment. 'That she had "tasted blood"?'
My visitor fairly admired me. 'How clever of you to guess! It's
exactly what he did say. She appeared—she continues to appear,
it seems—in a new character.'
I wondered a little. 'But that's exactly—don't you remember?
—what Miss Maria reported to us from them; that we "wouldn't
know her." '
My sister-in-law perfectly remembered. 'Oh yes, she broke out
from the first. But when they left her she was worse.'
'Worse?'
'Well, different—different from anything she ever *had* been or
—for that matter—had had a chance to be.' My reporter hung fire
a moment, but presently faced me. 'Rather strange, and free and
obstreperous,'

'Obstreperous?' I wondered again.

It's a peculiarly suggestive and sinister word in this context. But there is more to come:

> My companion met my eyes a moment. 'You don't know the queerest part. I mean the way it has *most* brought her out.'
> I turned it over; I felt I should like to know—to that degree indeed that, oddly enough, I jocosely disguised my eagerness. 'You don't mean she has taken to drink?'
> My visitor had a dignity—and yet had to have a freedom. 'She has taken to flirting.'

The last we hear of Jane abroad is that: 'She's bent on the East.' The situation has its aspects of comedy, but it is very tragic and macabre comedy. The story is one of James's most bitter and annihilating comments on those American deprivations and starknesses which—it is James's deliberate point—constitute exclusion from life. It is a grim but essentially poetic treatment of the nineteenth century American's deep longing for the values of Europe (and to read the story properly we must understand what a complex life-symbol Europe had become for James), and of his ultimate, tragic exclusion. The two sisters who remain behind, Rebecca and Maria, represent the tragedy in its roundness, and the closing pages in which they figure most largely are the finest in the story. The whole action is played out on its small and highly formal stage under the fixed, dead gaze of the mother whose presence becomes a richly symbolic one in the context:

> Though wasted and shrunken she still occupied her high-backed chair with a visible theory of erectness, and her intensely aged face—combined with something dauntless that belonged to her very presence and that was effective even in this extremity—might have been that of some immemorial sovereign, of indistinguishable sex, brought forth to be shown to the people in disproof of the rumour of extinction.

The image of the Mother, usually a life-symbol, is used in this story as a symbol of life-in-death, even to the point of giving her an indistinguishable sex. The three aged sisters represent a scale of maladjustments to life, symbolized by Europe. There is Jane, whose deep thirst drives her to what we can only recognize as a deranged and drunken grab at life. She stands, in her odd, macabre way, for a large group of James's characters whose desire for life overreaches itself in the extremities of immaturity and inexperience. And Jane's great age only gives lurid point to the double charge. There is Rebecca, the most attractive of the old sisters, for whom the deprivation of life means literal death. Finally, there is Maria, who will stay on in the old house outside Boston to take her place, at last, as a symbol of life-in-death in her turn.

I hope that the rather brief discussion of several of James's stories will have indicated the way in which his treatment of the international theme is simultaneously a treatment of 'life'. James is the first great American novelist to have been consciously and explicitly concerned with 'life' in the way that D. H. Lawrence, for example, was concerned with it. But to say this is to point, paradoxically, to the impassable abyss that separates them. We are not so much faced with a radical difference between two sensibilities (though there is certainly that) as with a radical difference between two traditions. Lawrence 'treated' life; it was for him the native, natural subject matter, the raw material that was simply there. But in the abstract, intellectualizing, democratic, American tradition, filled with disembodied ideas and aspirations, and empty of the concrete, man-soiled evidences of a living humanity, the first problem was to say what life was. In such a tradition, it is hardly remarkable that the artist, like the theologian proving God's existence, arrived at his positive concept by saying what life was not. James's art is deeply concerned with life, but, confronted with such a problem, 'life' in his fictions often ends up with a negative look. Among the major characters in his work, where is there one to whom we can point as having realized 'life' in larger terms than those supplied by a more deeply sensitized consciousness of the possibilities and values of an experience from which he is usually excluded? Strether, who may be taken as James's ultimate portrayal of the American who has discovered life in Europe, discovers it only to make sure that he keeps nothing for himself. His discovery enables him only to renounce more largely, and on the level of practical living I do not see how his final plight is much better than Bernard Longmore's. James's finest female character (apart from little Maisie), Isabel Archer, relates to Strether in these respects. The fuller life she finds in Europe is a matter of refining her consciousness by an ordeal of fire. If, in the end, she registers more finely, she is left with nothing to register but a life of wretchedness and emotional frustration. The best that James's Americans can do for themselves is to look for a moment at the young artist and his sweetheart in the French inn yard, and deeply recognize that life lies *there*. It is the moment in the rose garden recollected through a life of democratic abstraction and Puritan deprivation.

But this must not be construed as criticism of James. It is only a recognition of the character of his particular problem. I do not like critics who attack James for having 'failed' to treat life, for being sensuously thin, or for not dealing, in more blatant terms, with sexual love. These are the people who mistake the smell of the manured field for the harvested crop. James's fictions are the record of men and women, bleakly deprived through their Puritan, democratic, and American traditions of much that constitutes life for the European artist, searching for means to satisfy their spiritual and emotional needs without sacrificing the good that they already possess, and which Europe cannot provide. It is a search for life, but it is a search in which, by the nature of the case, most are bound to fail. It was only a single couple, after all, that Hawthorne permitted to glimpse the Great Carbuncle, although many began the search. And even for that couple, the vision of the mystic jewel forced them to recognize that the reality they sought was in their own hearts. Europe is a symbol that acts in James's fictions rather like Hawthorne's Great Carbuncle. It shows everybody up for what they really are. In the end, those characters discover life who look for it in themselves, and in this sense Strether and Isabel find it. But this leaves us with a version of 'life' in James that will be almost as unsatisfactory to most people as Hawthorne's 'inner sphere of reality'.

This is not James's fault. Life does not exist in a vacuum. It may be 'the force that through the green fuse drives the flower', but there has to be a pre-existent pattern of petals for it to actualize, and through which its radiance can glow greenly as the animating impulse sustained through a protracted creative moment. Such conventions as the American tradition could claim tended towards abstraction and speculativeness. Their direction was democratic and levelling, or puritan and repressive. The life of the senses contributed almost nothing. Love between the sexes is handled with a good deal of embarrassment in such a tradition, and the great loves in American literature are between Ishmael and Queequeg, Natty and Chingachgook, Huck and Jim, even perhaps Gatsby and Nick Carraway. For the artist intent on 'treating life', as James was, the American scene yielded few places for its cultivation. When the American artist dealt with it successfully, it was in the primitive wilderness, on a raft in the middle of the Mississippi, or on a whaling boat in the Pacific, and it is difficult to imagine James at home in any of these places.

James had to find a theme which would make life accessible to 'treatment' in the American world that was inevitably his subject, and with the impoverished materials at hand his great theme became that of deprivation—deprivation of life. And in James the theme *is* a great one because he knew what life was, and what his characters were being deprived of. He not only measured exactly their terrible loss, he understood as well the conditions that foredoomed them to suffer—those native conditions through which James's deprived Americans relate to Hawthorne's excluded ones. But James is far greater than Hawthorne because he possessed a positive knowledge of, and a feeling for, life that eluded the older novelist, and that feeling and knowledge is implicit in what he writes. The situation produces a paradox that sometimes gets out of hand. If, in the midst of all this deprivation, James wishes to suggest life, he has to present it as the positive focus of predominantly negative forces. He has to point, at times unbelievably, to a victory of life over losses and deprivations that may impress the reader as insuperable. One doesn't have to be unduly cynical to ask sometimes if James really expects a phoenix to rise out of such ashes as he gives us. And sometimes a phoenix doesn't. 'A Round of Visits' (1910), and 'Crapy Cornelia' (1909), are two examples of such failures.

'A Round of Visits' is concerned with the subject of spiritual metamorphosis. Newton Winch, who had once been a vulgarian and a rowdy at college, is encountered some years later by a former classmate of his, Mark Monteith, who in the old days had made a point of giving the insensitive Winch a wide berth.

Monteith becomes aware almost immediately that during the interval some inexplicable process of refinement has occurred in Winch:

> These facts were as nothing, however, in presence of his quick and strong impression that this pale, nervous, smiling, clean-shaven host had undergone since their last meeting some extra-ordinary process of refinement. He had been ill, unmistakably, and the effects of a plunge into clean plain living, where any fineness had remained, were often startling, sometimes almost charming. But independently of this, and for a much longer time, some principle of intelligence, some art of life, would discernibly have worked in him. Remembered from college years and from those two or three luckless and faithless ones of the Law School as constitutionally common, as consistently and thereby doubt-lessly even rather powerfully coarse, clever only for uncouth and questionable things, he yet presented himself now as if he had suddenly and mysteriously been educated. There was a charm in his wide, 'drawn,' convalescent smile, in the way his fine fingers—had he anything like fine fingers of old?—played, and just fidgeted, over the prompt and perhaps a trifle incoherent offer of cigars, cordials, ash-trays, over the question of the visitor's hat, stick, fur coat, general best accommodation and ease; and how the deuce, accordingly, had charm, for coming out so on top, Mark won-dered, 'squared' the other elements? For the short interval so to have dealt with him what force had it turned on, what patented process, of the portentous New York order in which there were so many, had it skilfully applied?

A straightforward and natural reading of this story leaves us with the interesting and significant question of what had happened to Winch to make him so much more intensely alive, refined, and intelligent, than he had been once. It is possible to bring deviously subtle interpretations to one's reading of this story, but James's answer is categorical and blunt enough. Newton Winch has become a swindler and has been 'refined' by his dishonesty. Literature is filled with charming rogues whose shady vocations sometimes seem to be offered as a badge of life. It is the way of things that it should be Autolycus, the vital cut-purse, who sings, '. . . the red blood reigns in the winter's pale'. But it is surely a little unusual to have embezzle-ment recommended to us as 'an art of life' and 'a principle of intelligence' capable of performing the metamorphosis we are shown in Newton Winch. And yet this is essentially what James does. Larceny is the convention he uses here to reveal life. It leaves one asking if it is the result of simple perversity on James's part, or if the 'deprived condition' of James's Americans is really so great that he is forced to coax a victory of life out of such an unpromising situation.

'Crapy Cornelia' might be treated as one of James's economic stories, for it was written after his last trip to America when his deepest economic recognitions were made. The handsome and rich widow, Mrs. Worthingham, to whom the hero White-Mason considers proposing in a reckless moment, has acquired a well-oiled ease of manner and an imperturbable assurance along with her recent acquisition of wealth. She is the representative of the new moneyed New York as opposed to the old social New York (about both of which Edith Wharton knew more than Henry James ever did), and she is well done. As a negative symbol of his values and his sense of life, James handles her with great control. By a number of deft touches James causes Mrs. Worthingham to embody all the anti-values that spelled out sterility and desiccation for him in early twentieth century America. She stands, though a little more softly, for the world that Undine Spragg took by storm in Edith Wharton's superb novel, *The Custom of the Country*. By the indirections Mrs. Worthingham offers, the reader discovers the directions of James's values, and one wishes he had left it at that. But Cornelia Rasch, the 'Crapy' of the story's title, appears at Mrs. Worthingham's one day when White-Mason has called. She and White-Mason have known each other in 'the old days', but have not met for ten years. In the gilded opulence of Mrs. Wothingham's Louis Quinze drawing-room, the two mutually recognize themselves as 'conscious, ironic, pathetic survivors together of a dead and buried society'. It is when James endeavours to give us his positive values straight that the story breaks down. Crapy Cornelia is not a suitable figure to embody any vigorous conception or tradition of life, either present or remembered. Without meaning to do so, James leaves the question open in the sentimentalized picture he gives of her of how truthfully or significantly she ever represented the vanished world she mourns. White-Mason says to her:

'But we can't afford at this time of day not to help each other
to have had—well, everything there was, since there's no more of
it now, nor any way of coming by it *except so*; and therefore let us
make together, let us make over and recreate, our lost world; for
which we have after all and at the worst such a lot of material.
You were in particular my dear sisters' friend—they thought you
the funniest little brown thing possible; so isn't that again to the
good? You were mine only to the extent that you were so much in
and out of the house—as how much, if we come to that, wasn't
one in and out, south of Thirtieth Street and north of Washington
Square, in those days, those spacious, sociable, Arcadian days,
that we flattered ourselves we filled with the modern fever, but
that were so different from any of these arrangements of pre-
tended hourly Time that dash themselves forever to pieces as
from the fiftieth floor of skyscrapers.'

Crapy Cornelia is not sufficiently realized in this story to
enable her to carry those values of life and society James would
endow her with. At best she is a tenderly rendered Miss Prism.
One knows of course the values James was aiming at, and in
any case the reference to 'those spacious, sociable, Arcadian
days' provides the clue. It carries us back to Chapter III of
The Europeans in which Felix describes the home of the Went-
worths to his sister, the Baroness, when he returns to their
Boston hotel after his first visit with their American relatives:

'Is it handsome—is it elegant?' asked the Baroness.
Felix looked at her a moment, smiling. 'It's very clean. No
splendours, no gilding, no troops of servants; rather straight-
backed chairs. But you might eat off the floors, and you can
sit on the stairs.'
'That must be a privilege. And the inhabitants are straight-
backed too, of course.'
'My dear sister,' said Felix, 'the inhabitants are charming.'
'In what style?'
'In a style of their own. How shall I describe it. It's primitive;
it's patriarchal; it's the *ton* of the golden age.'
'And have they nothing golden but their *ton*? A plain, homely
way of life; nothing for show, and very little for—what shall I call
it?—for the senses; but a great *aisance*, and a lot of money, out of
sight, that comes forward very quietly for subscriptions to institutions, for repairing tenements, for paying doctor's bills; perhaps
even for portioning daughters.'

In *The Europeans* James is able to realize these American values in the novel he is writing; there is no question of his simply telling us about them. The sureness of this realization largely depends on his having the help, through the persons of Felix and his sister, the Baroness, of a set of essentially European conventions and attitudes with which to define American values, and give them life. In the passage just quoted, the strength and positiveness of the simple New England virtues are rendered for us by the implicit cynicism and the quite explicit sophistication of the Baroness's pointed questions to Felix. And the spontaneous appreciation and warmth of Felix's answers are essentially those of a foreigner. He brings a detachment and a perspective that one would scarcely find in a native. Finally, James arrives at his final statement through a true dialectical process in which the European and the American values supplement each other. Even the stiffly Bostonian father seems spiritually enlarged by his younger daughter's marriage to Felix.

It is not extraordinary that James should have named his early novel in which he so positively rendered the American values that represent life, *The Europeans*. Without his European visitors James would hardly have known how to transpose that life, with its *ton* of the golden age, significantly into his art. It was too disembodied, too much a thing of the mind and too little a thing of the senses, too stripped of manners and sophisticated conventions, to be reproduced convincingly without the help that the Baroness and her delightful brother could bring from abroad.

A comparison between 'Crapy Cornelia' and *The Europeans* indicates how necessary it was for James to approach his American values obliquely, by way of the European tradition, in terms of which his insights were deeper and shrewder, his point of view more richly suggestive. Without the help of that, we are left face to face with such embarrassing 'cases' as Crapy Cornelia and Newton Winch, and although James seems to have believed that they somehow embodied life, it is a conviction that he is unable to communicate in terms of his art. The two later stories suggest how thin the unadorned American tradition could be for the novelist of manners who, in a given instance, might wish to eschew the assistance of the Old World in trying to give us the values of the New.

X

Henry James and
the Economic Age

AMONG those tensions that constitute 'the new American experience' it is the tension between Europe and America that predominates and controls the development of James's fictions. But like Cooper, James was much concerned with the sources of wealth, and he became more so after his final trip to America. However, certain difficulties discourage a full-scale discussion of the kind that Cooper's novels so obviously invited. For James, the horror of the economic age consisted in the way it corrupted the quality of life, and made 'fineness of living' in the Jamesian sense, impossible. But James's unfavourable reaction to the situation in America was hardly a definite one before his trip in 1904–5. In so far as it existed at all in the earlier years, it remained a somewhat bewildered gesture of spiritual dissent. After his sojourn in America, he learned enough, for example, never to place as high an estimation on Adam Verver's American City as he had appeared to do in *The Golden Bowl*. James's response to the economic age, while as much one of rejection as Cooper's, is not, at first, nor for a long time to come, a reasoned attitude based on observation of men and knowledge of institutions. It is an instinctive reaction which is operative only part of the time, and in a partial manner. To isolate such an attitude in his work is, therefore, not a work of intellectual analysis, as it is in Cooper—a matter of dealing with very palpable knowledge and economic theory; it is, rather, a matter of understanding and evaluating the Jamesian sensibility, a matter specifically for the literary critic rather than for the historian of ideas. And there is still another reason for abridging discussion of this aspect of James, important as it is. There has been widespread recognition of the economic factor in James's work, and a fairly wide appreciation of the way in which the Jamesian conscience wrestled with the moral problem of the unearned income: or, to be more accurate—for it was by no means the 'unearned' quality that disturbed him—the wealth which represented the spoils of the

245

new wealthy class. Most of the essential points have been made by others, and the most we can do is thread our way among their critical observations towards the little new that remains to be said.[1]

The fact to seize in the beginning about James's attitude to wealth is its contradictory nature, and here it resembles Cooper's rather closely. The life that James admired could only be supported by a large income: yet from where, in the economic world, could such an income innocently flow? He was as hard pressed to find an uncontaminated source as Cooper had been in the Littlepage novels. But if James grew to distrust the moneyed class, he looked for no infusion of virtue from the lower order. In 1886, the year in which he published *The Princess Casamassima*, he wrote to Charles Eliot Norton from Milan: 'I ought to have plenty of London news for you—but somehow I feel as if I had not brought it to Italy with me. Much of it, in these days, is such as there must be little profit in carrying about with one. The subject of the moment, as I came away, was the hideous —— divorce case, which will besmirch exceedingly the already very damaged prestige of the English upper class. . . . In England the Huns and Vandals will have to come *up*—from the black depths of the (in the people) enormous misery, though I don't think the Attila is quite yet found. . . . '[2] But if the upper class were hopelessly corrupt, it yet retained, and of necessity must, possession of all that James counted good in existence. It is this scale of values, so dependent on the leisure and luxuries that money can buy, that is often misunderstood when a case is stated against James. Essentially, the cultivated and leisured existence that recommended itself to him as an embodiment of the good life is intimately related to John Adams's realistic view of society, expressed in such a passage as: 'The great question will forever remain, who shall work? . . . Leisure for study must ever be the portion of the few.'[3] It is even closer to Cooper's: 'One man must labour, while another may live luxuriously on his means; one has leisure and opportunity to cultivate his tastes, to increase his information, and to reform his habits, while another is compelled to toil, that he may live. One is reduced to serve, while another commands, and, of course, there can be no equality in their social conditions.'[4] But Adams and Cooper were political theorists, and James was not. If one were to attempt a basic formulation of James's economic attitudes, they would prove to be practically identical with those of his distinguished predecessors; but such attitudes, incorporated in the novel of manners, may create a somewhat different effect from what they produce in a political or economic treatise. And even in Cooper's case, his arguments for a cultivated leisure class, so convincing in *The American Democrat*, appear distressingly illiberal when dramatized in the Effingham novels. It is because of this difficulty of keeping the inflection of theory perfectly under control when transposed to the level of fiction that a certain type of critic has misunderstood and condemned James's social attitudes in the past, when, in fact, they are in one of the great traditions of American thought. What James seeks is a state of civilization in which the finest faculties of the individual shall be given the maximum opportunity for development. But the wicked paradox that inevitably confronts such disinterestedness was bound, sooner or later, to confront James. Such a civilization, whose rarest product is the individual expressing himself at the highest pitch of his powers, can only be achieved and sustained at a more or less oppressive cost to the many. This is one of the first lessons of history, and it is the most bitter for a nation which talks more and more about the rise of the common man. But a choice between the minority and the many is inescapable.

For the intelligent democrat, whose integrity is matched by the refinement of his sensibility, this question is one of the most perplexing and difficult that life offers; and in the end there will be no answer, at least in the neatly trimmed and slickly packaged manner so favoured today. But James had an answer that, for the artist, was sufficient enough, and I think we come upon it, most at its ease and at its very best, in his beautiful Preface to *The Princess Casamassima*. James had an advantage over Hawthorne in that he found a warm and intimate welcome in English society. James was much aware of these advantages, and there is a certain feeling (or so one senses it) of democratic guilt when he comes to speak of how those advantages he had enjoyed might for another, his equal in all but economic privilege, he forever withheld:

> I arrived so at the history of little Hyacinth Robinson—he sprang up for me out of the London pavement. To find his

possible adventure interesting I had only to conceive his watching the same public show, and of his watching very much as I had watched; save indeed for one little difference. This difference would be that so far as all the swarming facts should speak of freedom and ease, knowledge and power, money, opportunity, satiety, he should be able to revolve round them but at the most respectful of distances and with every door of approach shut in his face. For one's self, all conveniently, there had been doors that opened—opened into light and warmth and cheer, into good and charming relations; and if the place as a whole lay heavy on one's consciousness there was yet always for relief this implication of one's own lucky share of the freedom and ease, lucky acquaintance with the number of lurking springs at light pressure of which particular vistas would begin to recede, great lighted, furnished, peopled galleries, sending forth gusts of agreeable sound.

That main happy sense of the picture was always there and that retreat from the general grimness never forbidden; whereby one's own relation to the mere formidable mass and weight of things was eased off and adjusted. One learned from an early period what it might be to know London in such a way as that—an immense and interesting discipline, an education on terms mostly convenient and delightful. But what would be the effect of the other way, of having so many precious things perpetually in one's eyes, yet of missing them all for any closer knowledge, and of the confinement of closer knowledge entirely to matters with which a connexion, however intimate, couldn't possibly pass for a privilege? Truly, of course, there are London mysteries (dense categories of dark arcana) for every spectator, and it's in a degree an exclusion and a state of weakness to be without experience of the meaner conditions, the lower manners and types, the general sordid struggle, the weight of the burden of labour, the ignorance, the misery and the vice. With such matters as these my tormented young man would have had contact—they would have formed, fundamentally, from the first, his natural and immediate London. But the reward of a romantic curiosity would be the question of what the total assault, that of the world of his work-a-day life and the world of his divination and his envy together, would have made of him, and what in especial he would have made of them. As tormented, I say, I thought of him, and that would be the point—if one could only see him feel enough to be interesting without his feeling so much as not to be natural.

This in fact I have ever found rather terribly the point—that the figures in any picture, the agents in any drama, are interesting only in proportion as they feel their respective situations; since the consciousness, on their part, of the complication exhibited forms for us their link of connection with it. But there are degrees of feeling—the muffled, the faint, the just sufficient, the barely intelligent, as we may say; and the acute, the intense, the complete, in a word—the power to be finely aware and richly responsible. It is those moved in this latter fashion who 'get most' out of all that happens to them and who in so doing enable us, as readers of their record, as participators by a fond attention, also to get most. Their being finely aware—as Hamlet and Lear, say, are finely aware—*makes* absolutely the intensity of their adventure, gives the maximum of sense to what befalls them. We care, our curiosity and our sympathy care, comparatively little for what happens to the stupid, the coarse and the blind; care for it, and for the effects of it, at the most as helping to precipitate what happens to the more deeply wondering, to the really sentient. Hamlet and Lear are surrounded, amid their complications, by the stupid and the blind, who minister in all sorts of ways to their recorded fate. Persons of markedly limited sense would, on such a principle as that, play a part in the career of my tormented youth; but he wouldn't be of markedly limited sense himself—he would note as many things and vibrate to as many occasions as I might venture to make him.[5]

This is a long quotation, but it is an enlightening one to study if we wish to know where James looked for his answer to the question of economic inequality. Lionel Trilling has pointed out that, to some degree, James identified himself with Hyacinth Robinson.[6] From the economic point of view this is important, for James is trying to imagine himself, not as the welcomed and pampered young American who was received so cordially into English society, but as one of the economically underprivileged and excluded. Tragic as such exclusion is, and as it proves to be very practically for Hyacinth Robinson, these terrible disadvantages are, in a sense, undercut by the possession, on the part of the protagonist, of those most formidable of Jamesian virtues, 'the power to be finely aware and richly responsible'. And it is no doubt significant that in this passage, dealing with the evolution of Hyacinth's character in James's imagination, the comparison he almost instinctively makes is with Lear and Hamlet. It is worthy of the American democrat at his best that he should see nothing incongruous in placing the poor little

Londoner bookbinder on a tragic equality with a King and a Prince.

If, for James, wealth and leisure were the medium in which the human faculties were refined, the medium could as readily prove the destructive element if the wrong sensibilities were immersed in it. James is the greatest master in the language when he describes the spiritual squalor of the vulgar and stupid rich. The charges of snobbishness that are brought against him[7] boil down to some such elementary proposition as this: he imagined that, other things being equal, a man or woman might achieve a more sensitive degree of awareness, a finer quality of mind and heart, if he lived among people and surroundings of taste than if he lived on a chicken farm in South Dakota or in a cold water flat on Rutgers Street.

The wealth which alone could guarantee such advantages had to be uncontaminated; but this was a recognition that James was too unfamiliar with contemporary conditions in America to make until after his visit in 1904–5. One of the first passages in his writings in which we have positive evidence of this recognition occurs in *The American Scene* in which he describes a visit to New York's lower East Side:

> One can speak only of what one has seen, and there were grosser elements of the sordid and the squalid that I doubtless never saw. That, with a good deal of observation and of curiosity, I should have failed of this, the country over, affected me as by itself something of an indication. To miss that part of the spectacle, or to know it only by its having so unfamiliar a pitch, was an indication that made up for a good many others. It is when this one in particular is forced home to you—this immense, vivid *general* life of poverty and general appreciation of the living unit's paying property in himself—that the picture seems most to clear and the way to jubilation most to open. For it meets you there, at every turn, as the result most definitely attested. You are as constantly reminded, no doubt, that these rises in enjoyed value shrink and dwindle under the icy breath of Trusts and the weight of the new remorseless monopolies that operate as no madnesses of ancient power thrilling us on the historic page ever operated; the living unit's property in himself becoming more and more merely such a property as may consist with a relation to properties overwhelmingly greater and that allow the asking of no questions and the making, for co-existence with them, of no conditions.

But that, in the fortunate phrase, is another story, and will be altogether, evidently, a new and different drama. There is such a thing, in the United States, it is hence to be inferred, as freedom to grow up to be blighted, and it may be the only freedom in store for the smaller fry of future generations. If it is accordingly of the smaller fry I speak, and of how large they massed on that evening of endless admonitions, this will be because I caught them thus in their comparative humility and at an early stage of their American growth. The life-thread has, I suppose, to be of a certain thickness for the great shears of Fate to feel for it. Put it, at the worst, that the Ogres were to devour them, they were but the more certainly to fatten into food for the Ogres.[8]

There is a well-known passage, also from *The American Scene*, in which James, remembering the Newport of his youth, filled with a group of the wealthy 'who confessed brazenly to not being in business', evokes for the imagination a picture of that economically privileged class whom he fondly liked to believe embodied, or had once embodied, those finer awarenesses and decencies that, for him, constituted civilization:

> Do I grossly exaggerate in saying that this company, candidly, quite excitedly self-conscious, as all companies not commercial, in America, may be pleasantly noted as being, formed, for the time of its persistence, an almost unprecedented small body—unprecedented in American conditions; a collection of the detached, the slightly disenchanted and casually disqualified, and yet of the resigned and contented, of the socially orthodox: a handful of mild, oh delightfully mild, cosmopolites, united by three common circumstances, that of their having for the most part more or less lived in Europe, that of their sacrificing openly to the ivory idol whose name is leisure, and that, not least, of a formed critical habit.[9]

But these had been an anomaly, even in the past, and by the time James wrote *The American Scene* he recognized that the Ogres of the Trusts and 'the new remorseless monopolies' had taken over. As he walked through the streets of the lower East Side, he recognized that the false prosperity of the poor he saw everywhere around him was the prosperity of the barnyard in which animals are fattened only to be slaughtered. The violence of James's image is softened by its elaborate, measured periods, but it is not the less, for that, indicative of the depth of his perception and the intensity of his reaction. When, addressing himself to the new American capitalists who had prospered so greatly in his long absence, he used the word 'Ogres', he meant it passionately.

The Jolly Corner, published in 1908, three years after he returned to England, is one of James's best 'economic' stories, and as an insight into his mind on this particular subject it may claim close attention. It tells the story of how Spencer Brydon, having left New York thirty-three years before, when in his early twenties, returns from Europe to oversee the remodelling of his two modest New York properties, on the rentals from which he has managed to live comfortably abroad during this long interval. One of these houses is the rather elegant and refined old house on the jolly corner, as he called it—'the one in which he had first seen the light, in which various members of his family had lived and had died, in which the holidays of his overschooled boyhood had been passed and the few social flowers of his chilled adolescence gathered, and which, alienated then for so long a period, had through the successive deaths of his two brothers, and the termination of old arrangements, come wholly into his hands'. Although the property is so comparatively small, the values other than financial which attach to it recall, on a minor scale, those which Cooper described in the Littlepage trilogy. But while cherishing his affection for the house on the jolly corner, and the values it represents, Brydon discovers, while overseeing the conversion of his other property into flats, an unexpected capacity for business in himself. As his old New York friend, Alice Staverton, puts it: 'If he had but stayed at home he would have anticipated the inventor of the skyscraper. If he had but stayed at home he would have discovered his genius in time really to start some new variety of awful architectural hare and run it till it burrowed in a gold mine.' It is this remark that is instrumental in starting a trend of thought in Brydon. As time goes on, he becomes consumed with a passionate curiosity to know what he would have been like if, instead of going to Europe against his father's wishes at twenty-three, he had stayed in New York and played his role in the American financial world. 'It comes over me,' he says to Alice Staverton while recalling his youth, 'that I had then a strange *alter ego* deep down somewhere within me, as the fullblown flower is in the small tight bud, and that I just took the course, I just transferred him to the climate, that blighted him for once and for ever.'

He develops, as the months pass, a curious habit of walking at night, by himself, through the deserted rooms in the old house: 'He knew what he meant and what he wanted; it was as clear as the figure on a cheque presented in demand for cash. His *alter ego* "walked"—that was the note of his image of him, while his image of his motive for his own pastime was the desire to waylay and meet him.' *The Jolly Corner* is, in fact, James's most impressive 'ghost' story, after *The Turn of the Screw*—if it is not too delimiting to designate it so. The actual encounter scene between Brydon and his *alter ego* in the grey light of early morning as the sinister figure stands, in full evening dress, at the foot of the staircase, is a splendid achievement. Confronted with that countenance, Brydon stares into his own face as it would have been had he not spent those thirty-three years in Europe:

> Horror, with the sight, had leaped into Brydon's throat, gasping there in a sound he couldn't utter; for the bared identity was too hideous as *his*, and his glare was the passion of his protest. The face, *that* face, Spencer Brydon's?—he searched it still, but looking away from it in dismay and denial. . . . It was unknown, inconceivable, awful, disconnected with any possibility——

This story is consummately done, and if it is not regularly grouped with James's masterpieces, it is because its meaning is not always apprehended in a perspective of sufficient depth. Coming as it does so soon after such 'pro-American' novels as *The Golden Bowl* and *The Wings of the Dove*, it appears to present an inexplicable reversal of values. To all appearances it is a profoundly anti-American story. But between *The Golden Bowl* and *The Jolly Corner* James's trip to America had intervened, and he had returned to England with a new awareness of the sinister side of the economic age. Spencer Brydon's *alter ego* is the symbol of that age in America, and for sheer intensity of loathing, it outstrips anything that had ever been within Cooper's range. But it may be unfair to say that *The Jolly Corner* is anti-American. Brydon is, after all, an American, and he remains uncontaminated, although it is Europe that has saved both him and his values. A significant note of those values has been, of course, that his income is derived from leases on New York property, and has nothing to do with commerce or Wall Street. James is quite as explicit about it as Cooper had been in the Littlepage trilogy. Brydon's *alter ego* has 'a million a year', but Brydon himself is saved precisely because he is comparatively poor. That is to say, he has enough to live, as James was to put it in his Notes to *The Ivory Tower*, 'in a quiet "European" way and on an income of an extreme New York deplorability'.

The values of Brydon as well as the economic background which alone was capable of explaining the horror of his *alter ego*, were to have been painted on a full-scale canvas in *The Ivory Tower*, which James never finished. The two old millionaire financiers, Abel Gaw and Frank Betterman, embody James's new vision of the American man of great wealth. To some extent they correct the mildness in Adam Verver's portrait of several years before. The values embodied in Spencer Brydon are recast, in a much younger actor, in Mr. Betterman's European-bred nephew, Graham Fielder, who returns to America to visit his dying uncle. In a similar manner, but on a larger stage, James planned to have Fielder also preserve his values, apparently at the cost of his income, so superfluously, so scandalously enlarged by the fact of his being his uncle's heir.

As the recipient of a vast fortune whose source is tainted, a moral problem of unusual complexity confronts Fielder. The problem is so difficult, in fact, that when Horton Vint, the young man to whom Fielder has entrusted the management of his inheritance, is discovered to be swindling him, he appears almost in the light of a 'solution'. 'The beauty', as James says in the Notes, 'is in the complexity of the question—which, stated in the simplest terms possible, reduces itself to Horton's practically saying to Gray [Fielder], or seeing himself saying to Gray should it come to the absolute touch:

"'You *mind*, in your extraordinary way, how this money was accumulated, and hanky-pankied, you suffer, and cultivate a suffering, from the perpetrated wrong of which you feel it the embodied evidence, and with which the possession of it is thereby poisoned for you. But I don't mind one little scrap—and there is a great deal more to be said than you seem so much as able to understand, or so much as able to want to, about the whole question of how money comes to those who know *how* to make it.'"

I remarked in the opening of this chapter that whereas Cooper was interested in the tensions of the American experience for their own sakes, and as they affected America, James was interested in them only as they affected the moral quality of men, not primarily as citizens, but as individual human beings. *The Ivory Tower* is an example of this. James was concerned with essentially the same impersonal economic problems that had concerned Cooper in those novels of his we have considered; the effect of great concentrations of wealth, more or less illegitimately acquired. But in James the final interest was focused on the consequences to the individual, not on the consequences to the political institutions or the character of the country at large. Towards such an end, James was intent on creating Fielder in a radically different pattern than any offered by contemporary America. He seems to hearken back to that delightful and unprecedented little group whom James nostalgically recalled when describing the Newport of the past. 'I have always', wrote James in the Notes, 'wanted to do an out-and-out non-producer, in the ordinary sense of non-accumulator of material gain. . . . ' It is perhaps difficult for a casual reader of James to appreciate fully the degree to which such a remark, so far from being an expression of social frivolity, is the register of a finely aware social conscience, too morally sensitive to accept, with the national complacency, those sinister economic possibilities into which the American 'promise' had degenerated —*had been* degenerating, in fact, ever since the early days of the Republic. The whole point of *The Ivory Tower* was to be the admirable, and wholly untypical way in which Graham Fielder would refuse to harmonize, in his sharper fineness and purer colour, with the background of tainted American gold:

> . . . I have felt my instinct to make him definitely and frankly as complete a case as possible of the sort of thing that will make him an anomaly and an outsider alike in the New York world of business, the N.Y. world of ferocious acquisition, and the world there of enormities of expenditure and extravagance, so that the real suppression for him of anything that shall count in the American air as a money-making, or even as a wage-earning,

or as a pecuniarily picking-up character, strikes me as wanted
for my emphasis of his entire difference of sensibility and of
association.

For James, the economic age was simply and merely monstrous, the age of the capitalistic Ogres of gold, and one had
one's salvation only in complete dissociation from all its ways,
and all its rewards. And dissociation implied a 'European'
moderation, a quietness and a scale as far removed as possible
from 'all the intensest modernity of every American description'. But James formulated the attitude I have described here
rather late in life, after the 1904–5 visit to America. Before that,
but still late enough to have entered into the novels of the so-
called 'major phase', the idea of American wealth, contemplated
from the safe and purifying distance of England, carried an
aura of New World glory. It symbolized those possibilities of
American life which evoked that narcotic phrase, the American
Dream. And where, in the economic age, could the American
hope to realize the dream save in 'ferocious acquisition' and
grotesque accumulation? The American millionaire to the
James of an earlier period had been symbolic of spiritual values.
He was Christopher Newman proving his moral superiority to
the decadent French aristocracy: he was Adam Verver virtu-
ously buying up the European past for transportation to a
purer air; or, with a change of sex, he was that remarkable
American heiress, Milly Theale, with the kingdoms of the earth
at her feet. What those kingdoms of the earth, under the
domination of American millionaires, would amount to, was the
shocked discovery of James's later years.

It is hardly too much to say that James's economic attitudes
are an expression, at the beginning of the twentieth century,
of the same basic economic conflict we have seen in America
at the beginning of the nineteenth, but existing now at an
advanced, and rather hopeless, stage. I am a little shy of a conclusion that will no doubt seem more irresistible to me than to
anyone else, but as Graham Fielder is an expression of James's
own economic attitudes, those attitudes, when we consider the
vastly changed conditions under which they are compelled to
express themselves today, seem to claim a continuity with the
regal republicanism of John Adams. And where, but from such
an emphatic (though remote) historical antecedent as Hamil-

ton, should old Abel Gaw and Frank Betterman have derived their unmistakably national colouring?

The role that economic considerations play in the development of James's work is important, but it is not always the same role. This, however, can be said of it in any period of his career: as the end of Jamesian art is the development of a consciousness that will be 'finely aware and richly responsible', this awareness and responsibility, as one of its conditions, must develop or sustain itself through the most delicate adjustments to that wealth which alone supports the medium of cultivated leisure that is the very element of life for the valued, sought-for consciousness. During the greater part of his career James had a tendency to *assume* that the wealth he so copiously provided for his more finely registering characters *was* uncontaminated. The ease with which he made the assumption, so far from being a snobbish withdrawal from his American past, was a measure of how generously, and how long, he read—in his European remoteness—economic innocence into American motives. When he discovered the facts were other than he had imagined, the economic problem was placed in a more complicated perspective, and it held, in its own identity, the very centre of the stage. But there was no contradiction, even implicit, in this reshifting of precedences. His values, from first to last, were the same.

The Ivory Tower is not finished. That, of course, was because of the interruption of the War; but even had that not occurred, one wonders, as one reads the Notes, how satisfactory the 'solution' offered in Graham Fielder's greater 'fineness' would really have been. At best, it is hardly of weight sufficient to balance, artistically, the terrible world of gold and ruthless competition that had been opened for James. In *The Jolly Corner*, Spencer Brydon, confronted by that ghastly symbol of the economic age that stood waiting at the foot of the stair, had given ground and fainted as the fearful figure had 'advanced as for aggression'. To fall back, to faint—preserving, it need hardly be added, one's values intact—does very well for a short story. But on the full field of a 'major' novel larger strategies are required. The passively resistant stance of Graham Fielder before an 'advance' so markedly *more* threatening, strikes one as likely to offer too little, in the way of formal balance, to offset the mere blatant mass arrayed against him.

I

The Ivory Tower is the last of James's works that calls for attention here. What these works have shown us is James's transition from a conception of the millionaire as a symbolic embodiment of those New World possibilities that sometimes go under the name of the American Dream, to the wistful figure of the 'good' American, preserving his 'fineness', finding salvation, in the rejection of his millions. James's work comes to an end at this point, leaving us with the feeling that much, along these lines, remained to be done.

XI

Scott Fitzgerald and the Collapse
of the American Dream

I

To say that Scott Fitzgerald's stories are uneven is not to say that he has not written some of the greatest ones in American literature. 'The Diamond as Big as the Ritz' is a story of very genuine originality, and I can think of no classic American writer with whose work to associate it with the possible exception of Hawthorne in some of his short stories. There are aspects of it that make one think of 'My Kinsman, Major Molineux'. Hawthorne's story gives us a dramatic parable of how the English and the New World traditions coalesce in the young hero, Robin, under the impact of the American Revolution, to produce a new type—the first American. It seems to me indubitably the greatest of Hawthorne's stories. I did not discuss it in the relevant chapter here because Q. D. Leavis's essay, to which I have already referred on several occasions, rescued the story from the oblivion into which critics had allowed it to fall, and gave it definitive treatment. The hero of Scott Fitzgerald's story, John T. Unger, enacts the parable of the young American who awakes from the American Dream. To suggest a tentative alignment with 'My Kinsman, Major Molineux', may be more misleading than useful in the end, however. The subject-matter of the two stories distantly relate, but there are important differences. Hawthorne's subject-matter is far more complicated in its political and historical ramifications; his theme is positive, and it is the greatest specifically American theme that a writer could discover. Hawthorne's mastery of it is so great that I am not sure that I wouldn't prefer doing without *The Scarlet Letter* to doing without 'My Kinsman, Major Molineux'. Moreover, Hawthorne has been able to confer a dimension of tragic greatness on Robin and Major Molineux which is no part of Fitzgerald's intention here, although it becomes so in *The Great Gatsby*. As the title of 'The Diamond as Big as the Ritz' suggests, it is in the tradition of the Western tall tale, and its Montana

setting underlines this; but this is important only as supplying a
traditional mould for a meaning and a seriousness that far
exceed anything the genre had ever held before. There is a story
called 'Absolution' which Scott Fitzgerald said that he had
originally meant to form a kind of introductory piece for *The
Great Gatsby*. Fortunately he saw in time the delimiting effect
the story would have if it were to be appended to his novel, and
he abstained. However, 'The Diamond as Big as the Ritz' is,
from one point of view, an excellent introduction to *Gatsby*,
and I should like to treat it so here, even though Fitzgerald
didn't intend it. It will help to clarify the nature and the extent
of Scott Fitzgerald's critical approach to the American experience, which is sometimes not admitted even though it is the
first, the most obvious thing, that one ought to take from his art.

But before considering 'The Diamond as Big as the Ritz' in
detail, I should like to digress for a few pages and consider Scott
Fitzgerald's work in general, and how it stands in relation to
the work of the other American novelists I have treated. More
than with any other writer in the American tradition, Scott
Fitzgerald's novels have been based on a concept of class. In
this respect he far exceeds James whose characters, if they
belong to an upper class, belong to one which is, as we have
seen, strangely disembodied, and not really related to any
economic structure at all—at least until his late years. Even
then, the recognition was one of pained, shrinking, and rather
superficial acknowledgement. The class role of Fitzgerald's
characters is possible because he instinctively realized the part
that money played in creating and supporting a way of life
focused in the Ivy League universities, country clubs, trips to
the Riviera, and the homes of the wealthy. He is the first
American writer who seems to have discovered that such a
thing as American class *really* existed—American class as an
endemic growth, to be distinguished from James's delightfully
mild Newport cosmopolities, united in the common circumstance of their having more or less lived in Europe. Fitzgerald
was enabled to make this discovery because he was almost
preternaturally aware of the reality that gold lent to the play
of appearances he loved so much. Because he immersed himself
so completely in this play of appearances—in swank parties,
jazz tunes, alcohol, and coloured lights—many have questioned

the fineness and the discrimination of his intelligence. But what he immersed himself in *was* the America of his time (and almost as much, perhaps, of ours), and just because he was as intelligent as any of the novelists treated here, he ended by making an evaluation of the life and wealth he seemed to love that was deeper, more richly informed, and at least as sensitive, as any ever made by James. The charge that Fitzgerald was 'taken in' by wealth is as irritating as it is untrue. There is a radical difference between coveting a 'tony' life that can only be supported by money—lots of money—and being critically and morally unable to assess the conditions under which the money must be acquired or its ultimate effects on character. As an artist, Scott Fitzgerald knew the worst there was to know about all these things, and he knew it with an inwardness and a profoundness. One admires James's instinctive recoil in the presence of the American economic age which the Republicans had fostered so neatly, but when one reads Scott Fitzgerald's treatment of it one is greatly relieved that he had found, in his better informed state, a more effective way of dealing with it than by Spencer Brydon's fainting fit.

I said that Scott Fitzgerald was the first of the great American writers to have found that a 'treatable' class, with its accompanying manners, really did exist in America—to have found it sufficiently, at any rate, to have been able to create characters who are representative of a socially solid and defined group rather than symbolic embodiments of the ultimate American solitude, or two-dimensional figures in the American morality play. As I shall point out later, Gatsby is an exception to this. He is a mythic embodiment in the great American tradition of Natty Bumppo and Huck Finn and Ishmael; but Fitzgerald's stories are populated by a type of rich or popular young man who, in a way that never really had happened in American literature before, carries a weight of representativeness. His manners, attitudes, and ideals, are shared by a large and important group, and have the admiring support of the influential members of the older generation. One may not like the group; its civilization may be a far cry from what one finds in Jane Austen's class structure (perhaps not if one looks into the fortunes of the great Whig peers who stood at the top of that structure), but one has to admit its existence, and its demands for 'treatment'. As the class had its origins in wealth, as its manners and way of life were nourished by gold, it was Fitzgerald's sense of, his feeling for, money, that enabled him not only to appreciate the surfaces, but to penetrate to the heart of the structure. But if that had been all it would certainly not have been enough. If Scott Fitzgerald loved wealth he was not taken in by it, and some of his gaudiest celebrations of it are simultaneously the most annihilating criticisms. And Scott Fitzgerald's rich young men *are* representative; they are representative in a way that Biron, Longaville, and Dumain were representative of the rich young men of Shakespeare's day; they are representative in a way that Hemingway's unpleasant tough young men are not. They may sometimes be a little silly or undiscriminating, but transposed to the level of actual living, they are no sillier than Bernard Longmore or White-Mason (who was, after all, forty-eight years old); and as for Roderick Hudson, he would certainly have preferred their company to Rowland Mallett's. To this extent at least, Scott Fitzgerald had begun to break through the abstracting and inhibiting American tradition, and this may have been one of the things that T. S. Eliot was thinking of when he wrote to Fitzgerald that he had taken the first important step in the American novel since James.

But to return to 'The Diamond as Big as the Ritz', this story is one in which Fitzgerald's attitude to wealth as a constituent part of the American dream is most clearly revealed. John T. Unger, the very young hero—just sixteen—is enrolled at St. Midas' School, half an hour from Boston, 'the most expensive and the most exclusive boys' preparatory school in the world'. But John T. Unger comes from Hades on the Mississippi, where his father 'held the amateur golf championship' and his mother played at politics. Although the story is fantasy, the overstatement given the native background is maintained at exactly the right pitch. It never balloons too high to miss the authentic note. At school John forms a friendship with an aloof and uncommunicative boy who asks John to spend the summer vacation with him at his home 'in the West'. John accepts, and during the long train trip into a remote part of Montana the dream quality that has been present from the first is intensified. The form of the story just a little resembles *Through the Looking-*

Glass. We don't quite know when the dream begins, but we are there for the awakening on the last page:

> 'It *was* a dream,' said John quietly. 'Everybody's youth is a dream, a form of chemical madness.'

But certainly the dream has begun by the opening of Part II when the Transcontinental Express stops at the forlorn village of Fish:

> The Montana sunset lay between two mountains like a gigantic bruise from which dark arteries spread themselves over a poisoned sky. An immense distance under the sky crouched the village of Fish, minute, dismal, and forgotten. There were twelve men, so it was said, in the village of Fish, twelve sombre and inexplicable souls who sucked a lean milk from the almost literally bare rock upon which a mysterious populatory force had begotten them. They had become a race apart, these twelve men of Fish, like some species developed by an early whim of nature, which on second thought had abandoned them to struggle and extermination.
>
> Out of the blue-black bruise in the distance crept a long line of moving lights upon the desolation of the land, and the twelve men of Fish gathered like ghosts at the shanty depot to watch the passing of the seven o'clock train, the Transcontinental Express from Chicago. Six times or so a year the Transcontinental Express, through some inconceivable jurisdiction, stopped at the village of Fish, and when this occurred a figure or so would disembark, mount into a buggy that always appeared from out of the dusk, and drive off toward the bruised sunset. The observation of this pointless and preposterous phenomenon had become a sort of cult among the men of Fish. To observe, that was all; there remained in them none of the vital quality of illusion which would make them wonder or speculate, else a religion might have grown up around these mysterious visitations. But the men of Fish were beyond all religion—the barest and most savage tenets of even Christianity could gain no foothold on that barren rock—so there was no altar, no priest, no sacrifice; only each night at seven the silent concourse by the shanty depot, a congregation who lifted up a prayer of dim, anaemic wonder.

These two paragraphs are strangely impressive, not only because they create the atmosphere of dream, but because the twelve men of Fish seem, in their shadowy way, to embody meanings that, as in a dream, are both insistent and elusive.

The Christian implications of the fish symbol are certainly intended by Fitzgerald, and these are enforced by the twelve solitary men who are apostles 'beyond all religion'. These grotesque and distorted Christian connotations are strengthened by their dream-like relation to Hades on the Mississippi where John was born. What we are given in these paragraphs is a queerly restless and troubled sense of a religion that is sick and expressing itself in disjointed images and associations, as if it were delirious. The landscape imagery helps build up this atmosphere. The religious imagery in these paragraphs is emphatic, but it stands here for spiritual desiccation, for the absence of any religion at all—even for the absence of the possibility of any religion. 'There was no altar, no priest, no sacrifice.' But even for the twelve spiritually dead Americans of Fish, a persistent capacity for wonder still survives, and the observation carries us to the great concluding page of *Gatsby* in which Nick Carraway thinks of those early Dutch sailors who must have held their breath in the presence of this continent, 'face to face for the last time in history with something commensurate to their capacity for wonder'. But no commensurate objects survive in the American world, for the American dream could feed only on material, and therefore exhaustible, possibilities. It was, as Scott Fitzgerald (a former Catholic who was never wholly at ease in his separation) very well knew, incompatible with any form of Christianity. The implicit contrast between the eternal promises of the old religion and the material promises of the American dream that had so largely taken the place of any orthodoxy in America provided the most dramatic and sinister note for Fitzgerald to strike as Percy and John descended from the Transcontinental Express at the forlorn, symbolic village of Fish.

What we have to bear in mind is that this story is an attack on that American dream which critics have so often imagined Fitzgerald was engaged in celebrating throughout his writings. The fevered religious imagery of the passage I have quoted presents it, in the very beginning, as a kind of gaudy substitute for a sterile orthodoxy whose promises cannot compete with the infinite material possibilities that the dream seems to hold out to the faithful Americans. This initial religious note indicates how deeply Fitzgerald understood the American tradition of which he was so profoundly a part. But having sounded it once, he moves on through the rest of the story to analyse those material possibilities on the secular level at which Americans have believed Heaven to be attainable. Before considering the story farther I should like to pause for a moment's reflection on just what, historically, this American dream is.

Essentially, the phrase represents the romantic enlargement of the possibilities of life on a level at which the material and the spiritual have become inextricably confused. As such, it led inevitably towards the problem that has always confronted American artists dealing with American experience—the problem of determining the hidden boundary in the American vision of life at which the reality ends and the illusion begins. Historically, the American dream is anti-Calvinistic—in rejecting man's tainted nature it is even anti-Christian. It believes in the goodness of nature and man. It is accordingly a product of the frontier and the West rather than of the New England and Puritan traditions. Youth of the spirit—youth of the body as well—is a requirement of its existence; limit and deprivation are its blackest devils. But it shows an astonishing incapacity to believe in them:

> I join you . . . in branding as cowardly the idea that the human mind is incapable of further advances. This is precisely the doctrine which the present despots of the earth are inculcating, and their friends here re-echoing; and applying especially to religion and politics; 'that it is not probable that anything better will be discovered than what was known to our fathers' . . . But thank heaven the American mind is already too much opened to these impostures, and while the art of printing is left to us, science can never be retrograde. . . . To preserve the freedom of the human mind . . . every spirit should be ready to devote itself to martyrdom. . . . But that the enthusiasm which characterizes youth should lift its parricide hands against freedom and science would be such a monstrous phenomenon as I could not place among the possible things in this age and country.

That is the hard kernel, the seed from which the American dream would grow into unpruned luxuriance, to become brutalized at last under the grossly acquisitive spirit of the Gilded Age and Republican capitalism. Jefferson's voice in the above passage is not remote from many European voices of his time, but it stands in unique relation to the country to whom he spoke. That attitude was bred into the bone of America, and in various, often distorted and corrupted ways, it has lasted. Perhaps this is where the trouble begins, for if the virtues of the American imagination which Jefferson singles out have the elements of greatness in them, they call immediately for discriminating and practical correctives. The reality in such an attitude lies in its faith in present life; the illusion lies in the undiscriminating multiplication of its material possibilities. The New England and puritan traditions saved Hawthorne and James from the pitfalls of the American dream, but in James we often feel that he would have believed in it if he could, and in the persons of Christopher Newman and Adam Verver he came dangerously close to doing so. *The Great Gatsby* is Scott Fitzgerald's great exploration of this theme, but first of all he explored its more degraded aspects as they had come to exist in the 'twenties in 'The Diamond as Big as the Ritz'.

From the moment that Percy and John leave the shanty depot of Fish in a buggy driven by a negro 'which had obviously appeared from nowhere', to the time they reach Percy's father's fantastic concealed chateau on the diamond mountain that makes him the richest man in the world, the imagery gradually changes in quality. The sick and portentous undertones that were struck by the twelve men of Fish, waiting under the poisoned sunset, give way to a riotous fantasy in a style that can only be called Babylonian-Hollywood. The implicit presence throughout of Hollywood criteria of values and taste (and Hollywood in its most barbaric age) is the technical means by which Fitzgerald makes his final point, and presses his condemnation. The boys change from the buggy into an immense limousine with jewel encrusted wheels, and in which 'the upholstery consisted of a thousand minute and exquisite tapestries of silk, woven with jewels and embroideries, and set upon a background of cloth of gold. The two armchair seats in which the boys luxuriated were covered with stuff that resembled duvetyn, but seemed woven in numberless colours of the ends of ostrich feathers.' The limousine is at last lifted by cables and cranes over a high ridge of rock into the little secret kingdom of Percy's father (a direct descendant of George Washington and Lord Baltimore). From this secret kingdom he sends out a discreet number of diamonds chipped from the mountain to be sold on the world market—not enough to flood it and lower the price, but enough to open up to him and his family all the material possibilities of life. By various fantastic means, Percy's father, Braddock Washington, has kept his diamond mountain a secret from the world so that it doesn't even appear on the official government maps of the area. Here, in this little circle of land that is quite literally out of the world, the Washington family lead a life as unrelated to any possible form of reality as the American dream itself.

The major part of the story is concerned with giving us a series of glimpses of life in this American dream—a fantasy on the theme of material possibilities run wild. Fitzgerald's treatment of the theme is completely successful. The sense of a colossal Hollywood movie set, and a 'plot' that unwinds along the lines of an old time movie scenario, keeps the question of reality implicitly to the fore of the reader's mind. In fact, the total effect of the story duplicates the odd ambivalence of response that one brings to the moving pictures of the period— disbelief neatly balanced by exhilarated acceptance. To have been able to do this is no small technical achievement, and in effect it adds up to a devastating comment on the experience it is presenting us in such an orgy of glamour. Here, for example, is a description of Percy's home and his mother as John first sees them as the limousine drives up:

> Full in the light of the stars, an exquisite chateau rose from the borders of the lake, climbed in marble radiance half the height of an adjoining mountain, then melted in grace, in perfect symmetry, in translucent feminine languor, into the massed darkness of a forest of pine. The many towers, the slender tracery of the sloping parapets, the chiselled wonder of a thousand yellow windows with their oblongs and hectagons and triangles of golden light, the shattered softness of the intersecting planes of star-shine and blue shade, all trembled on John's spirit like a chord of music. On one of the towers, the tallest, the blackest at its base, an arrangement of exterior lights at the top made a sort of floating fairy-land—and as John gazed up in warm enchantment, the faint acciaccare sound of violins drifted down in a rococo har- mony that was like nothing he had ever heard before. Then in a moment the car stopped before the wide, high marble steps around which the night air was fragrant with a host of flowers.

At the top of the stairs two great doors swung silently open and
amber light flooded out upon the darkness, silhouetting the figure
of an exquisite lady with black, high-piled hair, who held out her
arms toward them.

'Mother,' Percy was saying, 'this is my friend, John Unger,
from Hades.'

It is indeed the American dreamer's idea of Heaven, and
Hades is where all this is not. The implicit moving picture
imagery, as I have already said, opens on to the question of
appearance and reality, and relates in its own way to Hawthorne's search for the inner sphere and James's search for
life. What Fitzgerald is intent on here is a revelation of the
emptiness of those so-called values by which the American
world lived, and he makes it by revealing the grotesquerie in
which its implications, if extended far enough, would inevitably
end.

The grotesquerie, and also the inhumanity. The American
dream which had started innocently enough when there had
been a vast unexploited continent to support the possibilities
it seemed to promise, had become brutalized as the only means
of realizing them had more and more centred in money with
the passing of the frontier and the advent of the Gilded Age.
The Washingtons maintain their Hollywood existence on the
diamond mountain only at the price of the freedom of others
who have been unfortunate enough to stumble by accident into
this 'forbidden paradise'. And John learns that the friends they
invite must at last be put to death, lest returning to the world of
reality they betray what they have seen. Thus, in a literal sense
the American dream becomes the American nightmare with
naked negro executioners chasing John through the Babylonian-Hollywood corridors. The tempo quickens, as in an
ancient scenario, and United States bombers arrive in the nick
of time.

The scene in which Braddock Washington attempts to bribe
God on the mountainside to withhold the impending destruction with a gigantic diamond held by two negro slaves, brings
the dream sequence to its conclusion. Its symbolism is obvious
enough—too obvious to require comment; but it is a strong
scene, and visually impressive. This morning scene, during
which the giant diamond catches the first yellow light of the

sun, balances the sunset scene in the first two paragraphs of Part II. Whether it was explicitly intended or not—perhaps not —it is appropriate that the American dream (the particular dream of John T. Unger) which began under a poisoned sky, should dissolve in the clear light of day, and that the ominous note in the religious imagery of the opening should reach its climax in the blasphemous prayer of Braddock Washington.

Having 'escaped' the destruction of the diamond mountain, John 'awakens' on the hillside with his two companions, Kasmine and Jasmine, daughters of Braddock Washington who have figured largely in the dream. The descent here is from the 'unrealistic' heights of the American dream towards the banality of the typical American romance. John's last words are:

> 'At any rate, let us love for awhile, for a year or so, you and me. That's a form of divine drunkenness that we can all try. There are only diamonds in the whole world, diamonds and perhaps the shabby gift of disillusion. Well, I have that last and I will make the usual nothing of it.' He shivered. 'Turn up your coat collar, little girl, the night's full of chill and you'll get pneumonia. His was a great sin who first invented consciousness. Let us lose it for a few hours.'
>
> So wrapping himself in his blanket he fell off to sleep.

The sentimentality is mawkish, almost aggressive, but it is redeemed by being played off against the 'sentimentality' of the sequence of dream images to which we have just been exposed. Fitzgerald equates the emotional extravagance of the dream with the emotional cheapness of the romance—they are both equally the products of the same sensibility. In *The Great Gatsby*, the tawdry romance with Daisy, as we shall see, is the means Fitzgerald uses to show Gatsby the intolerable cheapness of his dream and illusion. Fitzgerald has sometimes been criticized for the inadequacy of his treatment of love, but on this point it would be difficult to find any writer in the American tradition who has treated the subject better, or even as well. Among the artists treated here, Cooper and Melville automatically exclude themselves; Hawthorne has given us moral parables in which the 'love interest', in so far as it can be said to exist at all, is incidental to the moral theme; and James, in his American novels particularly, seems to me to give the whole subject the lightest 'treatment'. Where the sentimentality and cheapness of the romance are most blatant, as here, they are used structurally (and perhaps not even with Fitzgerald's fullest consciousness) to illuminate the final meaning.

II

The Great Gatsby is an exploration of the American dream as it exists in a corrupt period, and it is an attempt to determine that concealed boundary that divides the reality from the illusions. The illusions seem more real than the reality itself. Embodied in the subordinate characters in the novel, they threaten to invade the whole of the picture. On the other hand, the reality is embodied in Gatsby; and as opposed to the hard, tangible illusions, the reality is a thing of the spirit, a promise rather than the possession of a vision, a faith in the half-glimpsed, but hardly understood, possibilities of life. In Gatsby's America, the reality is undefined to itself. It is inarticulate and frustrated. Nick Carraway, Gatsby's friend and Fitzgerald's narrator, says of Gatsby:

> Through all he said, even through his appalling sentimentality, I was reminded of something—an elusive rhythm, a fragment of lost words, that I had heard somewhere a long time ago. For a moment a phrase tried to take shape in my mouth and my lips parted like a dumb man's, as though there was more struggling upon them than a wisp of startled air. But they made no sound, and what I had almost remembered was incommunicado forever.

This is not pretentious phrase-making performing a vague gesture towards some artificial significance. It is both an evocative and an exact description of that unholy cruel paradox by which the conditions of American history have condemned the grandeur of the aspiration and vision to expend itself in a waste of shame and silence. But the reality is not entirely lost. It ends by redeeming the human spirit, even though it live in a wilderness of illusions, from the cheapness and vulgarity that encompass it. In this novel, the illusions are known and condemned at last simply by the rank complacency with which they are content to be themselves. On the other hand, the reality is in the energy of the spirit's resistance, which may not recognize itself as resistance at all, but which can neither stoop to the illusions nor abide with them when they are at last recognized. Perhaps it is really nothing more than ultimate immunity from the final contamination, but it encompasses the difference between life and death. Gatsby never succeeds in seeing through the sham of his world or his acquaintances very clearly. It is of the essence of his romantic American vision that it should lack the seasoned powers of discrimination. But it invests those illusions with its own faith, and thus it discovers its projected goodness in the frauds of its crippled world. *The Great Gatsby* becomes the acting out of the tragedy of the American vision. It is a vision totally untouched by the scales of values that order life in a society governed by traditional manners; and Fitzgerald knows that although it would be easy to condemn and 'place' the illusions by invoking these outside values, to do so would be to kill the reality that lies beyond them, but which can sometimes only be reached through them.

For example, Fitzgerald perfectly understood the inadequacy of Gatsby's romantic view of wealth. But that is not the point. He presents it in Gatsby as a romantic baptism of desire for a reality that stubbornly remains out of his sight. It is as if a savage islander, suddenly touched with Grace, transcended in his prayers and aspirations the grotesque little fetish in which he imagined he discovered the object of his longing. The scene in which Gatsby shows his stacks of beautiful imported shirts to Daisy and Nick has been mentioned as a failure of Gatsby's, and so of Fitzgerald's, critical control of values. Actually, the shirts are sacramentals, and it is clear that Gatsby shows them, neither in vanity nor in pride, but with a reverential humility in the presence of some inner vision he cannot consciously grasp, but toward which he desperately struggles in the only way he knows.

In an essay called 'Myths for Materialists' Mr. Jacques Barzun once wrote that figures, whether of fact or fiction, in so far as they express destinies, aspirations, attitudes typical of man or particular groups, are invested with a mythical character. In this sense Gatsby is a 'mythic' character, and no other word will define him. Not only is he an embodiment (as Fitzgerald makes clear at the outset) of that conflict between illusion and reality at the heart of American life; he is an heroic personification of the American romantic hero, the true heir of the American dream. 'There was something gorgeous about him,' Nick Carraway says, and although 'gorgeous' was a favourite word with the 'twenties, Gatsby wears it with an archetypal American elegance.

One need not look far in earlier American literature to find his forebears. Here is the description of a young bee hunter from *Col. David Crockett's Exploits and Adventures in Texas*, published in 1836:

> I thought myself alone in the street, where the hush of morning was suddenly broken by a clear, joyful, and musical voice, which sang. . . .
>
> I turned toward the spot whence the sounds proceeded, and discovered a tall figure leaning against the sign post. His eyes were fixed on the streaks of light in the east, his mind was absorbed, and he was clearly unconscious of anyone being near him. He continued his song in so full and clear a tone, that the street re-echoed. . . .
>
> I now drew nigh enough to see him distinctly. He was a young man, not more than twenty-two. His figure was light and graceful at the same time that it indicated strength and activity. He was dressed in a hunting shirt, which was made with uncommon neatness, and ornamented tastily with fringe. He held a highly finished rifle in his right hand, and a hunting pouch, covered with Indian ornaments, was slung across his shoulders. His clean shirt collar was open, secured only by a black riband around his neck. His boots were polished, without a soil upon them; and on his head was a neat fur cap, tossed on in a manner which said, 'I don't give a d—n' just as plainly as any cap could speak it. I thought it must be some popinjay on a lark, until I took a look at his countenance. It was handsome, bright, and manly. There was no mistake in that face. From the eyes down to the breast he was sunburnt as dark as mahogany while the upper part of his high forehead was as white and polished as marble. Thick clusters of black hair curled from under his cap. I passed on unperceived, and he continued his song. . . .

This young dandy of the frontier, dreaming in the dawn and singing to the morning, is a progenitor of Gatsby. It is because of such a traditional American ancestry that Gatsby's romanticism transcends the limiting glamour of the Jazz Age.

But such a romanticism is not enough to 'mythicize' Gatsby.

FITZGERALD AND COLLAPSE OF AMERICAN DREAM 273

Gatsby, for all his shimmer of representative surfaces, is never
allowed to become soiled by the touch of realism. In creating
him, Fitzgerald observed as high a decorum of character as
a Renaissance playwright: for although Gatsby's parents were
shiftless and unsuccessful farm people, Gatsby really 'sprang
from his Platonic conception of himself. He was a son of God—
a phrase which, if it means anything, means just that—and he
must be about His Father's business, the service of a vast,
vulgar, meretricious beauty.'

Fitzgerald created Gatsby with a sense of his own election;
but the beauty it was in his nature to serve had already been
betrayed by history. Even in the midst of the blighted earthly
paradise of West Egg, Long Island, Gatsby bore about him the
marks of his birth. He is a kind of exiled Duke in disguise. We
know him by his bearing, the decorous pattern of his speech.
Even his dress invariably touches the imagination: 'Gatsby
in a white flannel suit, silver shirt, and gold coloured tie. . . .'
There is something dogmatically Olympic about the combination. After Gatsby's death when his pathetic old father journeys
east for the funeral, one feels that he is only the kindly shepherd
who once found a baby on the cold hillside.

But so far I have been talking in general terms. This beautiful control of conventions can be studied more closely in the
description of Gatsby's party at which (if we except that distant
glimpse of him at the end of Chapter I, of which I shall speak
later) we encounter him for the first time. We are told later that
Gatsby was gifted with a 'hint of the unreality of reality, a
promise that the rock of the world was founded securely on a
fairy's wing'. Fitzgerald does not actually let us meet Gatsby
face to face until he has concretely created this fantastic world
of Gatsby's vision, for it is the element in which we must meet
Gatsby if we are to understand his impersonal significance:

There was music from my neighbour's house through the
summer nights. In his blue gardens men and girls came and went
like moths among the whisperings and the champagne and the
stars. At high tide in the afternoon I watched his guests diving
from the tower of his raft, or taking the sun on the hot sand of his
beach while his two motor-boats slit the waters of the Sound,
drawing aquaplanes over cataracts of foam. On week-ends his
Rolls-Royce became an omnibus, bearing parties to and from the

city between nine in the morning and long past midnight, while his station wagon scampered like a brisk yellow bug to meet all trains. And on Mondays eight servants, including an extra gardener, toiled all day with mops and scrubbing-brushes and hammers and garden-shears, repairing the ravages of the night before.

The nostalgic poetic quality, which tends to leave one longing for sterner stuff, is, in fact, deceptive. It is Gatsby's ordeal that he must separate the foul dust that floated in the wake of his dreams from the reality of the dream itself: that he must find some vantage point from which he can bring the responsibilities and the possibilities of life into a single focus. But the 'ineffable gaudiness' of the world to which Gatsby is committed is a fatal deterrent. Even within the compass of this paragraph we see how the focus has become blurred: how the possibilities of life are conceived of in material terms. But in that heroic list of the vaster luxury items—motor-boats, aquaplanes, private beaches, Rolls-Royces, diving towers—Gatsby's vision maintains its gigantic unreal stature. It imposes a rhythm on his guests which they accept in terms of their own tawdry illusions, having no conception of the compulsion that drives him to offer them the hospitality of his fabulous wealth. They come for their week-ends as George Dane in Henry James's *The Great Good Place* went into his dream retreat. But the result is not the same: 'on Mondays eight servants, including an extra gardener, toiled all day with mops and scrubbing-brushes and hammers and garden-shears, repairing the ravages of the night before'. That is the most important sentence in the paragraph, and despite the fairy-story overtone, it possesses an ironic nuance that rises towards the tragic. And how fine that touch of the extra gardener is—as if Gatsby's guests had made a breach in nature. It completely qualifies the over-fragility of the moths and champagne and blue gardens in the opening sentences.

This theme of the relation of his guests to Gatsby is still further pursued in Chapter IV. The cataloguing of American proper names with poetic intention has been an ineffectual cliché in American writing for many generations. But Fitzgerald uses the convention magnificently:

Once I wrote down on the empty spaces of a time-table the names of those who came to Gatsby's house that summer. It is an old time-table now, disintegrating at its folds, and headed 'This schedule in effect July 5th, 1922'. But I can still read the grey names, and they will give you a better impression than my generalities of those who accepted Gatsby's hospitality and paid him the subtle tribute of knowing nothing about him.

The names of these guests could have been recorded nowhere else as appropriately as in the margins of a faded timetable. The embodiments of illusions, they are as ephemeral as time itself; but because their illusions represent the distortions and shards of some shattered American dream, the timetable they adorn is 'in effect July 5th'—the day following the great national festival when the exhausted holiday crowds, as spent as exploded fire-crackers, return to their homes. The list of names which Fitzgerald proceeds to enumerate conjures up with remarkable precision an atmosphere of vulgar American fortunes and vulgar American destinies. Those who are familiar with the social registers, business men's directories, and movie magazines of the 'twenties might be able to analyse the exact way in which Fitzgerald achieves his effect, but it is enough to say here that he shares with Eliot a remarkable clairvoyance in seizing the cultural implications of proper names. After two pages and more, the list ends with the dreamily elegiac close: 'All these people came to Gatsby's house in the summer.'

Why did they come? There is the answer of the plotted story —the free party, the motor-boats, the private beach, the endless flow of cocktails. But in the completed pattern of the novel one knows that they came for another reason—came blindly and instinctively—illusions in pursuit of a reality from which they have become historically separated, but by which they might alone be completed or fulfilled. And why did Gatsby invite them? As contrasted with them, he alone has a sense of the reality that hovers somewhere out of sight in this nearly ruined American dream; but the reality is unintelligible until he can invest it again with the tangible forms of his world, and relate it to the logic of history. Gatsby and his guests feel a mutual need of each other, but the division in American experience has widened too far, and no party, no hospitality however lavish, can heal the breach. The illusions and the reality go their separate ways. Gatsby stands at the door of his mansion, in one of the most deeply moving and significant paragraphs of the novel, to wish his guests good-bye:

> The caterwauling horns had reached a crescendo and I turned away and cut across the lawn toward home. I glanced back once. A wafer of a moon was shining over Gatsby's house, making the night fine as before, and surviving the laughter and the sound of his still glowing garden. A sudden emptiness seemed to flow now from the windows and the great doors, endowing with complete isolation the figure of the host, who stood on the porch, his hand up in a formal gesture of farewell.

If one turns back to Davy Crockett's description of the elegant young bee hunter, singing while the dawn breaks in the east, and thinks of it in relation with this midnight picture of Gatsby, 'his hand up in a formal gesture of farewell', while the last guests depart through the debris of the finished party, the quality of the romanticism seems much the same, but the situation is exactly reversed; and from the latter scene there opens a perspective of profound meaning. Suddenly Gatsby is not merely a likeable, romantic hero; he is a creature of myth in whom is incarnated the aspiration and the ordeal of his race.

'Mythic' characters are impersonal. There is no distinction between their public and their private lives. Because they share their meaning with everyone, they have no secrets and no hidden corners into which they can retire for a moment, unobserved. An intimacy so universal stands revealed in a ritual pattern for the inspection and instruction of the race. The 'mythic' character can never withdraw from that air which is his existence—that is to say, from that area of consciousness (and hence of publicity) which every individual shares with the members, both living and dead, of his group or race. Gatsby is a 'mythic' character in this sense—he has no private life, no meaning or significance that depends on the fulfilment of his merely private destiny, his happiness as an individual in a society of individuals. In a transcendent sense he touches our imaginations, but in this smaller sense—which is the world of the realistic novel—he even fails to arouse our curiosity. At this level, his love affair with Daisy is too easily 'placed', a tawdry epic 'crush' of no depth or interest in itself. But Gatsby not only remains undiminished by what is essentially the meanness of the affair: his stature grows, as we watch, to the proportions of a hero. We must inquire how Fitzgerald managed this extraordinary achievement.

Daisy Buchanan exists at two well-defined levels in the novel. She is what she is—but she exists at the level of Gatsby's vision of her. Even Fitzgerald's admirers regard Daisy as rather a good, if somewhat silly, little thing; but Fitzgerald knew that at its most depraved levels the American dream merges with the American debutante's dream—a thing of deathly hollowness. Fitzgerald faces up squarely to the problem of telling us what Daisy has to offer in a human relationship. At one of Gatsby's fabulous parties—the one to which Daisy brings her husband, Tom Buchanan—Gatsby points out to Daisy and Tom, among the celebrated guests, one particular couple:

> 'Perhaps you know that lady,' Gatsby indicated a gorgeous, scarcely human orchid of a woman who sat in state under a white-plum tree. Tom and Daisy stared, with that peculiarly unreal feeling that accompanies the recognition of a hitherto ghostly celebrity of the movies.
> 'She's lovely,' said Daisy.
> 'That man bending over her is her director.'

Superficially, the scene is highly civilized. One fancies one has seen it in Manet. But in the context we know that it has no reality whatever—the star and her director can get no nearer reality than by rehearsing a scene. Our attention is then taken up by other scenes at the party, but by suddenly returning to this couple after an interval of two pages to make his point, Fitzgerald achieves a curious impression of static or arrested action. We have the feeling that if we walked behind the white-plum tree we should only see the back of a canvas screen:

> Almost the last thing I remember was standing with Daisy and watching the moving-picture director and his Star. They were still under the white-plum tree and their faces were touching except for a pale, thin ray of moonlight between. It occurred to me that he had been very slowly bending toward her all evening to attain this proximity, and even while I watched I saw him stoop one ultimate degree and kiss at her cheek.

'I like her,' said Daisy, 'I think she's lovely.'

But the rest offended her—and inarguably, because it wasn't a gesture but an emotion.

Daisy likes the moving-picture actress because she has no substance. She is a gesture that is committed to nothing more real than her own image on the silver screen. She has become a gesture divorced forever from the tiresomeness of human reality. In effect, this passage is Daisy's confession of faith. She virtually announces here what her criteria of human emotions and conduct are. Fitzgerald's illustration of the emptiness of Daisy's character—an emptiness that we see curdling into the viciousness of a monstrous moral indifference as the story unfolds—is drawn with a fineness and depth of critical understanding, and communicated with a force of imagery so rare in modern American writing, that it is almost astonishing that he is often credited with giving in to those very qualities which *The Great Gatsby* so effectively excoriates.

But what is the basis for the mutal attraction between Daisy and Gatsby? In Daisy's case the answer is simple. We remember that Nick Carraway has described Gatsby's personality as an 'unbroken series of successful gestures'. Superficially, Daisy finds in Gatsby, or thinks she finds, that safety from human reality which the empty gesture implies. What she fails to realize is that Gatsby's gorgeous gesturings are the reflex of an aspiration towards the possibilities of life, and this is something entirely different from those vacant images of romance and sophistication that fade so easily into the nothingness from which they came. But in a sense, Daisy is safe enough from the reality she dreads. The true question is not what Gatsby sees in Daisy, but the direction he takes from her, what he sees *beyond* her; and that has, despite the immaturity intrinsic in Gatsby's vision, an element of grandeur in it. For Gatsby, Daisy does not exist in herself. She is the green light that signals him into the heart of his ultimate vision. *Why* she should have this evocative power over Gatsby is a question Fitzgerald faces beautifully and successfully as he recreates that milieu of uncritical snobbishness and frustrated idealism—monstrous fusion—which is the world in which Gatsby is compelled to live.

Fitzgerald, then, has a sure control when he defines the

quality of this love affair. He shows it in itself as vulgar and specious. It has no possible interest in its own right, and if it did have the pattern of the novel would be ruined. Our imagination would be fettered in those details and interests which would detain us on the narrative level where the affair works itself out as human history, and Gatsby would lose his 'mythic' quality. But the economy with which Gatsby is presented, the formal and boldly drawn structural lines of his imagination, lead us at once to a level where it is obvious that Daisy's significance in the story lies in her failure to constitute the objective correlative of Gatsby's vision. And at the same time, Daisy's wonderfully representative quality as a creature of the Jazz Age relates her personal failure to the larger failure of Gatsby's society to satisfy his need. In fact, Fitzgerald never allows Daisy's failure to become a human or personal one. He maintains it with sureness on a symbolic level where it is identified with and reflects the failure of Gatsby's decadent American world. There is a famous passage in which Gatsby sees Daisy as an embodiment of the glamour of wealth. Nick Carraway is speaking first to Gatsby:

> 'She's got an indiscreet voice,' I remarked. 'It's full of——' I hesitated.
> 'Her voice is full of money,' he said suddenly.
> That was it. I'd never understood before. It was full of money—that was the inexhaustible charm that rose and fell in it, the jingle of it, the cymbals' song of it. . . . High in a white palace the king's daughter, the golden girl. . . .

Gatsby tries to build up the inadequacy of each value by the support of the other; but united they fall as wretchedly short of what he is seeking as each does singly. Gatsby's gold and Gatsby's girl belong to the fairy story in which the Princess spins whole rooms of money from skeins of wool. In the fairy story, the value never lies in the gold but in something beyond. And so it is in this story. For Gatsby, Daisy is only the promise of fulfilment that lies beyond the green light that burns all night on her dock.

This green light that is visible at night across the bay from the windows and lawn of Gatsby's house is the central symbol in the book. Significantly, our first glimpse of Gatsby at the end of

Chapter I is related to it. Nick Carraway, whose modest bungalow in West Egg stands next to Gatsby's mansion, returning from an evening at the Buchanans', while lingering on the lawn for a final moment under the stars, becomes aware that he is not alone:

> . . . fifty feet away a figure had emerged from the shadow of my neighbour's mansion and was standing with his hands in his pockets regarding the silver pepper of the stars. Something in his leisurely movements and the secure position of his feet upon the lawn suggested that it was Mr. Gatsby himself, come out to determine what share was his of our local heavens.
>
> I decided to call to him. . . . But I didn't . . . for he gave a sudden intimation that he was content to be alone—he stretched out his arms toward the dark water in a curious way, and, as far as I was from him, I could have sworn he was trembling. Involuntarily I glanced seaward—and distinguished nothing except a single green light, minute and far away, that might have been the end of a dock. When I looked once more for Gatsby he had vanished, and I was alone again in the unquiet darkness.

It is hardly too much to say that the whole being of Gatsby exists only in relation to what the green light symbolizes. This first sight we have of Gatsby is a ritualistic tableau that literally contains the meaning of the completed book, although the full meaning of what is implicit in the symbol reveals itself slowly, and is only finally rounded out on the last page. We have a fuller definition of what the green light means in its particular, as opposed to its universal, signification in Chapter V. Gatsby is speaking to Daisy as they stand at one of the windows of his mansion:

> 'If it wasn't for the mist we could see your home across the bay,' said Gatsby. 'You always have a green light that burns all night at the end of your dock.'
>
> Daisy put her arm through his abruptly, but he seemed absorbed in what he had just said. Possibly it had occurred to him that the colossal significance of that light had now vanished forever. Compared to the great distance that had separated him from Daisy it had seemed very near to her, almost touching her. It had seemed as close as a star to the moon. Now it was again a green light on dock. His count of enchanted objects had diminished by one.

Some might object to this symbolism on the grounds that it

is easily vulgarized, but if studied carefully in its full context it represents a convincing achievement. The tone or pitch of the symbol is exactly adequate to the problem it dramatizes. Its immediate function is that it signals Gatsby into his future, away from the cheapness of his affair with Daisy which he has vainly tried (and desperately continues trying) to create in the image of his vision. The green light is successful because, apart from its visual effectiveness as it gleams across the bay, it embodies the profound naïveté of Gatsby's sense of the future, while simultaneously suggesting the historicity of his hope. This note of historicity is not fully apparent at this point, of course. The symbol occurs several times, and most notably at the end:

> Gatsby believed in the green light, the orgastic future that year by year recedes before us. It eluded us then, but that's no matter —tomorrow we will run faster, stretch out our arms farther. . . . And one fine morning——
>
> So we beat on, boats against the current, borne back ceaselessly into the past.

Thus the American dream, whose superstitious valuation of the future began in the past, gives the green light through which alone the American returns to his traditional roots, paradoxically retreating into the pattern of history while endeavouring to exploit the possibilities of the future. There is a suggestive echo of the past in Gatsby's sense of Daisy. He had known her, and fallen in love with her, five years before the novel opens. During that long interval while they had disappeared from each other's sight, Daisy has become a legend in Gatsby's memory, a part of his private past which (as a 'mythic' character) he assimilates into the pattern of that historic past through which he would move into the historic future. But the legendary Daisy, meeting her after five years, has dimmed a little in lustre:

> 'And she doesn't understand,' he said. 'She used to be able to understand. We'd sit for hours——'
>
> He broke off and began to walk up and down a desolate path of fruit rinds and discarded favours and crushed flowers.
>
> 'I wouldn't ask too much of her,' I ventured. 'You can't repeat the past.'
>
> 'Can't repeat the past?' he cried incredulously. 'Why of course you can!'

He looked around him wildly, as if the past were lurking here in the shadow of his house, just out of reach of his hand.

By such passages Fitzgerald dramatizes Gatsby's symbolic role. The American dream, stretched between a golden past and a golden future, is always betrayed by a desolate present— a moment of fruit rinds and discarded favours and crushed flowers. Imprisoned in his present, Gatsby belongs even more to the past than to the future. His aspirations have been rehearsed, and his tragedy suffered, by all the generations of Americans who have gone before. His sense of the future, of the possibilities of life, he has learned from the dead.

If we return to the passage in which, linked arm in arm, Gatsby and Daisy stand at the window looking towards the green light across the bay, it may be possible to follow a little more sympathetically that quality of disillusion which begins to creep into Gatsby's response to life. It does not happen because of the impoverished elements of his practical romance; it happens because Gatsby is incapable of compromising with his inner vision. The imagery of this particular passage, as I suggested, is gauged to meet the requirements of Gatsby's young romantic dream. But two pages later Fitzgerald takes up the theme of Gatsby's struggle against disenchantment once again, and this time in an imagery that suggests how much he had learned from *The Waste Land*:

> When Klipspringer had played 'The Love Nest' he turned around on the bench and searched unhappily for Gatsby in the gloom.
> 'I'm all out of practice, you see. I told you I couldn't play. I'm all out of prac——'
> 'Don't talk so much, old sport,' commanded Gatsby. 'Play!'

> In the morning,
> In the evening,
> Ain't we got fun——

Outside the wind was loud and there was a faint flow of thunder along the Sound. All the lights were going on in West Egg now; the electric trains, men-carrying, were plunging home through the rain from New York. It was the hour of a profound human change, and excitement was generating on the air.

> One thing's sure and nothing's surer
> The rich get richer and poor get—children.
> In the meantime,
> In between time—

As I went over to say good-bye I saw that the expression of bewilderment had come back into Gatsby's face, as though a faint doubt had occurred to him as to the quality of his present happiness. Almost five years! There must have been moments even that afternoon when Daisy tumbled short of his dreams—not through her own fault, but because of the colossal vitality of his illusion. It had gone beyond her, beyond everything. He had thrown himself into it with a creative passion, adding to it all the time, decking it out with every bright feather that drifted his way. No amount of fire or freshness can challenge what a man can store up in his ghostly heart.

In view of such writing it is absurd to argue that Fitzgerald's art was a victim of his own attraction to the Jazz Age. The snatches of song that Klipspringer sings evoke the period with an immediacy that is necessary if we are to understand the peculiar poignancy of Gatsby's ordeal. But the songs are more than evocative. They provide the ironic musical prothalamion for Gatsby's romance, and as Gatsby listens to them an intimation of the practical truth presses in on him. The recognition is heightened poetically by that sense of the elements, the faint flow of thunder along the Sound, which forms the background of those artificial little tunes. And it is not odd that this evocation of the outdoor scene, while Klipspringer pounds at the piano inside, sustains in the imagination the image of that green light, symbol of Gatsby's faith, which is burning across the bay. This scene draws on the 'violet hour' passage from 'The Fire Sermon' in which 'the human engine waits Like a taxi throbbing waiting. . . .' It is the hour of a profound human change, and in the faint stirrings of Gatsby's recognition there is for a moment, perhaps, a possibility of his escape. But the essence of the American dream whose tragedy Gatsby is enacting is that it lives in a past and a future that never existed, and is helpless in the present that does.

Gatsby's opposite number in the story is Daisy's husband, Tom Buchanan, and Gatsby's stature—his touch of doomed but imperishable spiritual beauty, if I may call it so—is defined by his contrast with Tom. In many ways they are analogous in their characteristics—just sufficiently so to point up the differences. For example, their youth is an essential quality of them both. But Tom Buchanan was 'one of those men who reach such an acute limited excellence at twenty-one that everything afterward savours of anti-climax'. Even his body—'a body capable of enormous leverage'—was 'a cruel body'. In the description of Tom we are left physically face to face with a scion of those ruthless generations who raised up the great American fortunes, and who now live in uneasy arrogant leisure on their brutal acquisitions. But Gatsby's youth leaves an impression of interminability. Its climax is always in the future, and it gives rather than demands. Its energy is not in its body, but in its spirit, and meeting Gatsby for the first time, one seizes, as Nick Carraway did, this impression in his smile:

> It was one of those rare smiles with a quality of eternal reassurance in it, that you may come across four or five times in life. It faced—or seemed to face—the whole eternal world for an instant, and then concentrated on *you* with an irresistible prejudice in your favour. It understood you just as far as you wanted to be understood, believed in you as you would like to believe in yourself, and assured you that it had precisely the impression of you that, at your best, you hoped to convey. Precisely at that point it vanished —and I was looking at an elegant young rough-neck, a year or two over thirty, whose elaborate formality of speech just missed being absurd.

This passage is masterly in the way in which it presents Gatsby to us less as an individual than as a projection, or mirror, of our ideal selves. To do that is the function of all 'mythic' characters. Gatsby's youth is not simply a matter of three decades that will quickly multiply themselves into four or five. It is a quality of faith and hope that may be betrayed by history, may be killed by society, but that no exposure to the cynical turns of time can reduce to the compromises of age.

Again, Gatsby and Tom are alike in the possession of a certain sentimentality, but Tom Buchanan's is based on depraved self-pity. He is never more typical than when coaxing himself to tears over a half-finished box of dog biscuits that recalls a drunken and illicit day from his past, associated in memory with his dead mistress. His self-pity is functional. It is sufficient to condone his most criminal acts in his own eyes as long as the crimes are not imputable. But Gatsby's sentimentality exists in the difficulty of expressing, in the phrases and symbols provided by his decadent society, the reality that lies at the heart of his aspiration. 'So he waited, listening for a moment longer to the tuning fork that had been struck upon a star'—Gatsby's sentimentality (if it *is* sentimentality, and I rather doubt it) is as innocent as that. It has nothing of self-pity or indulgence in it —it is all aspiration and goodness; and it must be remembered that Fitzgerald himself is *outside* Gatsby's vocabulary, using it with great mastery to convey the poignancy of the situation.

Tom Buchanan and Gatsby represent antagonistic but historically related aspects of America. They are related as the body and the soul when a mortal barrier has risen up between them. Tom Buchanan is virtually Gatsby's murderer in the end, but the crime that he commits by proxy is only a symbol of his deeper spiritual crime against Gatsby's inner vision. Gatsby's guilt, in so far as it exists, is radical failure—a failure of the critical faculty that seems to be an inherent part of the American dream—to understand that Daisy is as fully immersed in the destructive element of the American world as Tom himself. After Daisy, while driving Gatsby's white automobile, has killed Mrs. Wilson and, implicitly at least, left Gatsby to shoulder the blame, Nick Carraway gives us a crucial insight into the spiritual affinity of the Buchanan couple, drawing together in their callous selfishness in a moment of guilt and crisis:

> Daisy and Tom were sitting opposite each other at the kitchen table, with a plate of cold fried chicken between them, and two bottles of ale. He was talking intently across the table at her, and in his earnestness his hand had fallen upon and covered her own. Once in a while she looked up at him and nodded in agreement.
>
> They weren't happy, and neither of them had touched the chicken or the ale—and yet they weren't unhappy either. There was an unmistakable air of natural intimacy about the picture, and anybody would have said that they were conspiring together.

They instinctively seek out each other because each recognizes the other's strength in the corrupt spiritual element they inhabit.

There is little point in tracing out in detail the implications of the action any further, although it could be done with an exactness approaching allegory. That it is not allegory is owing to the fact that the pattern emerges from the fullness of Fitzgerald's living experience of his own society and time. In the end the most that can be said is that *The Great Gatsby* is a dramatic affirmation in fictional terms of the American spirit in the midst of an American world that denies the soul. Gatsby exists in, and for, that affirmation alone.

When, at the end, not even Gatsby can hide his recognition of the speciousness of his dream any longer, the discovery is made in universalizing terms that dissolve Daisy into the larger world she has stood for in Gatsby's imagination:

> He must have looked up at an unfamiliar sky through frightening leaves and shivered as he found what a grotesque thing a rose is and how raw the sunlight was upon the scarcely created grass. A new world, material without being real, where poor ghosts, breathing dreams like air, drifted fortuitously about. . . .

'A new world, material without being real.' Paradoxically, it was Gatsby's dream that conferred reality upon the world. The reality was in his faith in the goodness of creation, and in the possibilities of life. That these possibilities were intrinsically related to such romantic components limited and distorted his dream, and finally left it helpless in the face of the Buchanans, but it did not corrupt it. When the dream melted, it knocked the prop of reality from under the universe, and face to face with the physical substance at last, Gatsby realized that the illusion was *there*—there where Tom and Daisy, and generations of small-minded, ruthless Americans had found it—in the dreamless, visionless complacency of mere matter, substance without form. After this recognition, Gatsby's death is only a symbolic formality, for the world into which his mere body had been born rejected the gift he had been created to embody— the traditional dream from which alone it could awaken into life.

As the novel closes, the experience of Gatsby and his broken dream explicitly becomes the focus of that historic dream for which he stands. Nick Carraway is speaking:

> Most of the big shore places were closed now and there were hardly any lights except the shadowy, moving glow of a ferryboat across the Sound. And as the moon rose higher the inessential

houses began to melt away until gradually I became aware of the old island here, that flowered once for Dutch sailors' eyes—a fresh, green breast of the new world. Its vanished trees, the trees that had once made way for Gatsby's house, had once pandered in whispers to the last and greatest of all human dreams; for a transitory enchanted moment man must have held his breath in the presence of this continent, compelled into an aesthetic contemplation he neither understood nor desired, face to face for the last time in history with something commensurate to his capacity for wonder.

It is fitting that this, like so many of the others in *Gatsby*, should be a moonlight scene, for the history and the romance are one. Gatsby fades into the past for ever to take his place with the Dutch sailors who had chosen their moment in time so much more happily than he.

We recognize that the great achievement of this novel is that it manages, while poetically evoking a sense of the goodness of that early dream, to offer the most damaging criticism of it in American literature. The astonishing thing is that the criticism —if indictment wouldn't be the better word—manages to be part of the tribute. Gatsby, the 'mythic' embodiment of the American dream, is shown to us in all his immature romanticism. His insecure grasp of social and human values, his lack of critical intelligence and self-knowledge, his blindness to the pitfalls that surround him in American society, his compulsive optimism, are realized in the text with rare assurance and understanding. And yet the very grounding of these deficiencies is Gatsby's goodness and faith in life, his compelling desire to realize all the possibilities of existence, his belief that we can have an Earthly Paradise populated by Buchanans. A great part of Fitzgerald's achievement is that he suggests effectively that these terrifying deficiencies are not so much the private deficiencies of Gatsby, but are deficiencies inherent in contemporary manifestations of the American vision itself—a vision no doubt admirable, but stupidly defenceless before the equally American world of Tom and Daisy. Gatsby's deficiencies of intelligence and judgment bring him to his tragic death—a death that is spiritual as well as physical. But the more important question that faces us through our sense of the immediate tragedy is where they have brought America.

The Americanness of the
American Novel

THE last nine chapters have attempted to make explicit the general propositions advanced in the first chapter. If they have not done so I can scarcely hope to compensate now by an elaborate conclusion. But there are certain observations I should like to make about my general argument. The subject I have been treating in these pages is a slippery one by its very nature, and to keep it steadily in sight I have had to give it at times an unduly rigorous formulation. In bringing my argument to a close I should like to make sure that my emphases are correctly distributed and my intentions in the foregoing chapters perfectly clear. Despite several chapters which might lend support to the thought, I have not meant this to be a study in the history of ideas, a Discrimination of American Experiences in the novel. Nor have I wished to expose a mouldering skeleton in a show-case and label it the Structure of American Fiction. Such an exhibition would be a fossil indeed, and a fraud at that. What I have wished to do is more important, and more difficult. It is more important because, in Sir Herbert Read's words, it is concerned with the form of life rather than the life of form: because it is an attempt to trace the specifically national quality in the artistic life of the American novel to its multiple source, and this is not a matter simply of planting the American flag in easily marked out territories. To do that is the function of literary imperialism, not of criticism. In a national tradition which is in the flowering of its vigour, its native strength and flavour are communicated to the artists it produces. This is a commonplace. No one believes that Texas could have produced Shakespeare or the Tonga Islands, Proust. It is equally obvious that national characteristics colour speech habits and rhythm, and that the historical moment dictates the popular type of hero. In a period of ebullient nationalism Shakespeare will produce Henry V, or when the Americans want to murder the Indians along the frontier with a clear conscience, Robert Montgomery Bird will rise to fame with Bloody Nathan, the Indian-killing Quaker. The relation between art and a national context is so easy at these levels that it is hardly worth discussing. But such relations are entirely extrinsic; they explain nothing about the creative motive itself, that inner urgency to discover in art a resolution of deeply felt problems which, however much they may be shared among all men, will also differ in greater or less degree according to the national tradition in which they are experienced.

The American tradition differs from western European ones in that it is to some degree artificial. It was more or less legislated into existence in the beginning. I do not mean that it does not possess a life of its own, or is not an organic, growing thing. But like a new vegetable, it owes its existence to some artificial grafting. This factor, together with the provincialism and other conditions I discussed earlier, make it a particularly tractable field in which to study the interaction between creative activity and national existence at fairly inaccessible levels: I mean the levels below patriotic and personal expediency, below jingoism, below a nostalgic interest in native folklore and history, below the preachments and parables of literary axe-grinders and demagogues. I have tried to reach to that level at which the American artist confronts his own spiritual needs in all the terrible deprivation of his stark American condition, and struggles towards the resolution of those problems that only the artist of genuine fineness can ever *feel* as problems at all. It is a depth at which only the *great* American writers could exist, and for that reason I have dealt here with a very restricted number. At the same time it is a very *American* depth, an underworld of complex tensions that are of specifically native growth. In my brief historical chapter I tried to suggest the intellectual and political grounding of these tensions. Simply because the American tradition is so circumscribed and, in a sense, concocted, I believe such a chapter to be far from irrelevant; but it would not be possible to write a similar chapter prefatory to a study of the major writers of any century in English literature without a sense of futility.

As each tension I have treated reflects only a facet of the total reality through which they are all related, so there are doubtless many others. But I think it demonstrable that the

K

ones I have discussed are the ones which have shaped the creative impulses of the novelists considered here. I do not mean that this 'new American experience' levelled them to a common pattern, but through it they claim a recognizable fellowship among themselves. It is in this underworld of tensions that we find the common roots of those three great symbolic embodiments in American literature, the Scarlet Letter, Natty Bumppo, and the White Whale. The very diversity among these symbols should prove adequate protection against the charge of being too schematic. My attitude towards this simultaneous similarity and diversity is suggested by the two epigraphs from Wallace Stevens I have appended to this volume: the one in which he speaks of 'a law of inherent opposites, of essential unity', and the lines,

> It was when the trees were leafless first in November
> And their blackness became apparent, that one first
> Knew the eccentric to be the base of design.

It is through what they have in common that the great American artists have always expressed their uniqueness; and it is perhaps because it is so often November in American art, because there is so little leafage of shared manners, inherited institutions, and traditional attitudes, that we tend to regard the singularity of the great American novelists as almost absolute. But to carry the tree image farther, they all draw their nourishment from one deep, dark soil.

The number in this select circle is necessarily small. The only other American novelist in the nineteenth century who belongs with those I have treated is Mark Twain. But I have not discussed Twain because he is not a writer who comes to terms easily with literary analysis. When he is great it is with a purity that makes analysis irrelevant; and when his materials offer ground for analytic comment, his art is likely to be at such low ebb that discussion seems hardly worthwhile. What there is to say positively of his achievement has been registered by T. S. Eliot, F. R. Leavis, and Lionel Trilling in their respective introductions and essays, and there is no point in rephrasing it here. As for Mark Twain's 'case', Van Wyck Brooks's classic analysis of it is definitive.

I have ended my 'tradition' of American novelists with Scott

Fitzgerald simply because it seems to me to end with him. I believe Scott Fitzgerald *is* a great American writer, and fully deserves the company I put him in. He deals with 'the new American experience' more critically than anyone in this tradition since Cooper, and at times it seems to me that he has a finer sense of the inherent tragedy in the American experience than any of the others. The alcoholic haze in which he spent so much of his time has obscured for us how intelligent he really was in his best writing. If he had some of the characteristic weaknesses of his decade and his country, he knew them with a rare inwardness, and his writing is not a celebration of them but a judgement on them. His one great figure, Gatsby, is the only symbolic figure in American literature who descends to the depth of the American Dream and comes back to tell us it is a nightmare.

There is one final problem I should like to mention. This 'tradition' as I have set it up here has no room for the so-called realists and naturalists. I hardly suppose that anyone would think of advancing the claims of Dreiser anyway; but collectively the realist writers in American fiction carry some weight. I agree with D. H. Lawrence in finding a certain impressiveness in Frank Norris's *The Octopus*, and I think I can indicate very briefly why the realists cannot belong with the writers discussed here by a reference to this novel. Mr. Robert E. Spiller has written of *The Octopus*: 'Since *Moby Dick*, by then virtually forgotten, there had been nothing like it in American literature.' [1] Mr. Spiller may be only referring to the fact that Norris's book gives a detailed account of wheat growing and that *Moby Dick* gives us the whaling industry on an even more panoramic scale, but the remark reminds one that both are symbolic novels. The Octopus is the Railroad, whose tentacles squeeze the wheat growers to death, its killing force being the high rates for transport that it charges. The novel is heavily laden with symbolism throughout. The Railroad symbolizes our machine civilization; wheat, of course, symbolizes life. Typical of its technique is the rather effective and quite upsetting scene in which a locomotive, racing through the night with its headlight ablaze like a single eye, rips into a flock of sheep who have strayed through a broken fence on to the track. The destructive economic power of the Railroad over the wheat growers is dramatized effectively enough, but symbolism of this kind at best resembles Ibsen rather than Melville, and it is not often at its best. Norris's and Melville's symbolism point in quite different directions. Melville's symbols move inward, or downward, towards primordial depths of consciousness. Their meanings are not limited by the boundaries of the material world. But Norris's symbols, effective as they sometimes are within their small limits, are little more than marginal illustrations to his dramatized economics and sociology. The symbols explore nothing, discover nothing. They merely lend an obvious kind of structure and emphasis to the story and the meaning.

The extreme realists and naturalists among American writers are always concerned with these outside surfaces. Even their symbolism is an exterior frosting, and hence can hardly be considered symbolism at all. There is no point in speculating here about the reasons for this externality, whether it was because of the example of the French naturalists, or of Darwinism and the physical sciences, or was merely the effect of the gross materialism of America after the Civil War. 'The new American experience' that Cooper, Hawthorne, Melville, and James had dealt with had been, above all else, an inward thing: and it was inward, not with the professional curiosity of the Freudian, who came later, nor the impertinent inquisitiveness of the sociologist, but with the deeply humane recognition that the problems that tormented them as American artists had first to be confronted in the solitude of their own souls. They were all great moralists, great critics in their art, and, in their own way, metaphysicians; and the reality they sought to explore was where the sociological novelists, the naturalists and the documentarians, could never follow them.

I think it will be desirable to bring this account of the great American novelists to a close with a summary recapitulation of those characteristics I have sought to reveal in their work. *Great* artists everywhere are those who have been most seriously and intensely concerned with life. But the writers I have dealt with here suggest that 'life' for the serious American artist has a distinctive quality and set of interests of its own, and that these have traditionally been determined and conditioned by the deprivations and confinements of the American condition, and directed by a specific set of problems or tensions growing out of the historical circumstances of America's existence. Obviously no generalizations can be offered that will apply equally to all the novelists treated here, nor even to as many as two of them in the same way. But this much, at least, is worth hazarding: the novelists treated here are, as a group, extraordinarily non-sensuous. I do not mean that sensuous experience is closed to them, nor that they are inept at treating it when the occasion requires: but the occasion will almost always be for the sake of making an abstract point. Hawthorne handles Hester's and Dimmesdale's meeting in the forest with rare imaginative control, but he is not interested in their emotional natures nor their love except in so far as they illuminate a moral meaning that is essentially unrelated to them as individuals and as sexual beings. If one can imagine this great scene rewritten by D. H. Lawrence, one will begin to have some sense of the distance that lies between American and English fiction, for I take the genius of Lawrence to be the polar opposite of the artists I have dealt with. Sexual love as a subject carrying its own intrinsic interest is almost completely absent from their writing, and when it is attempted, as it was with Poe, it is an embarrassment and a disease. Because the American tradition provided its artists with abstractions and ideas rather than with manners, we have no great characters, but great symbolic personifications and mythic embodiments that go under the names of Natty Bumppo, Jay Gatsby, Huckleberry Finn, Ahab, Ishmael—all of whom are strangely unrelated to the world of ordinary passions and longings, for the democrat is at last the loneliest man in the universe. The great American novelists can, in their way, give us Lear, and make a decent attempt at Hamlet; but Othello, and even Romeo, are beyond their range. The urgencies that have always spurred them to their greatest efforts have been less of the senses than of the spirit, and less of the spirit than the mind. As artists they are thinkers and a species of metaphysician: and a passion of intelligence is the virtue we most often find in their work. They analyse endlessly—not, indeed, the human psyche, but the impersonal moral problems of men, and they analyse them towards abstract ends. At the close of *The Scarlet Letter* we have to sacrifice Hester and Dimmesdale for the sake of the impersonal moral truth they illustrate and dramatize, and Hawthorne expects us to rest in that truth with no backward glance. If the European experience qualified all this in Henry James, we still have to ask what other tradition on earth could ever have produced the role of 'the restless analyst'. The tensions I have spoken of are, in the end, merely so many channels by which we are able, however stumblingly, to reach the depth of meaning and the roots of creative impulse in these writers. It was here that they sometimes encountered problems that seemed insoluble, and which deflected them towards despair, and hence those strangely nihilistic glooms that sometimes darken the pages of America's greatest novelists. Taken *en masse*, these problems that they coped with were an attempt to discover, or perhaps create, a reality beyond the aery speculativeness of their intellectual and historical heritage which endowed them with ideas, but no tangible vesture of manners, traditions, institutions, and earth-bound history by which their abstractions might live with significant and personal meaning. James's famous list of all the American novelists did not possess in the way of subject matter is, in the end, a description of those conditions that gave rise to symbolism in American art. It is, then, in the light thrown by the tensions I have treated here that we can see what a different breed of artists these American novelists are in their deepest hearts and motives from their European fellows, but how, under their wide diversities, they all bear a resemblance to each other.

APPENDIX A

Hamilton's Financial Reforms

THE three measures by which Hamilton imposed a financial aristocracy on the United States are the funding of the national debt, the assumption of state debts, and the establishment of the National Bank. In support of certain statements made in the text of my discussion of Hamilton, it will be necessary to describe these measures here, however briefly. Of these measures, the funding of the national debt raised least resistance. The new government was heavily in debt, and this way, whatever might be said against funding at another time, was obviously the best way to meet the emergency which confronted Congress and the Treasury. The wisdom of the assumption of state debts was debated more vigorously, but the real fight was precipitated by Hamilton's Report on a National Bank, which was communicated to the House on December 14, 1790. Its constitutionality was immediately challenged, and Hamilton's reply was his doctrine of implied or inherent powers. From the time Hamilton realized, at the Constitutional Convention, the impossibility of imposing his own scheme of elective monarchy on the states, he withdrew from active participation in the Convention, but he actively, and with great success, campaigned for the acceptance of the Constitution when it was submitted to the country. He foresaw from the first the possibility of forming the Constitution, during the course of applying it, into something like his original design. James Truslow Adams quotes a remark of Madison's which indicates how early Hamilton's strategy was recognized (*The Living Jefferson*, New York, 1936, p. 218): 'I deserted Colonel Hamilton, or rather Colonel H. deserted me; in a word, the divergence between us took place—from his wishing to *administration*, or rather to administer the Government . . . into what he thought it ought to be; while, on my part, I endeavoured to make it conform to the Constitution as understood by the Convention that produced and recommended it, and particularly by the State conventions that adopted it.' Hamilton's great admirer, Senator Henry Cabot Lodge, put it more delicately when he wrote (*Alexander Hamilton*, New York, 1909, p. 87):

> The intellect and personality of Hamilton have not left their stamp and superscription upon the Constitution as it went from the Philadelphia convention, but upon the government, the public policy, the political system which grew up under the Constitution, they made an indelible impression in those early and plastic years, and one which has never been effaced.

Whatever one may think of Hamilton's motives, the importance of his measures to the new government can scarcely be exaggerated. In *The Works of Alexander Hamilton* (edited by Henry Cabot Lodge, New York, 1904), Lodge remarks of the First Report on Public Credit (Vol. II, pp. 89–90):

> In his first report he embodied the financial policy which organized and brought out our resources, rendered us strong and prosperous at home, established our credit, and made us respected in every money market in Europe. But the first report was far more than a vigorous and able piece of financing. It was the corner stone of the government of the United States, and the foundation of the national movement.

As the new national government swung into operation the debt that it inherited from the old Confederation was immense. The foreign debt amounted to $11,710,378; the domestic debt to $42,414,085; and in addition to this national debt there was about $25,000,000 owed by the individual states as the result of the Revolution. When one reflects that as Secretary of State Jefferson conducted his whole Department on something less than $3,000 a year, the relative enormity of the national debt is clear. Opening his First Report with some decorous remarks on the moral propriety of preserving good faith by a punctual performance of contracts, Hamilton moved rapidly to the heart of his plan, the funding of the national debt—that is to say, selling the debt in the form of interest bearing bonds. Some years later he was to define funding succinctly when he said in an address to the electors of New York (quoted by William Graham Sumner, *Alexander Hamilton*, New York, 1890, p. 93): 'What is the funding system? It is nothing more nor less than the pledging of adequate funds or revenues for paying the interest, and for gradual redemption of the principal of that

very debt which was the sacred price of independence.' In his
First Report he discussed it at much greater length, arguing
that it answered most of the purposes of money, and would
therefore increase the capital of the country.

The funding system was associated in everybody's mind with
the English system. Sumner exonerates Hamilton's version of
funding from the vices of the English system ('... as it was
applied here by Hamilton, it had none of the vices of the English
system, which, after all, could be resolved into allowing
expenditures to exceed revenue'), but this was not the popular
view in Hamilton's day. In an early life of Hamilton by John
Williams we have this more representative view (*Hamilton Club
Series*, No. 1, New York, 1865, p. 12):

> We know of few traits among considerable men, that is so
> much and so frequently overcharged with praise, as this finan-
> ciering faculty; and Mr. Hamilton deserves as little of this praise
> of office as most men; all he did was borrowed from the precedent
> of Mr. Pitt, and a more obnoxious precedent he could not have
> selected. He perused the British Acts of Parliament relative to
> loans and the Funding System, and endeavoured to introduce
> their scrofulous and contaminating influence into the Republican
> constitutions of America.

The basic objection against funding was, of course, that it
taxed the agricultural population, and the non-security-
holders generally, for the sake of paying the interest on the
bonded debt. A passage from John Taylor's pamphlet, *An
Examination of the Late Proceeding in Congress Respecting the Conduct
of the Secretary of the Treasury* (1793, p.7) indicates how generally
Hamilton's class favouritism was understood and resented:

> The experience of other countries has shown that the dealers in
> the public funds, and especially those whose fortunes consist prin-
> cipally in that line, have no interest and of course feel but little
> concern, in all those questions of fiscal policy which particularly
> affect the landholder, the merchant, and the artist. Although
> these classes should groan under the burden of government, yet
> the public creditor will be no otherwise affected by the pressure,
> than as he receives what has been gleaned by their industry. The
> tax never reaches him, till the money is counted out quarterly
> from the public coffers, in discharge of his claim. The disparity of

their interests, and the difference of their situations, respecting the objects to which they point, in great measure separate them in society. . . . And having one common interest which consists simply in the imposition of high taxes and their rigid collection, they form a compact body and move always in concert.

Besides the inherited debt which the Federal government had from the Confederation, there was also a large number of state debts contracted during the course of the Revolution. Some of these had been largely paid off, but other states had done very little towards diminishing their obligations. Hamilton therefore proposed that the Federal government should assume the obligations for these individual states. The fight opposing assumption was particularly bitter. This was due to the reluctance of states who were nearly in the clear to undertake the burden of the still heavily indebted states. But beyond this, assumption ominously augmented the size of the funded debt, and gave even greater power and influence to those who dealt in public securities. And there was still another objection which the Jeffersonians entertained. Most of their spokesmen felt that it was corrupt and fraudulent for members of Congress to own national or state bonds, for in their capacity as legislators it was necessary for them to enact laws affecting the value of government stock, and it was thought—probably quite correctly—that such legislation could not be disinterested. John Taylor is quite explicit (op. cit., pp. 8–9):

If then the certificate-holders or dealers in the funds in general, are subservient to the views of a department faithful to their interests, is it reasonable to expect that such as have, or may hereafter become, members of Congress will prove less so? Being on the great theatre of speculation and gain, and possessed of more correct information, with the means of turning it to better account, will they abandon their occupation and slight the opportunity offered of becoming thrifty? In what condition would the landholder, the merchant, and the artist, find themselves if they should be represented in the national legislature by persons of this description only? Might they not count at least on high taxes and their rigid collection? This is the first principle of free government, that those who impose the tax should feel the effect, but here it would be not only violated but reversed. What security would the people have in any of the departments of government whose checks were destroyed by an interest which supervened every consideration of public good?

Hamilton's Report on a National Bank was communicated to the House on December 14, 1790, and it is the keystone of his whole financial structure. There is no need to consider its organization here except to say that it was essentially a private enterprise, independent of the government, and yet so powerful that at last, under Nicholas Biddle, it entered into dangerous competition with the Federal government itself. Sumner (op. cit., pp. 163-4) gives a brief characterization of the Bank that is worth quoting:

> This bank was very much more like the Bank of England than either of the previous projects which Hamilton had put forward. In the fundamental principles of its constitution it was, as the Bank of England originally was, a syndicate of holders of the public debt who were incorporated and granted a monopoly of issuing notes, as far as the power of the Federal government could control that monopoly. There was no need in the case of the Bank of the United States, of allowing subscriptions in the public debt. This was only a measure for carrying out another notion which was stigmatized as English, with more reason than in other cases; namely, that of interweaving the interests of the wealthy men with those of the government.

James Thomson Callender published a rather unusual book of the muck-raking variety, *The Prospect before Us* (Richmond, Va., 1800) which gives us, unsavoury as the book is in most respects, a remarkably clear insight into the currents of feeling of the time. Callender has one passage (p. 11) concerning Hamilton's ruling that three-fourths of the public subscription in the bank stock should be paid in six per cent funded government shares which indicates the manner in which the new financial class legislated themselves into profit and power:

> Of the eight millions subscribed by private individuals the holders were allowed to deposit one-fourth in gold and silver, and three-fourths in six per cent stock; that is to say, they drew six per cent with one hand for their paper from the treasury, as a debt, and eight per cent from the public for the very same stock, as bankers, by the charter for circulating their bank notes. This class of creditors, did, therefore, clear in the issue, fourteen per cent by their own making; for the matter was driven through

Congress by a majority, of whom the greater part, or perhaps the whole, were destined to be future partners.

The number of Congressmen who owned stock in the national debt and in the National Bank was a source of concern to many, but John Taylor was particularly indignant because several members of Congress had been made directors of the Bank. In Taylor's eyes this was a deliberate attempt to bring the legislature into intimate contact with the new moneyed machine for the purpose of assailing more effectively the integrity of the law-makers. He saw in this dual role of Congressman and Bank Director a powerful mechanism organized for supporting and justifying the policy of the Secretary of the Treasury (op. cit., p. 11):

> Thus organized the game becomes more easy. In all operations upon the legislature, whether for the particular emolument of the bank, the fiscal corps in general, or any other purpose, in which the views of the party are interested, the prospect of success is greatly improved. And in all enquiries relative to the conduct of the officer, in the management of the public monies, these members of Congress, *bank directors*, and the bank itself, give him their firm and uniform support. In *their eyes* his conduct will appear *immaculate, angelic*, and partaking of something still more divine.

Taylor's choice of words in the last sentence was not accidental. The Federalist devotion to Hamilton was intense, and was characterized even then by that piety and righteousness that still sanctify their descendants today. This passage from an elegy written at the time of his death is fairly representative of the new speculators' sense of themselves (*Hamilton Club Series*, No. 3, op. cit., p. 56):

> How sad we mourn his loss, how deep deplore,
> One brightest star that's set to rise no more,
> Till the last trump shall sound on that great day,
> When Hamilton—disrobed of mortal clay,
> At God's right hand shall sit with face benign,
> And at his master cast a look divine.

It is evident from this brief analysis of Hamilton's financial measures, and the reaction to them among the non-Federalists, that there was a widespread fear that a tight and insidious organization of merchants and speculators was about to be created which would form a financial aristocracy. This view is very neatly summed up by William Findley in *A Review of the Revenue System adopted by the First Congress under the Federal Constitution* (Philadelphia, 1794, pp. 52-3). Having spoken of the financial machinery created by Hamilton, Findley says:

> By these means an aristocracy formerly unknown in the United States, has been created. The feudal aristocracy that long prevailed in Europe, tyrannical as it was, had some leading features in it preferable to this. Their wealth consisting in land, their titles and habits inspiring them with a high sense of honour, their interest in land secured their attachment to the general interests of their country, and their own interest, and high sense of honour, secured protection to their vassals. They seldom acquired money to hoard up, or put to usury. But an aristocracy supported by the public revenue, is not attached to any interest except promoting oppressive taxes.

As expressed here, Findley's sentiments are near to John Adams's, and as we have seen, to Fenimore Cooper's. This view of the financial aristocracy in America persisted, and we find this representative view nearly forty years later in William Gouge's widely read *A Short History of Paper Money and Banking in the United States* (Philadelphia, 1833, p. 44):

> The difference between England, and the United States, is simply this: in the former country, exclusive privileges are conferred on individuals who are called *Lords*; in the latter, exclusive privileges are conferred on corporations which are called *Banks*. The effect on the people of both countries is the same. In both the many live and labour for the benefit of the few.

Hamilton now brought his financial programme to a close and integrated the whole wide-flung scheme by his Report on Manufactures (*Works*, Vol. IV, pp. 70-198). This Report, which is sometimes considered the greatest of the series, is important because it makes it quite explicit that the chief beneficiaries of the programme will be the commercial and capitalist classes. Hamilton does not, of course, say this. Indeed, he goes out of his way to argue the benefits to agriculture that will spring from the growth of industry in the United States, but it is evident that his whole financial organization is geared to support that rapid growth and augmentation of industry

that he boldly envisages as the future America. There is no need
to go into Hamilton's specific recommendations for the encouragement of industry here. They were what one would have
expected—protective duties, exemption from import duties on
raw materials not produced in America, the building of
strategic roads and canals, and so on. But Hamilton had made
his real contribution to the American capitalist class by
stabilizing public credit, and providing a financial machinery
adequate to meet the demands of the new capitalistic enterprises when they should begin to grow.

APPENDIX B

The Genteel Tradition

As described by Santayana in his lecture, 'The Genteel Tradition in American Philosophy', the genteel tradition in America was the consequence of the decline of Calvinism, with its sense of human depravity, and its exultation in its own misery as a proof of God's infinity and 'irresponsibility'. 'Serious poetry, profound religion (Calvinism, for instance), are the joys of an unhappiness that confesses itself; but when a genteel tradition forbids people to confess that they are unhappy, serious poetry and profound religion are closed to them by that; and since human life, in its depths, cannot then express itself openly, imagination is driven for comfort into abstract arts, where human circumstances are lost sight of, and human problems dissolve in a purer medium. The pressure of care is thus relieved without its quietus being found in intelligence.' Calvinism declined and Transcendentalism prevailed:

> The sense of sin totally evaporated. Nature, in the words of Emerson, was all beauty and commodity; and while operating on it laboriously, and drawing quick returns, the American began to drink in inspiration from it aesthetically. . . . Good will became the great American virtue; and a passion arose for counting heads, and square miles, and cubic feet, and minutes saved—as if there had been anything to save them for. . . . If you told the modern American that he is totally depraved, he would think you were joking, as he himself usually is. He is convinced that he always has been, and always will be, victorious and blameless.

Santayana's essay is brilliant and delightful, but it postpones rather too late, I think, the development of the genteel tradition in America, which hardly waited for the exhilarating release provided by Transcendentalism. Before Calvinism grew moribund in America, it grew cynical under the pressure of the new business interests in the country, who used it (with how much hypocrisy, who can say?) to buttress the conservative mercantile interests. The men of property became the men of sound morals, and sound morals were what, in the long run, protected property interests. While the New England pulpits reviled

Jefferson, Hamilton proposed (*Works*, Vol. X, p. 435) the formation of an organization called 'The Christian Constitutional Society', which was ostensibly to promote the Christian religion, but which, under that guise, was to disseminate Federalist doctrine. He planned a complex organization of officers suggesting an ecclesiastical hierarchy, and the whole scheme savours of the union of Church and state. Thus, the Calvinist sense of sin, even before the Transcendentalist reaction, was losing serious interest in man's universal wretchedness for the sake of identifying human depravity with those Republican (that is to say, Democratic) interests which were critical of the accumulations of wealth acquired in trade and commerce. A Calvinism that surveyed the national blessings God conferred through the channels of business was bound to modify its former pessimistic views, and bless that class of great and good merchants whose co-operation with the Divine Will had worked such public weal for America.

As an intense but unimpassioned orthodoxy came to the support of the pro-British mercantile interests, so the arts were also conscripted, and, on the practical level, it was this alliance of literature and business that generated the genteel tradition with which we are concerned—a tradition essentially servile, imitative, timid, and observing all those proprieties which the men of property recognize as the useful defences of wealth and illicitly acquired position. Santayana's title for it is admirable, for the genteel tradition can no more be aristocratic than the business man millionaire can be an aristocrat.

The Port Folio, published in Philadelphia from 1801 by Joseph Dennie, and after Dennie's death by Nicholas Biddle, who was later to become Director of the Bank of the United States, represents a full scale attempt to build up an American culture in support of Hamilton's programme—a culture that followed British precedent on all fronts. *The Port Folio* was the first successful American literary magazine of any stature, and it remains by far the most amusing to read among the country's early periodicals.

This is partly because Dennie's personality, which was really rather extravagant, leaves its touch everywhere during the first decade of publication. Dennie was a dandy, and perhaps the greatest Anglophile America ever produced. It is impossible to resist giving this elegant description of him which is quoted by H. M. Ellis, *Joseph Dennie and His Circle* (Austin, Texas, 1915, p. 91):

> I have a vivid recollection of Dennie's personal appearance, in 1796. . . . In person he was rather below than above the middle height, and was of a slender frame. He was particularly attentive to his dress, which, when he appeared in the street on a pleasant day, approached the highest notch of the fashion. I remember, one delightful morning in May, he came into the office dressed in a pea-green coat, white vest, nankin small-clothes, white silk stockings, and shoes, or pumps, fastened with silver buckles, which covered at least half the foot from the instep to the toe. His small-clothes were tied at the knees, with ribbons of the same colour, in double bows, ends reaching down to the ankles. He had just emerged from the barber's shop. His hair, *in front*, was well loaded with pomatum, frizzled, or *craped*, and powdered; the ear locks had undergone the same process; *behind*, his natural hair was augmented by the addition of a large queue (called vulgarly, the *false tail*), which, enrolled in some yards of black ribbon, reached half-way down his back.

It is pleasant to recall that this figure was private secretary to the dyspeptic Timothy Pickering while the latter headed the State Department. William Charvat in *The Origins of American Critical Thought* (Philadelphia, 1936, p. 10) has given a neat summary of Dennie's views as they are expressed in *The Port Folio*:

> *The Port Folio* was founded by Dennie in a spirit of antagonism to the mob and in its prospectus he said, 'We will not strive to please the populace at the expense of their quiet by infusing into every ill-balanced and weak mind a jealousy of rulers, a love of innovation, an impatience of salutary restraint.' Oberholtzer quotes him as saying, 'For more than fifteen years we have published in periodical papers our sentiments in complete defiance of the choice or dictation of the many,' and toward the end of his career the patrician note came out even stronger in his declaration that he had 'aimed to serve only the most illustrious descriptions of American society—the liberal, the ladies, the lawyers, the clergy, and all the gentlemen and cavaliers of Columbia.

Dennie would have rejoiced in Mr. Charvat's attribution of 'patrician' to him, but the rather suffocating list of illustrious

K*

Americans ('the liberal' is, of course, meaningless in this context) Dennie enumerates indicates that the only patriciate available to him was the party of Hamilton, whose death he commemorated in an issue of *The Port Folio* in which every page was bordered with a half inch of black. It is *The Letters of Joseph Dennie 1768–1812* (edited by L. G. Peddler, Orono, Me., 1936) that gives the best insight into his character. A letter to his parents, May 20, 1800, a year before Dennie undertook the publication of *The Port Folio*, indicates the policy his critical journal would follow, and it reveals with great clarity the alliance between British and American commercial interests as they came to a focus in one of the country's leading literary men and propagandists (pp. 185–6):

> The British merchants are attentive to me, and I find them very sensible and honest men. I take this opportunity, if you do not already know this prejudice, to express my strong, well grounded, and settled attachment to *Englishmen* and English principles. Independently of my family benefits and favours, I can declare with emphasis that the best friends I have proved for many years are either Englishmen or men of British attachment, partialities, generosity, and honour. . . . Putting this aside, the English character, abstractly considered, is the most honest, the most generous, the most frank and liberal and foul is that day in our Calendar, and bitterly are those *patriotic*, selfish and Indian traitors to be cursed who instigated the *wretched* populace to declare the 4th day of July, 1776, a day of Independence. We are now tasting the bitter fruit of that baleful tree, which our forefathers planted at Plymouth, which Sam Adams and Deacon Newell watered, and to which the natural malignancy of our rascal populace has given the increase.

Although many of the articles in *The Port Folio* have a good deal of interest and show intelligence (there is even a long article on John Donne in the second issue), the intellectual framework that is consistently developed is an unmistakable forecast of the genteel tradition. There is that decorous coupling of good taste and good morals which we associate with it (Second Series: Vol. IV, no. 6, p. 489):

> In promoting the refinement of a people, the formation and diffusion of a correct taste constitute the step next in importance to the establishment of sound morals.

Morals and taste (the lesson was inculcated in every issue) were both fostered by the commercial ties joining the two countries (Vol. I, no. 23):

> Fortunately, the two countries are now, in the forcible phrase of a great writer, 'on terms like a bride and groom'—Heaven grant, that nothing may sever our commercial interests, or chill our mutual attachment. The two countries are one. The powers of RELIGION, NATURE, INTEREST, LANGUAGE, and HABIT, loudly proclaim our natural and necessary union; and what 'GOD HATH JOINED let no man put asunder'. Let no mean jealousy or fanatic rage or French coquetry, incite or direct America *to forget her first love*.

The British writers who were most favoured and recommended by *The Port Folio* were the polite essayists, Addison, Steele, Goldsmith, Shenstone, Johnson's *The Rambler*, and so on. And a concern for the decorous pattern of American English was a perpetual theme in the magazine. Dennie was particularly fond of indulging a somewhat heavy irony at the expense of English in America, and in this he was representative of the genteel tradition in full flower. The articles in *The Port Folio* were anonymous, but one of the essays called 'The American Lounger', printed over the pseudonym of Samuel Saunter (Vol. I, no. 3, pp. 33–5) is almost certainly by him. The essay is a satire describing the social and educational disadvantages of being born and reared in America. 'My first effort in the imitative arts was to mimic the gutteral accent of an Oneida chief.' Sent to the university, he did not read classics, mathematics or natural philosophy, but preferred to memorize Hubbard's *History of the Indian Wars*:

> Among the archives of my college there were innumerable Indian manuscripts; and whole alcoves in the library were devoted to pamphlets and tracts in the Indian tongue. To these I confined myself. . . . While the declaimers and the rhetoricians were drowning the college bell, and deafening the chapel with their noisy speeches from Tully, or Mr. Webster's selection, I was more profitably and more pleasingly engaged in acquiring the Indian vocabulary, and tiring all the echoes of Cambridge, while I repeated aloud the flowing and harmonious words of Hobbamock, Wessagusset, Mohekunah, Awasuncks, and Umbagog.
>
> After I had received what are commonly called the honours of

the university. . . . I mingled with the American world at large
and instantly found reason to congratulate myself on the judicious
direction of my studies. I found the Indian language pretty
generally spoken.—Most of the classics of the New World were
written in some of the aboriginal dialects. Indian manners were
fashionable. Men drank and smoked like Indians. At the commencement of the last war, at Lexington and many other places,
men fought gallantly, like Indians, behind walls, beside trees, and
beneath coverts. Whenever I had the happiness to peruse a
sermon of New England, or a letter from a Committee of Correspondence and Safety, or a Humble Remonstrance and Petition,
or a Non-importation Agreement, or the divine speeches of
Samuel Adams and of John Hancock, or the diviner Declaration
itself, I could not help observing, with the most pleasurable
emotions, how finely the savage style was copied. Whenever it
was my rare good fortune to talk with some of our politicians, and
to mark the course of their policy, I could not help discerning . . .
their scheme was adopted on Indian principles, and for an Indian
interest.

Ill-natured and narrow, such writing nevertheless has an
energy that was not always present in the less vigorous examples
that came later. But it marks a direction. Dennie was out to
embellish the wealthy American commercial classes with *tone*,
and here perhaps his touch is most deft of all (Vol. I, no. 3,
p. 22):

> Such gentlemen, as carry small canes, in modish language
> called *canees*, ought to put them in a horizontal position, under
> their left arm, taking especial care, that the ferrule end, which
> must be carried behind them, be sufficiently dirty. This, with a
> jerk of the gait, and a frequent whisk, as if to look about them, will
> prevent that crowd of busy people, who infest the public streets,
> from pressing too close.

As I have said above, there is much that is attractive about
The Port Folio and Dennie himself. As an example of intelligence
applied to the defects and limitations of the United States, I
would point to his fine analysis of the American publishing
world and the sad lot of American writers (Vol. I, no. 37,
pp. 291–2). The description is pertinent to the difficulties of
publishing that confronted the younger Hawthorne years later,
and to the misfortunes that overtook Melville. And this level of
insight and intelligence is often achieved, especially during the

earlier years of the publication. If we trace the shortcomings of the magazine, we should not lose sight of its virtues and its genuine cultural significance for the America of that day. And in view of the tone that undoubtedly prevailed in popular American society, the violence of Dennie's reaction should be understandable at least. But a summary statement of Dennie's position reveals the whole genteel tradition, its snobbishness and overestimation of the values of wealth, its imitativeness of England, its uncreative conservatism, in embryo. His 'New Prospectus of *The Port Folio*,' printed in 1806, provides such a summary; and the whole is sealed by a kind of bloodless moral delicacy (so common later on among the exponents of this tradition). Henry Adams in his history of Jefferson's administrations quotes this representative bit from an issue for February, 1803:

> I heard from married ladies, whose stations as mothers demanded from them a guarded conduct,—from young ladies, whose age forbids the audience of such conversation, and whose using it modesty must disclaim,—indecent allusions, indelicate expressions, and even at times immoral innuendoes. A loud laugh or a coarse exclamation followed each of these, and the young ladies generally went through the form of raising their fans to their faces.

There are so many attitudes in the genteel tradition that, superficially, are also shared by Cooper, Hawthorne, and James, it is difficult to quote or generalize briefly without unfairly appearing to involve them also in the indictment. But it is rather in the *way* these attitudes were held that we must distinguish between the serious creative artist and the sterile practitioners of the genteel tradition. I must let my discussions of Cooper, Hawthorne, and James speak for themselves. If their attitudes sometimes appear to resemble those of Barrett Wendell, quoted below, the similarity is an illusion only that would dissolve under critical examination.

Like Dennie, Wendell detested the lower classes, and declaimed against those Americans who 'held it a superstition that kings, nobles, and gentlemen are in any aspect lovelier than the mob', or 'that virtuous women are inherently better than street walkers' (op. cit., p. 468). The kind of literary values this regard for status and 'morality' led to in Wendell's case were embalmed in the more imitative productions of American writers. But it is difficult not to sympathize with Wendell's description of the American in love with England (ibid., p. 178):

> A modern Londoner, however, who can walk in a forenoon from Westminster Abbey to the Temple Church and so to the Tower, can never dream of what such monuments mean to an imagination which has grown up amid no grander relics of antiquity than King's Chapel or Independence Hall, than grey New England farmhouses, and the moss-grown gravestones of Yankee burying grounds. To any sensitive nature, brought up in nineteenth-century America, the mere sight of anything so immemorially human as a European landscape must have in it some touch of that stimulating power which the Europe of the Renaissance found in the fresh discovery of classical literature and art.

It might be Cooper or James; but from Wendell's attitude a different perspective opens, converging at last on genteel imitation. And as the growth of the genteel tradition, according to Santayana, forbade people to confess they were unhappy, the American Calvinistic conscience, deprived of its normal field of operation, became preoccupied with non-human and abstract subject-matter. Wendell provides an excellent illustration of this (ibid., p. 177):

> The American conscience, in fact, always a bit over-developed, has sometimes seemed evident in our attempts at literary art. No one who lacks artistic conscience can write an effective short story; and it is doubtful if anyone troubled with much artistic conscience can write in less than a life-time a three-volume novel.

This attitude is ultimately the antithesis of that conception of aesthetic form as 'the form of life' we have followed here. The enormous production of James, the greatest master of form among American artists, is enough to 'show up' Wendell's remark. This kind of insistence on form is merely a safeguard against any disturbing intrusion of life into art. It is the genteel tradition at its most rotten.

APPENDIX C

The International Novel

IT is tempting to trace the origin of the international novel back to such early examples of a dialectical exchange between England and America as occur, for example, in *A Pretty Story*, 1774, by Francis Hopkinson (*The Miscellaneous Essays and Occasional Writings of Francis Hopkinson, Esq.*, Philadelphia, 1792, Vol. I, pp. 65–92), or Jeremy Belknap's *The Foresters, an American Tale*, 1792 (reprinted, Exeter, 1834). But it would prove pedantic and silly to suppose that the international novel in the fullness of its development has any direct genealogical relation with these dull allegorical barebones. At most, they point to the presence of 'an interest' in the American mind that was to find more satisfactory modes of expression. If such 'novels' do indeed have a progeny at all, it had better be traced, I think, through James K. Paulding's irritating and spiteful *The Diverting History of John Bull and Brother Jonathan*, 1812, and Cooper's *The Monikins*, 1835, terminating at last, perhaps, in Melville's *Mardi*, 1848, whose hero, Taji, during his voyage through the Mardian archipelago, visits the islands of Dominora (Great Britain) and Vivenza (the United States). All of these books are concerned with relating and contrasting the manners and attitudes of the two countries. But they remain a tissue of abstractions, whose interest at best, in Cooper's case, is political, and superficially ironical in Melville's. The mode of this writing insulates its characters from the moral effects of the contrast described, whereas the Revolutionary novel, as developed by Cooper, has the merit of placing its characters between the poles represented by England and America, as on a field of discrimination and choice.

There are, of course, other places in which we can look for the antecedents of the American international novel. Gilbert Imlay's *The Emigrants*, first published in 1794, contrasts England and America in a way that suggests the international novel of seventy years later, and the development of the characters themselves is partly controlled by their relations with the two cultures; and, as was to be characteristic of the later international novel, the New World comes out ahead.

Attempts are sometimes made to put Washington Irving in the pre-Jamesian tradition, but Irving's attachment to England was essentially different from the international one of James, which left ample room for the qualifications, ambiguous ironies, and caustic insights, as well as the exhilarated enthusiasms of the American. James's Americanness added a whole dimension to his relation with England that is totally lacking in Irving. Irving, as James Russell Lowell remarked, was 'wholly English', and it was not a very stimulating type of Englishness at that. The English sketches in *Bracebridge Hall* might have been written by a second-rate Addison.

Much nearer to the excited and self-conscious tone of the international novel as it was to develop is a passage like this from that genuine precursor of the tradition, Nathaniel P. Willis (*The Complete Works*, New York, 1846, p. 360):

> . . . *the Atlantic is to us a century.* We picture to ourselves England and Victoria as we picture to ourselves England and Elizabeth. We relish an anecdote of Sheridan Knowles as we should one of Ford or Marlowe. This immense ocean between us is like the distance of time; and while all that is minute and bewildering is lost to us, the greater lights of the age and the prominent features of society stand out apart, and we judge of them like posterity. Much as I have myself lived in England, I have never been able to remove this long perspective from between my eye and the great men of whom I read and thought on the other side of the Atlantic.

Willis's enthusiasm for England and Europe did not prevent his taking a critical view of what he observed, but his criticisms were enlivened and sweetened by his love of the Old World: 'I love my country, but the *ornamental* is my vocation, and of this she has none' (quoted by Robert E. Spiller, *The American in England*, New York, 1926, p. 366).

Nothing by Willis seems to be read any more, but it is a pity that a charmingly extravagant little story like *Wigwam versus Almack's* should have dropped into oblivion. As one reads it today, it seems a delightful cross between *The Deerslayer* and *Lady Barberina*. The story is recounted by an elegant young detached observer, and is concerned with a beautiful innkeeper's daughter on the American frontier who loves a handsome young

Indian brave. But a marriage is prevented when the girl proves
to be an heiress to an immense fortune in England through one
of those conventional genealogical mix ups that were popular
in the fiction of the day. She is adopted by a socially prominent
aunt who lives in London. Several years elapse before our young
detached observer meets her again, quite unexpectedly, at a
ball at Almack's. She has become the rage of London society,
and is courted like a Duchess—and lives, and looks like one too.
Willis gives some very pretty and convincing pictures of high
London society that remind one inevitably of James. Several
years pass once more, and the travels of our young observer
lead him again to the American wilderness, where he meets the
heroine again. She has returned to marry her Indian brave.
There, in a wigwam which Willis manages to make sound like
a London drawing-room, the young lady, no less elegant than
at Almack's, is so utterly at ease that one concludes that
Almack's is the best training in the world for life in an American
wigwam.

Fantastic as this story is, it contains in a highly developed
form all the elements that we become familiar with in the
international novel a few years later. The characteristic note of
this form seems to have been in an attitude towards the Old
World held by the writer, rather than in any narrowly defined
set of conventions. Although *The Marble Faun* is, strictly speaking, an international novel, and follows many of its conventions,
that exhilarated note we find in Willis is absent, and it does not
commonly occur to us to group it with this form.

Notes

CHAPTER I

[1] Sir Herbert Read, *The True Form of Feeling*, New York, 1953, p. 9.
[2] Lionel Trilling, *The Liberal Imagination*, New York, 1953, p. 206.
[3] Ibid., 249.
[4] Allen Tate, *On the Limits of Poetry*, New York, 1948, p. 135.
[5] Conrad, Letter to Arthur Symonds, 1908.
[6] Joseph Conrad, *Notes on Life and Letters*, London, 1949, p. 56.
[7] Ibid.
[8] He has been, by implication at least, excluded from the symbolist phase of literature by Charles Feidelson, *Symbolism and American Literature*, Chicago, 1953.

CHAPTER II

[1] Op. cit., p. 20.
[2] Maxwell Geismar, *Writers in Crisis*, London, 1947, p. vii.
[3] Adrienne Koch in *Literary History of the United States*, edited by Spiller, Thorp, Canby, Johnson, New York, 1948, Vol. I, p. 602.
[4] *National Gazette*, April 10, 1793.
[5] John Adams, *Defense of the Constitutions of Government of the United States of America*, New York, 1787, Vol. I, p. 59.
[6] Thomas Jefferson, *The Writings of Thomas Jefferson*, edited by Paul L. Ford, New York, 1892–9, Vol. IV, p. 153.
[7] Adams, *The Works of John Adams*, edited by Charles Francis Adams, Boston, 1850–6, Vol. IV, pp. 417–18.
[8] *Defense*, op. cit., Vol. III, p. 282.
[9] This, at any rate, was the belief of the makers of the American Constitution. However, Walter Bagehot in *The English Constitution* (World's Classics edition, p. 195) writes:

> But there are two classes of government. In one the supreme deter-mining power is upon all points the same; in the other, that ultimate power is different upon different points—now resides in one part of the constitution, and now in another. The Americans thought that they were imitating the English in making their constitution upon the last principle —in having one ultimate authority for one sort of matter, and another for another sort. But in truth, the English constitution is a type of the opposite species; it has only one authority for all sorts of matters.

[10] *Works*, Vol. IV, p. 234.
[11] *Works*, Vol. VI, p. 241.

[12] *Works*, Vol. VI, p. 243.

[13] *Works*, Vol. VI, p. 285.

[14] *Works*, Vol. IV, p. 392.

[15] *Works*, Vol. VI, p. 530.

[16] *Works*, Vol. III, p. 124.

[17] *Works*, Vol. VI, p. 530.

[18] *Works*, Vol. IV, p. 395.

[19] 'There is less disposition to congratulation with genius, talents, or virtue, than there is with beauty, strength, and elegance of person' (*Works*, Vol. IV, p. 253).

[20] March 20, 1790.

[21] *Works*, Vol. VI, pp. 502–3.

[22] *Works*, Vol. VI, p. 271.

[23] *Works*, Vol. X, p. 12.

[24] *Works*, Vol. VI, p. 470.

[25] Quoted in *Literary History of the United States*, op. cit., Vol. I, p. 150.

[26] *Memoir concerning the commercial relations of the United States with England*, Philadelphia, 1805, p. 5.

[27] *Correspondence of John Adams and Thomas Jefferson*, edited by Paul Wilstach, Indianapolis, 1925, p. 27.

[28] *The American People*, London, 1949, p. 137.

[29] Zoltán Haraszti, *John Adams and the Prophets of Progress*, Cambridge, Mass., 1952, p. 137.

[30] Quoted by Parrington, op. cit., Vol. I, p. 302.

[31] Hamilton, *Works*, Vol. III, pp. 207–8.

[32] *An Enquiry into the Principles and Tendency of Certain Public Measures*, 1794; quoted by Charles A. Beard, *Economic Origins of Jeffersonian Democracy*, New York, 1915, p. 209.

[33] Henry Adams, *History of the United States of America During the Administration of Thomas Jefferson*, New York, 1889–90, Vol. IV, p. 136.

[34] For the information in these two paragraphs I have relied on Louis M. Hacker, *The Triumph of American Capitalism*, New York, 1940, pp. 374–400.

[35] Henry Adams, *Democracy*, New York, 1953, p. 185.

[36] Russell Kirk, *The Conservative Mind*, Chicago, 1953, p. 68.

[37] John Fiske, *Essays Historical and Literary*, New York, 1907, Vol. I, pp. 169–70.

[38] Jefferson, *Writings*, Vol. VII, pp. 149–50.

[39] Vol. IV, no. 107, June 8, 1793.

[40] Jefferson, *Writings*, Vol. VII, pp. 201–3.

[41] Jefferson, Ibid., Vol. VI, p. 153.

[42] Arthur M. Schlesinger, Jr., *The Age of Jackson*, London, 1946, p. 8.

[43] Jefferson, *Writings*, Vol. III, p. 269.

[44] Claude G. Bowers, *The Young Jefferson*, New York, 1945, p. vi.

[45] Op. cit., Vol. I, p. 9.

CHAPTER III

[1] See F. R. Leavis, 'The Europeans', *Scrutiny*, Vol. XV, No. 3, pp. 209–21.

[2] Robert E. Spiller, *Fenimore Cooper; Critic of His Times*, New York, 1931, p. 220.

[3] R. H. Tawney, *Religion and the Rise of Capitalism*, London, 1926, p. 87.

[4] *Hamilton Club Series*, No. 1, New York, 1865, pp. 24–5.

[5] *The American Democrat*, intro. by H. L. Mencken, New York, 1931, pp. 19–20.

[6] Brooks Adams, *The Law of Civilization and Decay*, New York, 1951, p. 217.

[7] Ibid., p. 201.

[8] Ibid., p. 203.

[9] Ibid., p. 240.

[10] Op. cit., pp. 326–7.

[11] Quoted by Zoltán Haraszti, op. cit., p. 233.

[12] John Adams, *Works*, Vol. IV, pp. 354–5.

[13] 'Cooper and the European Puzzle', *College English*, Vol. VII, p. 199.

[14] Yale University Press, 1938.

[15] Quoted by Henry Christman, *Tin Horns and Calico*, New York, 1945, p. 10.

[16] Dixon Ryan Fox, *The Decline of Aristocracy in the State of New York*, 1918, p. 136.

[17] Adams, *Works*, Vol. VI, p. 280.

[18] Op. cit., p. 64.

[19] Ibid., p. 32.

[20] Cited in Waples, op. cit., p. 206.

The recognition of this tension in Cooper is general among all biographers and critics who have written on him. Thomas R. Lounsbury, whose biography (*James Fenimore Cooper*, New York, 1900, p. 82) was first published in 1882, more or less sets a pattern:

He was an aristocrat in feeling, and a democrat by conviction. To some this seems a combination so unnatural that they find it hard to comprehend it. That a man whose tastes and sympathies and station connect him with the highest class, and to whom contact with the uneducated and unrefined brings with it a sense of personal discomfort and often of disgust, should avow his belief in the political rights of those socially inferior, should be unwilling to deny them privileges which he claims for himself, is something so appalling to many that their minds strive vainly to grasp it. But this feeling was so thoroughly wrought into Cooper's nature that he almost disliked those of his countrymen whom he found not to share it.

[21] *Gleanings in Europe*, edited by Robert E. Spiller, New York, 1928–30, Vol. I, p. 36.

²² The most recent and exhaustive study of these land laws and the agitation that led to their repeal is to be found in Henry Christman, op. cit. The laws are discussed in relation to the Littlepage novels in 'Landlord Cooper and the Anti-Renters', by Granville Hicks, *Antioch Review*, Vol. V, pp. 95–109. An account narrowly sympathetic to the land-owners is given by Edward P. Cheyney, *The Anti-Rent Agitation in the State of New York, 1839–46*, Philadelphia, 1887. The style and tone of life on these old estates are described by Cooper in *The Pioneers*. A visually suggestive account is given in an article by General Egbert L. Viele, 'The Knickerbockers of New York Two Centuries Ago', *Harper's New Monthly Magazine*, December, 1876:

> The early Dutch residents of Albany and its vicinity constituted a kind of landed aristocracy, and, with their numerous retainers and slaves, held a sort of feudal court in the grand mansions which may still be found dotted here and there in the interior of the State. The family seat of the Knickerbockers at Schagticoke is one of these ancestral homes. . . . The spacious edifice is built in the Flemish style of architecture, with its steep pyramidally shaped roof. . . .
>
> The principal entrance is reached through an avenue of ancient trees, time-worn and scarred, that climb high above the roof. . . . The main hall is in itself a room. Quaint settees and an antique bookcase, with rare old engravings on the walls, constitute the furniture, while over all an air of quiet comfort and repose prevails. The principal stairway is in the second hall, separated from the first by folding doors. On either side of the main hall are the reception and drawing-rooms, while the dining-room and library open into the rear hall. In the olden time the dining-room contained the historic fireplace, with its tiled front and sides representing the scenes and events in Bible History. . . . Beyond the dining-room, in the large wing, are the kitchen and servants' apartments. The great cellar, which extends under the entire building, was the slaves' quarters in winter.

This description of the Knickerbocker ancestral estate reminds one of the description given by Henry Walcott Boynton (*James Fenimore Cooper*, New York, 1931, p. 8) of Otsego Hall, in which much of Cooper's boyhood was spent: a stately mansion made of brick, two stories high, above an enormous cellar, the entrance opening into a great central hall flanked by large rooms. The lands attached to the estate numbered 40,000 acres in 1786.

The aristocratic tone which pervaded wealthy New York society, which still thought in terms of land, is described by D. R. Fox (op. cit., pp. 130–3):

> The gentry who centred in the drawing-rooms of those fashionable streets running eastward from Broadway, all had their coats of arms, and history of knights and squires and manor houses with wide stretching acres in the counties of old England. To lord it over docile tenantry, and ride at hunt through one's own forest, made up a part of what was most attractive in the family legends of a storied past. . . .
>
> So these families came, bringing in a spirit of aristocracy which left its

mark, as we have seen, upon the county politics. That now they have for the most part disappeared adds a touch of pathos to the story. Theirs was a spirit foreign to the custom of the country; while others made their way into the wilderness to be rid of every vestige of the feudal system, these came to perpetuate so much of that tradition as could be saved. But the aloofness of this gentry, so proper to their social theory, could not be comfortably preserved, and, bound by an inflexible endogamous rule, these branches of the families slowly withered and passed into memory, though leaving after them an influence that increased respect for 'the few, the rich, and the well-born'.

This was essentially the class that Cooper admired, and with which he identified himself; and as I have remarked elsewhere in Chapter III, the intensity of his loyalty to it blinded him to the fact that the men of wealth in New York were no longer the old aristocrats, but men whose wealth came from speculation and business, and who, for that very reason, were pleased to identify themselves with the more honoured tradition of land, which not only shed a lustre of dignity over them, but proved profitable as well. Thus, the character of the old landowning class was gradually sapped by its fusion with those very elements Cooper distrusted. As Fox describes it (ibid., pp. 122–4):

> The men of wealth in New York City had no settled prejudice against holding real estate; not only were there close connections with the Schylers and the Van Rensselaers, but in most families of the gentry there were large-acred cousins, of whose prosperity there could be no doubt. . . . The attention of large investors was already fixed on these lands while they were still dispensed by the colony land office, and the bidding grew far brisker in the early days of statehood. As one glances down the pages of the *Calendar of Land Papers* one sees many familiar Federalist names, William Bayard, the Bleeckers, C. D. Colden, Duane, James Emott, Nicholas Fish, and many others. Alexander Hamilton invested all his surplus earnings in the lands about Oswego which would pay a rich dividend only after years of waiting, so that his tragic death left his widow 'landpoor'.

CHAPTER IV

[1] George E. Hastings, 'How Cooper Became a Novelist', *American Literature*, Vol. XII, pp. 20–51.

[2] For those to whom this juxtaposition does not seem convincing, I would suggest that Cooper's Revolutionary novel, *Lionel Lincoln*, would be a good place to make the comparison, and particularly Chapters XXVI and XXVII, which record the death by smallpox of the idiot boy, Job. These chapters illustrate particularly well Cooper's ability to manipulate a great number of characters in the scene at once, all of them operating at high levels of emotional intensity; and they point towards a fascination for and

pity of human misery one does not ordinarily associate with Cooper. It has been remarked that *Lionel Lincoln* has a very Hawthornian tone long before Hawthorne evoked it (Grossman, *James Fenimore Cooper*, London, 1950, p. 41). This is true; but the accidental similarities with Dostoevski seem to me more revealing in defining the character of Cooper's imagination.

Despite Cooper's rigorous social and theological orthodoxy which increased as he grew older, one is frequently aware in his writings of the imponderable character reality carried for him. The immensity of wilderness that stretches endlessly through so many of his novels is itself a symbol of this. One of his favourite devices is to shatter the primitive forest silence by causing some ancient oak or elm to collapse suddenly under its own weight of years and size. Only so loud a noise could disturb so ancient a stillness. The violence of Cooper's action, as he creates it in his novels, is sometimes rather like that. The imagination penetrates reality deepest, if at all, only through a violence of drama and character that stands at the farthest remove from Jane Austen. And it is here that one finds, for a moment, a valuable suggestiveness in the comparison with Dostoevski.

Cooper was not always an accomplished creator of character, although his abilities in this direction have sometimes been underestimated. It is worth remarking here that he scored some of his most successful points with aberrational types that, in a few cases, might have sprung from the pages of the Russian novelist. For example, in his first novel on an American theme, *The Spy*, in Chapter XXXII we are given a harrowing episode in which the leader of a gang of Skinners, those marauders who infested the country during the Revolution, and committed all kinds of crimes under the guise of patriotism, is hanged in a deserted barn by a brutal officer of a band of Cow-boys—the opposite number of the Skinners on the British side—whom he has casually encountered in the countryside. The contrasting characters of these two men, the treacherous degeneracy of the Skinner, the clod-like insensibility of the Refugee officer, smoking his pipe as he searches for a beam from which to hang his prisoner, is done with an insight into the terrifying squalor of which the human personality is capable that inevitably evokes a comparison with the later Russian novelist. And as so often with Dostoevski, although it is extraneous to the main action, the episode is one of those vignettes of violence and psychological terror without which the novel would collapse in significance.

[3] The historical identity of Harvey Birch has created a good deal of unnecessary speculation for many years. The problem is irrelevant to any but an antiquarian's interest in Cooper. The best consideration of Birch's historical antecedents occurs in a Note by James S. Diemer, 'A Model for Harvey Birch' (*American Literature*, Vol. XXVI, No. 2, pp. 242-7).

[4] We can see how Cooper's concept of the American gentleman passed over into the hands of the genteel tradition by comparing it with this

passage by an exponent of the tradition, James Lane Allen ('The Gentleman in American Fiction', *The Bookman*, Vol. IV, p. 118):

> It is our honest persuasion, however provincial, that, take him all in all, his like has never been seen elsewhere; and when this has been admitted, surely enough has been said to make it clear that in the practice of our national life, in its theory, at the very heart of our towering ideals, we as a nation regard the gentleman, and the gentleman alone, as the utmost embodied excellence of our social institutions.

[5] The English title was *Eve Effingham*. It was with the publication of these books that Cooper's unpopularity in America got under way in earnest. Reviewing *Homeward Bound* in *The North American Review* for October, 1838, Francis Bowen wrote:

> Professing to be a sturdy republican, he has exhausted his powers of invective upon the manners and characters of his countrymen, who are, taking his own descriptions for truth, ignorant of the first principles of social refinement, and no better than a nation of brutes and savages. If such are the friends of Republicanism, she may well pray heaven to save her from them.

From this point on, Cooper's quarrel with his countrymen was almost constant. It is, in fact, Cooper's indignant refusal to be bullied by the prejudices and ill nature of the Americans that makes him, merely on the personal level, the most winning of American writers. But this, of course, was not the popular verdict. As Lounsbury puts it (op. cit., p. 78): 'The most intense lover of his country, he became the most unpopular man of letters to whom it has ever given birth.'

[6] Quoted by Richard Hofstadter, *The American Political Tradition*, New York, 1951, p. 209.

[7] A notable instance of this is the immensely popular novel by Robert Montgomery Bird, *Nick of the Woods; or the Jibbenainosay: a Tale of Kentucky*, first published in 1837. It tells of an epileptic Quaker, Bloody Nathan, whose family had been murdered by Indians before his eyes. He himself had been scalped, but lived to bear the horrifying scar as a reminder to kill as many Indians as possible. He became a kind of avenging agent, known as the Red Devil of the Indians. 'Often would the snakelike creeping files of Indians, while seeking the peaceful habitations of the Kentuckian or emigrant for blood and plunder, stumble in their path upon the cold and stiffened corpse of some Shawnee warrior, the leaves glued to his scalped head with gore; with two long and deep gashes cut in the form of a cross, the certain and fatal mark of the avenging spirit.' The Indian was regarded as a barrier to national growth, and a threat to frontier security, and the cult of Indian-killing which the swashbuckling heroes of the backwoods professed had to be condoned. Melville's chapters on Colonel Moredock in *The Confidence Man* (Chapters XXV, XXVI, XXVII) presents a deadly picture of the mentality.

[8] In discussing form in Cooper in this chapter I have been concerned with aesthetic form as the 'form of life'. There were, in addition to Cooper's superb conception of an action as the form of a novel, a number of minor innovations that he achieved in dealing with the fictional conventions of his day. A good analysis of them will be found in Henry Nash Smith's *Virgin Land: the American West as Symbol and Myth*, Cambridge (U.S.A.), 1950, pp. 69–70.

CHAPTER V

[1] Edmund Wilson, *Axel's Castle*, New York, 1936, p. 12.

[2] Charles Feidelson, Jr., *Symbolism and American Literature*, Chicago, 1953, p. 49.

[3] Ibid., p. 1.

[4] We enjoy the symbol, but we also penetrate to the meaning. The symbols do not create their meaning: the meaning, in the form of actual effective beings acting upon us, exists for us in its own right. But the symbols discover this meaning for us. They discover it because, in the long course of adaptation of living organisms to their environment, nature taught their use (Alfred North Whitehead, *Symbolism: Its Meaning and Effect*, New York, 1927, p. 57).

[5] Op. cit., p. 48.

[6] Henry James, *The Art of Fiction and Other Essays*, New York, 1948, p. 15.

[7] Henry James, *The Art of the Novel*, edited by R. P. Blackmur, pp. 33–4.

[8] *Letters from an American Farmer*, Everyman edition, pp. 172–3.

[9] James Grossman, *James Fenimore Cooper*, London, 1950, p. 149.

CHAPTER VI

[1] Quoted in Henry Adams, *History of the United States of America During the Administration of Thomas Jefferson*, New York, 1889–90, Vol. I.

[2] Mark Van Doren, *Nathaniel Hawthorne*, New York, 1949, pp. 138–9.

[3] *Hawthorne's Fiction: The Light and the Dark*, Norman, Oklahoma, 1952, p. 58.

[4] Op. cit., p. 256.

[5] Quoted from *The Melville Log*, edited by Jay Leda, New York, 1951, Vol. II, p. 529.

[6] Op. cit., p. 40.

[7] Henry James, *Nathaniel Hawthorne*, New York, 1901, p. 63.

CHAPTER VII

[1] Henry James, *The Art of Fiction and Others Essays*, edited by Morris Roberts, New York, 1948, p. 14.

[2] Henry James, *Hawthorne*, p. 130.

[3] *The Sewanee Review*, Vol. LIX, Nos. 2 & 3, Spring & Summer, 1951. The discussion of *The Blithedale Romance* occurs in the second part.

[4] Hyatt H. Waggoner, *Hawthorne: A Critical Study*, Cambridge, Mass., 1955, p. 178.

[5] Ibid., p. 186.

[6] Op. cit., p. 128.

[7] Ibid., p. 133.

[8] Op. cit., *S.R.*, Vol. LIX, p. 453.

[9] *The Complex Fate*, p. 61.

[10] F. O. Matthiessen, *The American Renaissance*, New York, 1941, pp. 318–19.

[11] *Jefferson*, New York, 1926, pp. 68–70.

[12] Jefferson, *Writings*, Vol. V, p. 121.

[13] See Hyatt Waggoner, op. cit., pp. 151–73.

CHAPTER VIII

[1] *The Degradation of the Democratic Dogma*, New York, 1919, pp. 30–2.

[2] I have discussed this in the *The Complex Fate*, pp. 79–113 and 145–9.

[3] Lawrance Thompson, *Melville's Quarrel with God*, 1952, Princeton, p. 153.

[4] D. H. Lawrence, *Studies in Classic American Literature*, London, 1937 (Pocket Edition), 145.

[5] Giovanni Giovanini has remarked in 'Melville's *Pierre* and Dante's *Inferno*' (*PMLA*, March, 1949, p. 70) that 'Melville, like many of his contemporaries, apparently did not extend his reading of Dante beyond the *Inferno*'. But the reason for such a surmise is merely that no allusions to the *Purgatorio* and *Paradiso* have been recognized.

[6] For example, H. B. Parkes, *The American People*, London, 1949, p. 202: 'In Melville's Ahab the drive of the American will is carried to its furthermost limits;' Richard Chase, *Herman Melville*, New York, 1949, p. 101: 'Ahab is the epic transmutation of the American free enterprise;' Newton Arvin, *Herman Melville*, New York, 1950, p. 176; 'He is modern man, and particularly American man, in his role as "free" and "independent" individual. . . .'

[7] The role of Ishmael and the positive values represented by Queequeg have recently received excellent treatment in *Ishmael* by James Baird, Baltimore, 1956.

[8] Alexander Cowie, *The Rise of the American Novel*, American Book Company, p. 398.

⁹ *Pierre*, Edited by Henry A. Murray, New York, 1949.

¹⁰ Newton Arvin, *Herman Melville*, New York, 1950, p. 227.

¹¹ See, for example, Leo Mark's 'Melville's Parable of the Walls', *The Sewanee Review*, Autumn, 1953, pp. 602–27.

¹² *The Philosophy of Santayana*, edited by Irwin Edman, New York, 1936, pp. 55–6.

¹³ Op. cit., pp. 185–209.

¹⁴ Allen Tate, *The Forlorn Demon*, 1953, pp. 75–6.

CHAPTER IX

¹ *Scrutiny*, Spring, 1948, pp. 209–21.

² *Partisan Review*, Vol. XI, pp. 436–55.

³ *The Notebooks*, New York, 1947, p. 57.

⁴ Ibid., p. 191.

CHAPTER X

¹ An early consideration of James's economic viewpoint is Newton Arvin's 'Henry James and the Almighty Dollar' (*The Hound and Horn*, Vol. VII. pp. 434–43), Arvin sums up James's economic world in these terms:

> It is a world . . . in which men have their eyes sharply fixed on the main chance and women know how to add and multiply, a world in which buying is done in the cheapest market and selling in the dearest, a world obsessed by the nervous craving for acquisition and haunted by the fear of penury. James's scene is one in which greed plays something like the same role as snobbishness in Thackeray's scene, or sentimentality in Meredith's. It is not an aristocratic scene in any real sense: it is something more modern than that.

A recent article by Bradford A. Booth, 'Henry James and the Economic Motif,' (*Nineteenth Century Fiction*, Vol. VIII, pp. 141–50) analyses a number of stories and novels to prove that:

> James clearly saw to what extent the ruthless pursuit of wealth deadens not only the aesthetic but the moral sense, and he returned to his task as writer with a renewed desire to dramatize the spiritual blight that feeds on the love of money.

The best critic on this subject is F. O. Matthiessen (*Henry James: the Major Phase*, New York, 1944). Chapter V, which deals with *The American Scene* and *The Ivory Tower*, is by far the best in the book. I have tried as far as possible to keep from duplicating his material, but as some of his points are central to the theme itself it has been a little difficult.

[2] *The Letters of Henry James*, edited by Percy Lubbock, London, 1920, Vol. I, p. 125.

[3] Adams, *Works*, Vol. VI, p. 280.

[4] *The American Democrat*, op. cit.

[5] Henry James, *The Art of the Novel*, edited by R. P. Blackmur, New York, 1941, pp. 60–2.

[6] Lionel Trilling, 'Introduction', *The Princess Casamassima*, New York, 1948, Vol. I, pp. xxx ff.

[7] See, for example, *Henry James*, F. W. Dupee, London, 1951, pp. 142–3.

[8] Henry James, *The American Scene*, New York, 1946, pp. 136–7.

[9] Ibid., 222.

CHAPTER XII

[1] *Literary History of the United States*, op. cit., Vol. II, p. 1031.

Index

Printed in Great Britain by
Butler & Tanner Ltd.,
Frome and London